HUDDERSFIELD TOWN

Champions of England
1923-24, 1924-25, 1925-26

DESERT ISLAND FOOTBALL HISTORIES

HUDDERSFIELD TOWN
Champions of England
1923-24, 1924-25, 1925-26

Series Editor: Clive Leatherdale

Jim Brown

DESERT ISLAND BOOKS

First published in 2003
by
DESERT ISLAND BOOKS LIMITED
89 Park Street, Westcliff-on-Sea, Essex SS0 7PD
United Kingdom
www.desertislandbooks.com

© 2003 Jim Brown

The right of Jim Brown to be identified as author of this work has been
asserted under The Copyright Designs and Patents Act 1988

British Library Cataloguing-in-Publication Data
A catalogue record for this book is available from the British Library

ISBN 1-874287-66-X

Printed in Great Britain
by
Biddles Ltd

Photographs in this book are reproduced by kind permission of:
Clem and Marie Stephenson, Andrew Earnshaw, Robert and Liz Smith,
Kirklees Community History Service, Tony Trotman, Pat Armer, Mick Hesp

CONTENTS

~ AUTHOR'S NOTE ~

Only four teams have won a hat-trick of League championships. Most football fans could probably name three of them: Arsenal, Liverpool and Manchester United. But, outside West Yorkshire, few are aware that the first team to achieve this memorable feat was Huddersfield Town. This was made all the more amazing, partly because of the comparatively small size of the West Riding town, partly because the town was a Rugby League stronghold, and partly because of the relative youth of the club at the time.

Before I was offered this project by Clive Leatherdale of Desert Island Books, I had no great understanding of that wonder-team, apart from a vague knowledge of key personalities – Herbert Chapman, Clem Stephenson and Billy Smith – and that the 1924 championship had been the closest in history. I did not know that my researches would uncover one of the most extraordinary tales in British football history. In a modern age, when football is dominated by multi-million pound transfers, and salaries and TV money go to the rich whilst the poor go to the wall, it is refreshing to discover that, in the 1920s, clubs like Huddersfield could dominate the English game and, probably, the world scene, had they been given the chance.

Several excellent books have been written about Huddersfield Town, but none has probed the glorious three-year championship period in detail. I am indebted to Terry Frost, author of *Huddersfield Town: A Complete Record* (1990), George Binns, author of *Huddersfield Town 75 Years On* (1984) and Ian Thomas, author of *Leeds Road: Home of My Dreams* (1994). Their works helped me greatly as a starting point for my research.

Other books which have proved invaluable include: John Harding's *Alex James: Life of a Football Legend* (1988), Stephen Studd's *Herbert Chapman: Football Emperor* (1981), *Kicking and Screaming: An Oral History of Football in England* (1995) by Rogan Taylor and Andrew Ward, Simon Inglis's *Football Grounds of Britain* (1996) and *League Football and the Men Who Made It* (1988), Geoffrey Green's *The History of the Football Association* (1953), Brian Tabner's *Through the Turnstiles* (1992), John Graves' (ed) *Herbert Chapman on Football* (1934), Charles Buchan's autobiography, *A Lifetime in Football* (1955), and other books from Breedon's Complete

Record series and Yore Books' History series. Apologies to those whose material has been used where copyright has not been identified, and who are invited to contact the author and publishers.

In the statistical section, all the line ups have been gleaned from contemporary newspaper match reports and checked against the relevant Breedon or Yore book. Attendances have been taken either from match reports or published histories. Unfortunately, prior to 1925, clubs were not required to report gate figures to the Football League and many of these attendances may be estimates. It was common practice in those days for journalists to estimate the gate as best they could, and that is why, if looking at the Sunday newspapers of the era, you will notice the gates quoted to the nearest thousand spectators. It appears that only Cup gates were properly and accurately recorded.

I have tried to follow the trail of all the Huddersfield players in the wake of the championship years – where they went, what they did, how they died – and whilst I succeeded with many I failed with a few. I would like to hear from anyone who might shed more light on the movements of these ex-Town heroes.

During the writing of this book I have developed a strong affinity with this marvellous football club. My wish is that they will once again grace England's top division and, who knows, emulate their forebears from the 1920s.

Thanks to everyone who has helped me – Clem Stephenson (grandson of the maestro) and his mother, Marie, Andrew Earnshaw and his wife Liz, (granddaughter of Billy Smith), Robert Smith (grandson of Billy Smith), Pat Armer (granddaughter of Jack Chaplin), Sue Gillooley of Kirklees Cultural Services, Mick Hesp, a Town fanatic, George Binns and Jayne Lee at the Kirklees Stadium and Doug Thomson of the *Huddersfield Examiner*. Numerous others have given me assistance. These include, in no particular order, Gerald Mortimer, Alex Smith, Nellie Green, David and Ron Ramsden, Harold Whitaker, Paul Joannou, Rich Smart, Chris Collings, Peiter Verhagen, Richard Whitehead, Stanley Gilling, Alan Stevenson, Ken Davy, Richard Monteith, Gill Shearer, Julie Simpson and the staff at the British Newspaper Library, and the public libraries of Huddersfield and Leighton Buzzard.

Last, but not least, thank you to my family. My wife Doreen and children Lisa and Alastair have all given me wonderful support in this and my other writing projects.

Jim Brown
October 2003

~ PREFACE ~

It is a great privilege for me to be Chief Executive of Huddersfield Town Football Club. The recent past of the club has been tumultuous, to say the least, and I believe that, with the club's financial situation now on a much firmer base, the future of Huddersfield Town is assured and that the club will go from strength to strength from here.

As I delved into this fascinating book to read about the club's glorious period in the 1920s, it underlined what a unique club we have here in the town. Not only was winning the Football League three years running a 'first', but the achievement also put our town on the map. Back then England was undoubtedly the centre of world football and I am sure that, if there had been a Champions League competition, Town would have won it.

As a Huddersfield lad, I was brought up on tales of the great Town team of the 1920s. The book brings back to life the era and the characters, such as Clem Stephenson, Billy Smith and Herbert Chapman, and although there will be few fans alive today who actually saw the Triple Champions, younger supporters will be able to enjoy a nostalgic journey back to Town's golden period.

Our greatest desire is for Town to rise from its current position and recreate some of the glory enjoyed in its famous past.

I am pleased to have the opportunity to write the preface of this excellent book, *Huddersfield Town: Champions of England*, and I wish it every success.

ANDREW WATSON
Chief Executive
Huddersfield Town FC

Introduction

~ THE CLOSEST FINISH EVER ~

(MAY 1924)

Shortly after 4.40pm on Saturday, 3 May 1924, Rochdale referee Harold Hopkinson put his whistle to his lips to signal the end of the match at Leeds Road. With that brief, shrill sound, he ended Huddersfield Town's season on a winning note. Town had completed a 3-0 victory over visitors Nottingham Forest. But neither he nor anyone else in the stadium knew whether Huddersfield were Champions of England for the first time. Everything depended on the outcome of Cardiff City's game at St Andrews in Birmingham. This was the state of play at kick-off:

	P	W	D	L	F	A	Pts
Cardiff	41	22	12	7	61	34	56
Huddersfield	41	22	11	8	57	33	55

On this, the last day, the destiny of the championship lay between just two clubs. Whichever way it went, there would be a new name carved on the trophy, as neither club had achieved the feat before. Huddersfield had started the day a point behind, following a 1-3 midweek defeat at Aston Villa. That result meant that all Cardiff had to do was win at St Andrews to clinch the title, and if they did, the Football League trophy would leave England for the first time in its 36-year history.

As their team's fate was now out of their hands, most Huddersfield folk had resigned themselves to missing out on the big prize. Manager Herbert Chapman and his players must have been kicking themselves after winning only one of the last seven games, when Town had only to keep their nerve over the final hurdles to be home and dry.

One hundred miles away, Cardiff had spent 90 minutes battering away at Birmingham's defence, without success. The game ended goalless to leave Cardiff and Huddersfield level on points. But that was just the simple bit. In those days, teams finishing level on points were separated by the archaic mechanism of goal average. Unlike goal difference – which was introduced in 1976 and can be calculated by basic arithmetic – goal average meant dividing the number of goals scored by the number conceded. This could run to any number of decimal places, and in those pre-computer, pre-calculator days, required pencil, paper, and a working knowledge of long division.

Compared to the modern 'goal difference', 'goal average' favoured defensive sides, which is one of the reasons it was abandoned. For example, goal figures of 100 for, 40 against, produce a goal difference of +60, but a goal average of 2.50. Figures of 30 for, 10 against, presents a smaller goal difference (+20), but an inflated goal average (3.00).

But this is to run ahead of events. News of the final score from St Andrews did not permeate through to Leeds Road for some minutes, which must have seemed like a lifetime to those involved. It was, said the *Huddersfield Examiner*, 'an unusual sight to see the crowd hanging about after the match instead of rushing for the tramcars back to town.'

In those days, radio was in its infancy and television was a twinkle in someone's eye. There were few means of communicating football results across the country. Most spectators relied on the half-time scoreboard situated on the Bradley Mills end of the ground. This wooden construction had white numbers painted on black metal plates, which were hung up on rows of nails alongside the letters of the alphabet. The numbers could be decoded via the key in the matchday programme, which on the day in question showed that Birmingham v Cardiff was match 'B'. At half-time the scoreboard indicated that match 'B' was 0-0, but no update had been available since the interval. Was it still all square at St Andrews?

Leeds Road at that time had a little office at the end of the 'paddock' – the standing area in front of the main grandstand – in which was housed the telephone which received scores from elsewhere. This tiny room now became the centre of fevered waiting. The phone sat there, silent, while officials sat nervously, head in hands, beside it. What happened next is described in Herbert Chapman's biography:

'Then suddenly the door was flung open and Mr Chapman dashed out with his face one huge smile and shouting "we've won!"' The score from Birmingham had come through, someone had done their sums, and Town had become the first club to win the Football League on goal average. *Athletic News*, the definitive weekly national newspaper dedicated to sport in general and football in particular, reported that, 'Cardiff … immediately dispatched a telegram congratulating the victors. It was almost worth losing the prize to act so nobly.'

The mathematics showed that Town were the new champions with a superior goal average of 0.024 of a goal. That still stands as the closest winning margin in the League's history. For example, had Town beaten Forest 4-1 instead of 3-0, Huddersfield and Cardiff would have been locked together on points, goals scored, and goals conceded. Nowadays, that unlikely eventuality would have to be settled by a play-off decider, as almost happened with Rangers and Celtic in the Scottish Premier League in 2003. In 1924, it is not clear from the Football League's regulations what, if any, contingencies were in place in the event of a dead-heat. What is clear is that under today's rules, Cardiff's final goal figures would have placed them above Town on 'goals scored', though that would have been rendered meaningless because Town had won one game more. Since 1981, wins have earned three points instead of two, so Huddersfield would have topped the table by one point.

With goal figures of 61-34, Cardiff's goal average at the start of play was 1.794. Huddersfield, with figures of 57-33, had a minutely inferior average of 1.727. Every possibility was raked over in the minds of players, officials and supporters of both clubs. Clearly, Town had to get at least one point more than Cardiff but, if they did, then every goal would be crucial. The permutations were endless, and to spare readers with a phobia for figures, they won't be pursued here. Suffice to say, that, were the situation to be repeated today, any change in score would be instantly transmitted to those playing in the other game, whose priorities would change accordingly. In 1924, Leeds Road and St Andrews might have been on different planets, so cumbersome was it to communicate from one to the other.

Equally important was the attitude of the opposition. Cardiff's opponents, Birmingham, would finish just below halfway whatever the outcome. Nothing rested on the score. For Nottingham Forest, however, the result was every bit as important as it was for Town. At the start of play Forest stood twentieth of 22, level on points with Chelsea – who had completed their programme – but above them on goal average. Prior to 1973, only two teams went down from the English top division, and Forest knew they had to avoid defeat by eleven goals to avoid slipping below Chelsea and into Division Two.

Athletic News' reporter at Leeds Road, 'Harricus', gave short shrift to those who believed that Forest would offer no resistance: 'For the benefit of those cynical people who profess to know about these matters, I desire at the outset to state that Nottingham Forest fought most strenuously, not exactly to prevent Huddersfield Town from securing the League championship, but to comply with the spirit of the league rules by striving conscientiously to secure the two points at stake. That they failed to do so was due entirely to the fact that that their conquerors won on their merits.'

Huddersfield had eventually run out easy winners after looking nervous in a tense first half, with 'spectators not in a very happy mood and constantly urging their pets to score'. Town's combative David Steele had a 'goal' disallowed before George Cook netted a rebound after Forest goalie Bennett had saved from George Brown. After half-time, as the rain started to pour down, Town turned up the heat on the fragile Forest defence. Cook headed in Billy Smith's cross and Eddie Richardson's jinking dribble set up Brown for a third ten minutes later. It was just as important for Town not to concede a goal as to score more themselves, but near the final whistle Steele, not renowned for his dribbling skills, went on a mazy scurry that took him past several Forest men. He arrived in the penalty area with just the goalie to beat, but the tension of the moment went to his head and he shot wildly and wide.

Only later did details of the remarkable happenings at St Andrews emerge. With 56 minutes played, Cardiff's Jimmy Gill's header was goalbound when Percy Barton, the Birmingham half-back, fisted it away. A penalty was awarded. Two of Cardiff's most experienced players, Jack Evans and Gill, were too affected by the occasion to accept responsibility for the kick, which was taken by the young and less-experienced Welsh international forward Len Davies. Facing him in the Birmingham goal was Dan Tremelling. With 23 goals already, Davies had been one of the stars of the Welsh club's amazing season which, as *Athletic News* pointed out, 'had put Cardiff City into the front rank of football.' The Welsh club's rise to the top was even more spectacular than Huddersfield's; they had only entered the Football League in 1920, winning promotion to Division One in their first season.

The sports newspaper described the penalty: 'He [Davies] shaped for the kick with the aplomb of an experienced marksman, very sure of himself but not shrewd. The ball rose scarcely wide of Tremelling and he arrested it. In that magnetic moment Cardiff City lost the League Championship.' A collective groan went up from the large Welsh contingent in the near-capacity 49,000 crowd. Despite ever increasing pressure, Cardiff could not find a way through Birmingham's stubborn defence. As *Athletic News* described proceedings, 'Cardiff had the ball of fortune at their feet and spurned it in the wrong direction.'

Len Davies wasn't to know that, at the time of his miss, Huddersfield were still only one goal up against Forest. Even when Town scored a second, it would not have been enough to deprive Cardiff of the crown. It was George Brown's third that made Davies rue the costliest miss of his life.

Cardiff, in reality, should not have had to rely on results from the final day of the season. They had started with an eleven-match unbeaten run and only suffered their second defeat, at Villa Park, on Boxing Day. By St

David's Day, 1 March, when they travelled to Huddersfield for the league meeting, City had a five-point lead over their West Riding rivals, but somehow in the intervening weeks their advantage slipped away. They lost four games in a row in a dreadful run which saw them go seven games without a win. Injuries hampered them in the run-in. Half-back Harry Evans broke his leg at Blackburn and missed the last ten games, and leading scorer Len Davies – who would waste that climactic penalty – missed four crucial games. Davies' absence was a killer blow to Cardiff. Many realised how important he was to the side when, without him, they gained just one point from those four games. Despite everything, manager Freddie Stewart appeared to have got the wheels back on the rails. Cardiff stayed unbeaten in the final nine games, and were where they wanted to be, with their noses in front, at the final showdown.

Huddersfield, too, had been up with the leaders virtually all season. They were up there by virtue of an outstanding home record — Town lost only one home game all season – and a miserly defence which conceded only 33 goals in 42 matches. Only deposed champions Liverpool, with 31, had conceded fewer since Division One had been expanded to 22 clubs in 1919.

But suppose Huddersfield had failed to score that all-important third goal against Forest, or Len Davies' penalty for Cardiff had been more accurate. What then? In many respects football supporters were as unforgiving then as they are now. Had Town finished runners-up instead of Cardiff, Chapman might have found himself vilified for allowing his team to squander their games in hand earlier in the season. Psychologically it would have been a hammer-blow to the club and it is hard to imagine the next two seasons turning out as they did. Far from stamping himself as the first great English football manager, Herbert Chapman could have become the great loser, the man who choked when the title was within his team's grasp. Football reputations hang on one match, one goal, and one decision. Would Arsenal have been so keen to employ Chapman a year later? Just one goal on that fateful May afternoon might have changed the face of English football.

This is not just idle speculation, for the fate of Cardiff City showed what might easily have happened to Huddersfield. Although they reached two Cup finals (losing in 1925, winning in 1927), Cardiff – having missed by a whisker – never again challenged for the League championship. A year after Davies' penalty miss they finished eleventh, and their downward spiral continued until they were relegated in 1929.

Huddersfield Town were champions in only their tenth season in the Football League. The biggest element of their success was undoubtedly the manager, Herbert Chapman. Chapman had arrived at the club in 1921, just twelve months after it had come close to extinction. Chapman was one of the first managers to have total control over playing matters at a British football club and he was credited with introducing many innovations, both to Huddersfield and to the game in general. Praise for his appointment should be given to his chairman, Joseph Barlow, and the other directors, who somehow kept the club afloat in the financial crisis of 1919-20. They had faith in Chapman and backed their faith with financial support to enable him to build one of the greatest sides in the history of English football.

The winning team he created was one with few stars. Sam Wadsworth, Ted Taylor and W H (Billy) Smith were already England internationals, but the man who was arguably the architect of success on the pitch, Clem Stephenson, would gain only one England cap in an eighteen-year career. None of these players, however, matched the celebrity of the game's glittering lights – Charlie Buchan of Sunderland and Arsenal, Hughie Gallacher of Newcastle United, Dixie Dean of Everton and Billy Walker of Aston Villa.

That team-spirit did not happen by chance. Chapman encouraged everyone at the club to pull together and fostered a spirit of co-operation by consulting with his directors on team matters. He worked hard at developing a close-knit camaraderie among players, taking every opportunity to bring them together for sport (cricket, billiards, bowls and golf) or socialising (theatre and music hall visits). Allied to this was Chapman's ability to make his players feel they belonged to a great club, where even playing for the reserves was considered an important and worthwhile enterprise. As the *Huddersfield Year Book 1925-26* put it, he controlled his players in a 'firm but kindly manner'. He saw to it that they had decent changing rooms (by contemporary standards) and 'expert and scientific training methods' to 'preserve and lengthen their careers'. At Leeds Road, Chapman and his club trainer, Jack Chaplin, prepared a side for battle each Saturday that never knew it was beaten. To defeat Huddersfield Town in this era required a super-human effort.

Chapman's team retained their title a year later, after which the great man was lured to Arsenal, where his impact endures to this day. At Leeds Road his banner was picked up by Cecil Potter, whereupon Town became champions for a third time. Huddersfield's reputation as triple champions spread around the world. This is the remarkable story of an apparently ordinary team that went on to achieve extraordinary greatness. Huddersfield Town were Champions of England.

Chapter 1

~ FOUNDATIONS ~

(1907 – 1923)

In the late nineteenth century, Huddersfield gave little indication of one day having a world-famous football team. Its fame lay in its textiles. Local historians insist that the worsted cloth produced in the town's mills was the best in the world. By the 1920s the other principal industries were chemicals and dyes, closely related to the colour needs of textile manufacture. The company established by Read Holliday, for example, is credited with discovering the colour mauve. By 1919, British Dyestuffs, in addition to being a major employer in the town, was belching out fumes which would surely breach government regulations today. Textile machinery and associated engineering trades provided the town with another major focus. Firms like William Whiteley of Lockwood, Thomas Broadbent, and J Hopkinson were some of the largest in the area. In 1921 Hopkinsons employed 1,500 workers in the manufacture of valves and boiler fittings.

The 1921 Official Handbook of Huddersfield Corporation stresses the variety of textile and chemical manufacture but also lists a range of auxiliary trades, including valves and boiler fittings, electrical machinery, motor vehicles, sheet metal goods, leather working, tool making, wood working and furniture, boots and shoes, bricks and cardboard boxes. The earlier industrial base of textiles and chemicals had by this time diversified into a broader industrial structure, within which many firms built strong reputations.

Today, the town boasts over 200 protected buildings – more than any other English town, with the exception of Bath. One, the grand Victorian Railway Station, was described by the poet John Betjeman as 'the most splendid station facade in England'. By the 1920s, however, industrial dirt and grime caked many of these princely buildings A Pathe News clip showing Huddersfield Town's return from winning the 1922 FA Cup exposes many black and grubby building facades.

Across the square from the now-restored railway station stands the George Hotel. It looks cleaner these days than the blackened building it was in the 1920s. Inside, you will find a plaque marking the spot of a historic meeting in 1895, at which the Northern Rugby Football Union was established. In time it became the Rugby Football League, and Huddersfield Rugby League Club were founder members. Like so many areas in the industrial West Riding, Huddersfield was a stronghold of the handling code. Association Football was of lesser importance in the textile town until the last few years of the nineteenth century.

By 1897 there were enough amateur soccer clubs to merit the formation of a Huddersfield and District Football Association. Over the next few years enthusiasm for the round-ball game continued to expand locally. In 1903 Bradford City became the first West Riding club to be admitted to the Football League and they were followed by Leeds City in 1905. Soccer enthusiasts in Huddersfield harboured dreams of emulating their neighbours and having a senior club in the League, but many sporting people in the town believed this to be a flight of fancy.

However, in 1906 circulars were distributed far and wide, convening a meeting at the Imperial Hotel. It was there, on 7 February 1907, that the Huddersfield Town Football Club Limited was formed. Its first need was somewhere to play. One possibility was Fartown, the home of Huddersfield's Rugby League club. This idea was scotched by the Northern Union, which would not countenance ground sharing. They were not to know that 90 years later both sports would happily co-habit within the McAlpine Stadium.

Rebuffed by Fartown, the soccer club settled on an expanse of recreational land, part of which was once used as a pitch by the local technical college. It was situated on Leeds Road and was squeezed between a row of Victorian tenement housing and Bradley Mills. The Huddersfield & District Football Association had used the pitch for local Cup finals for some years, but the enclosure was modest and unprepossessing. There were no turnstiles or covered areas, and no dressing rooms. Players changed in an old tramcar or a local public house. Faced with these ramshackle conditions, the club paid £600 to erect a covered stand to accommodate 2,000 spectators. In 1908 the new club was admitted to the North Eastern League, which mainly comprised clubs from distant Tyneside. The records show that Huddersfield Town's first fixture was at South Shields Adelaide. Town lost 0-2.

It proved costly having to travel so far so often that first season. For their second season they were admitted to the Midland League, and held their own against the likes of Worksop Town, Castleford Town, Mexborough, and reserve sides of Football League clubs – Hull City, Leeds City, Notts County and the two Sheffield clubs. But the standards in the Midland League were high, and several members had graduated from it to the Football League.

Once again Town were soon on the move. In 1910, the Babes – as they were soon to become known – were elected to the Football League. The hard-working and persuasive chairman Hilton Crowther, a local woollen-mill owner, led a campaign to have Town elected in place of one of the two clubs up for re-election – Grimsby Town and Birmingham. Grimsby had actually finished higher than Birmingham, but it was they who were voted out at Huddersfield's expense.

To celebrate admission to the highest level of the professional ranks, the club adopted new colours – a white shirt with a blue 'yoke', and white shorts, or 'knickers' as they were known. The directors planned further ground improvements costing £6,000. This involved much more than a revamp of the old ground. The pitch was turned around by 90 degrees so that it ran parallel with Leeds Road, and provision for a modern grandstand was entrusted to the famous football architect Archibald Leitch, whose designs at Manchester United, Chelsea and Fulham were widely admired. Between 1900-39, Leitch's firm helped develop 27 League stadia, a record no modern design company is likely to approach.

The new west grandstand (modelled on that at Stamford Bridge and Craven Cottage) would accommodate 4,000 seated spectators, plus a further 3,500 standing in a paddock area to the front. The term 'paddock' is normally associated with horse racing. But it also refers to an enclosure, usually covered, at a football stadium, for which clubs charged a slight premium over normal terrace prices.

Tons of earth were covered with ash and cinders from local factories to form the steep bank that would become known as the 'Terrace', which occupied the east side of the stadium. It was open to the elements until a roof was erected in the 1950s. Railway sleepers were inserted up to halfway to act as fixed steps. Metal crush barriers were concreted into the bank in a staggered formation to halt any excessive swaying of the crowd. The Leeds Road end, behind the north goal, was covered at the back by a rickety wooden roof, and steps carved out by means of bricks and railway sleepers. The small roof was, in 1929, replaced by a larger one that covered the whole end. The Bradley Mills end, behind the south goal, was also an ash-covered terrace – though dwarfed by the East Terrace – and remained virtually unchanged until the stadium was demolished in 1994. When all was done, the capacity of Leeds Road was increased to around 34,000. Its prize asset, the Main Stand, took many months to complete and was opened in 1911 at a cost of £3,047.

The first two seasons of Division Two football were hard for Town, with tough battles to avoid finishing in the bottom two places. Having to apply for re-election so soon after admission would have been humiliating. But losing teams mean smaller crowds and, in 1912, with gates having slumped to under 3,000, the club could no longer balance the books and sank into liquidation.

The Crowther family stepped in to pay off the debts and a new club emerged later that year on a new financial footing. The club also acquired a new manager, Arthur Fairclough, fresh from leading Barnsley – then also in the Second Division – to a famous FA Cup final victory over West Brom. According to board minutes, Fairclough was tempted by a wage of '£7 per week'. The following season Town posted their first FA Cup giant-killing feat when they beat First Division Sheffield United 3-1. Gates were only marginally up, but a fine home record, which saw just one defeat, ensured the club's best finish to date – fifth in Division Two.

The 1913-14 season saw the introduction of the blue and white striped shirts for which Huddersfield Town would become famous. It also saw the arrival of Billy Smith, who would grace the team for over twenty years and establish a record 574 appearances. But Smith nearly said no. Hailing from the County Durham village of Tantobie, Smith impressed in a trial against Bury reserves. However, when asked to attend a further trial, the precocious 17-year-old – who played for Hobson Wanderers – stated that he would not accept a weekly wage of less than 50 shillings (£2.50) and would not subject himself to a second trial.

Fortunately this proved to be a storm in a teacup and, four days later, on 4 October 1913, Billy Smith signed. By the end of the year he was in the first team. A natural left-winger, Billy could not immediately displace the incumbent, Joe Jee, and for two seasons he played on the other flank. Over the years Smith's form ebbed and flowed, and there were times when he was close to being sold. The board minutes of November 1920 report that 'Sheffield United had asked for the transfer of WH Smith but it was resolved not to part with Smith'. Then, two years later, the minutes state: 'if any offers for WH Smith's transfer was forthcoming the same should be considered'.

1914-15 was a surreal season, for it was played out against the backdrop of the Great War. The financial situation at Leeds Road worsened to the extent that, without the financial input of the Crowther family, the club would have folded again. Gates were no more than 5,000, often far smaller, which meant the club could not operate on a viable basis. The only ray of sunshine came when the reserve team unexpectedly won the Central League (reserve teams from the North and the Midlands).

Unlike World War II when football was immediately brought to a halt, the Government in 1914 saw no pressing reason to intervene. There were no enemy aircraft capable of dropping bombs at that time, and football could offer much by way of leisurely distraction for the masses. The problem was that, as players and spectators went off to fight, there were not too many left to play or to watch, and a year later the curtain came down.

Before it did so, another hero of the triple championship side grabbed his chance. Billy Watson came into the first team in the spring of 1915. A native of Bolton-on-Dearne, Watson had briefly peeped into the team at right-back in 1912, soon after arriving at Leeds Road. He was, however, a natural wing-half and made his first appearance in that position in a 3-0 win at Woolwich Arsenal. When League football was suspended, and regional, makeshift leagues took its place, Watson wore Town's colours against other Yorkshire and North Midland sides. Arthur Fairclough stayed at the helm throughout the years of artificial wartime competition and should be credited for assembling the basis of the Huddersfield side that Chapman would take to glory.

The Football League resumed in 1919, a year after the Armistice that ended hostilities. Considering the massive loss of life for young men of fighting age, it is remarkable to note that of the 22 players who appeared for Huddersfield in that first post-War season, seventeen had worn the stripes five years previously, seven of whom had been first-team regulars. Only two Town players, both reserves, lost their lives in the Great War.

Radical changes had been made to the structure of the League, both divisions having been increased from twenty to 22. The two extra places in the senior division, however, were not filled by reprieving those clubs due for relegation in 1915. One of them Chelsea, retained their place, the other, Tottenham, after much lobbying and jiggery-pokery, were replaced by their north London rivals Arsenal, who had finished sixth in Division Two in 1914-15 (just one point ahead of Huddersfield). The whole sordid business left a bad taste for years afterwards, but Spurs accepted their new status and would quickly prove their detractors wrong.

As far as Town were concerned, ambitions were high. In those days football club bosses were customarily called 'secretary-managers', as their duties were twofold. In April 1919 Fairclough asked to be released from his 'manager's' responsibilities in order to concentrate on the 'secretarial'. According to board minutes, he was now retained as part-time secretary at an annual salary of £150. Within weeks, Ambrose Langley had been appointed manager, in charge of team affairs. Langley, a former Sheffield Wednesday and Aston Villa left-back, had managed Hull City before the War and had built a reputation for discovering young talent, especially in the North East, a football breeding ground which had already been farmed by Huddersfield in the form of Billy Smith and Tommy Wilson.

In his time at Hull, Langley was reputedly so determined to fend off rival interest in a player, that he once rowed a small boat across the Humber in order to secure his signature. Langley's wages at Leeds Road were £6 a week (£312 per annum).

Until the 1960s, British football operated a players' maximum wage. It has been said that in the 1920s Town's directors were not deterred from paying that maximum to attract and keep the best. The club minutes confirm that in August 1919 Billy Smith was earning £6 a week, but how widespread this practice was at Leeds'Road is open to conjecture. In view of the fact that the club had twice flirted with extinction, burdened by the weight of its debts, it is doubtful that many team-mates could match Smith's wages.

Hopes that Town's experienced squad could make a challenge for promotion to Division One had to be quickly reassessed. Two months into the season, leading scorer Jack Cock – who had just become Town's first England international player and scored the winning goal against Ireland – was transferred to Chelsea for the substantial fee of £2,500. But behind the scenes seismic changes were afoot. With gates at Leeds Road averaging only 4,300 and match receipts barely £100, the club's financial backers were struggling to balance the books. They also had another agenda, to uproot Huddersfield Town – lock, stock and barrel – to Leeds, sixteen miles away.

Three weeks earlier, on 13 October, Second Division rivals Leeds City had been expelled from the Football League for 'financial irregularities'. It appears the club had made illegal payments to players during the War. In consequence, Leeds City now became the first club to suffer expulsion from the Football League. To fill the void, the League installed Port Vale – next on the list of hopefuls when the divisions were expanded – to take over Leeds City's fixtures. This led to the extraordinary situation whereby the ten points Leeds had earned from their eight matches were transferred to Vale.

This was manifestly unfair. Never before or since has the Football League replaced one club by another mid-season and transferred results in this way. Port Vale's own results were poor; those of Leeds City had been good. Teams facing Leeds were therefore penalised, none more so than Coventry City, who were beaten twice by the strong Elland Road team, and who were unable to pick up easier pickings against Port Vale, and survived having to apply for re-election by just two points.

But the crisis had a human dimension as well. Amongst the Leeds City officials suspended from football *sine die* were the club's directors and secretary-manager Herbert Chapman. Chapman always denied involvement on the grounds that the alleged improper payments took place during a period when he was not involved with the club. He had taken a job as a manager in a local munitions factory between 1916 and 1918. These are murky waters, for if matters were as clear-cut as Chapman claimed, he is unlikely to have been accused, never mind suspended. It was also accepted that (like today) several – perhaps many – clubs were guilty of 'illegal payments'. In fact, Leeds City were not expelled for that offence, but for refusing to produce their financial ledgers for inspection. Those books might have exonerated Chapman from any wrong-doing.

As it was, Chapman lost not only his job but his team. A week after Leeds' expulsion, the players were auctioned off at the Metropole Hotel in the city. Though none were snapped up by Huddersfield, four of them – Billy Kirton, Billy Ashurst, Bill Pease and George Stephenson (brother of Clem) – would later play for England.

With their club banished, effectively disbanded, influential voices in Leeds were desperate for first-class football to return. A proposal to form Leeds United from the ashes of Leeds City was quickly approved. The trouble was, the new club would have to play in the Midland League. The only quick route back to the Football League was by riding piggy-back on another club. It was at this point that secret talks – initiated, it seems, by Huddersfield Town, not by Leeds – took place with the aim of amalgamating the two clubs.

The plan was 'the transfer of the Town club in its entirety over to Leeds'. Had it succeeded, Elland Road would have Second Division football; Huddersfield would have nothing. The composition of the new nine-man board would include five Huddersfield Town directors, among them Hilton Crowther and chairman WL Hardcastle.

News of the merger exploded like a bombshell in Huddersfield. 'Town Club Dead,' screamed the headline in the *Examiner*. The club could not survive without the financial subsidies injected by the Crowther family, which had kept it afloat in troubled times past.

In one sense it is difficult to be too critical of the Town directors. Local support had always been pitifully poor and, in a town where Rugby League had such a strong foothold, there was little sign that spectators would support the round-ball game in large numbers. Soccer crowds at Elland Road, on the other hand, averaged 10,000. In Huddersfield, the rugby and soccer teams generally played on alternate Saturdays. But in the autumn of 1919 crowds at Fartown – the home of Huddersfield Rugby League club – were more than double those at Leeds Road. Whatever the arguments, it seemed that Huddersfield Town would follow clubs like Middlesbrough Ironopolis and Bootle into Football League oblivion.

Planned mergers of this kind were, and are, uncommon and the board at Leeds Road could not have anticipated the level of popular outrage that it provoked. Local businessmen and civic dignitaries rushed to the rescue, pooled their resources, and took steps to save the club. If the merger was somehow to be halted, the Crowther family would have to be reimbursed.

The Crowthers were owed some £25,000 (the better part of £1 million in today's terms). That was just the start, for further funds were necessary to keep the club afloat. A public meeting was convened. In an age without radio or television, it was advertised by means of telegrams to prospective benefactors and slides shown at local cinemas. Within days, protest meetings were taking place all over Huddersfield and in the surrounding villages. Appeals were made for cash donations, which flooded in to the club.

Attendances increased at Leeds Road. In late November, the visit of Bristol City drew almost 8,000, three times the crowd for the previous game. Afterwards it was announced that £4,000 had already been raised. However, time was running out. A deadline of 31 December had been set for the Crowthers to be repaid their money. Failure to meet that deadline meant that the Football League would have no objection to Crowther taking his team to Elland Road.

Just before Christmas, Hilton Crowther's brother, Stonor, served a writ on the club, seeking to recover £10,000. He proposed that a receiver be appointed, and suggested that club secretary Arthur Fairclough assume the role. The club's affairs were darkening by the hour, as Fairclough had already agreed to take up secretarial duties at the proposed merged club at Elland Road. He now promptly quit his position at Huddersfield, which was filled by manager Ambrose Langley.

Astonishingly, amidst the financial mayhem around them, the players blocked out fears for their future, carried on playing and reeled off win after win. From early December they lost just one of 25 League games, and that was at leaders Spurs, who had lost their place in Division One to Arsenal in dubious circumstances and were now rushing to reclaim it.

Gates at Leeds Road, already boosted by the merger crisis, now shot up with the spur of a winning team. In January a record crowd of 27,000, paying receipts of £1,500, saw a 1-1 draw with Spurs. The sale of Jack Cock had been forgotten, as his replacement, Sammy Taylor, scored 35 League goals, a total never bettered by any Town player, and a further six in the FA Cup. Taylor had debuted on the opening day of the season at inside-left, but switched to the middle after Cock's departure. A one-season wonder, Taylor was sold to Sheffield Wednesday during 1920-21.

Langley had also introduced Tommy Wilson at centre-half. Wilson, who hailed from Seaham in Durham, had failed to shine with Sunderland and returned to play for Seaham Colliery. He had been signed by Arthur Fairclough in June 1919 as the long-term replacement for the evergreen Fred 'Tiny' Fayers who, Fairclough felt, at 5ft 5in was too small to play at centre-half.

Against the odds, and with the merger fiasco rumbling on in the background, it looked increasingly likely that Huddersfield would accompany Spurs in gaining promotion. Not only that, Town were marching ever onwards in the FA Cup. Brentford were dismissed 5-1 in the first round, First Division Newcastle in the second, and Plymouth in the third in front of another record home crowd of 35,000. Division One title-chasers Liverpool were then drawn at Leeds Road in the quarter-finals. Town's players were whisked off to Northumberland's Whitley Bay to prepare and to escape the hullabaloo in Huddersfield.

To cater for the expected capacity crowd, the club imported ashes and soil to make the Terrace yet higher. Town also increased admission prices. General ground admission stayed at one shilling (5p), but the paddock enclosure was doubled to three shillings (15p). The biggest hike was reserved for centre seats in the grandstand, from four shillings (20p) to ten shillings (50p). The Leeds Road attendance record was smashed yet again; this time 47,570 paid record receipts of £4,094. They saw Swann and Taylor score in a 2-1 victory over the Merseysiders.

Before the semi-final with Second Division Bristol City at Stamford Bridge, Town went off again, this time to Hornsea in Lincolnshire, where once again the sea air proved to be to their liking. Town won 1-0. The players adopted a lucky charm in the form of a lamp presented at a Christmas pantomime. Before each round the players would rub the lamp in turn as they left the dressing room.

To prepare for the final, on 24 April, the players returned to Whitley Bay. The board minutes report that Langley was given a 50 per cent pay rise to £9 per week in recognition of his success. Crystal Palace, the setting for FA Cup finals since 1895, had become a War service depot and Wembley had not yet been built. Chelsea's Stamford Bridge, scene of Town's semi-final, was now selected to host its first final. Town's opponents in the first post-War Cup final – watched by 50,018 spectators – were doughty Aston Villa, who had already won the trophy five times. Snippets of the game can be viewed on old Pathe News clips, but watching the grainy footage it is still possible to recognise the Chelsea ground that endured until the 1960s. The location of the cameras, however, high on the terraces, makes it impossible to follow any details of the game.

Without their prized winger, Billy Smith – suspended after being sent off at Stoke a few weeks earlier – Town struggled against their costly, star-studded First Division rivals, for whom Clem Stephenson had an outstanding game. Villa snatched the only goal eight minutes into extra-time, denying Town the feat of becoming the first club to win the FA Cup and promotion in the same season. For their part, Aston Villa became the first club to win the trophy six times.

Losers or not, on their return to Huddersfield the players received a huge welcome, with 10,000 well-wishers packing St George's Square. Forging a path across the square to the George Hotel proved almost impossible, and the size of the reception offered final confirmation that the planned move to Leeds had been scuppered; nor would the club sink into receivership and oblivion.

As a footnote to this crazy season, one final bizarre incident is worthy of mention. Two days after the semi-final, Huddersfield travelled to Port Vale, who had been parachuted into the League in the autumn. Regular goalie Alex 'Sandy' Mutch had been hurt in the semi-final with Bristol City. Realising he would not be fit to play against Vale, the club despatched a telegram – the most reliable and quick means of communication in those days – summoning reserve custodian Edwin Davis. Davis never received it. Manager Ambrose Langley was forced to field right-half Charlie Slade in goal. The match ended goalless.

In June 1920, after three months of complex negotiations, Amos Brook Hirst and his backers paid the Crowther family £17,500 of the £25,000 owed, plus an allocation of 12,500 shares. Brook Hirst rejoined the board, whilst Hilton Crowther ploughed money into the new Leeds United, who were voted into Division Two under the management of former Town manager Arthur Fairclough.

The following month Town elected a new board of directors, the nucleus of which would preside over the glory years to come. Among the new faces were the club's saviours – Joseph Barlow, Wilfred Dawson and Rowland Mitchell. Also on board were the Huddersfield Town Retention Committee – Amos Brook Hirst, Dick Parker and Harry Rayner. The only old faces were Stonor Crowther, who retained shares in the club, and Norman Robinson, an original director from 1908.

This was a good time to be a top footballer, for the Football League now doubled the maximum wage from £4 10s to £9 a week. The caveat was that there was no obligation for clubs to pay the maximum, and no minimum wage was defined. The League had even proposed abandoning all wage restrictions, but that was merely a sop to the Players Union and was quickly rejected by the clubs.

At least the better players would be better rewarded, something for which they had lobbied strongly. Across the country, gate receipts had soared as war gave way to peace, and entertainment took priority in people's lives. Added to which, the peacetime cost of living had also soared, with many players struggling on their existing wages. That same meeting saw the introduction of the Third Division, raising the number of clubs to 66. The new division was effectively the old Southern League. A year later it would be renamed Division Three (South), when 22 more clubs were invited to form Division Three (North).

For players and supporters of Huddersfield Town, it must have seemed that they had awakened from a nightmare. The winning ways continued. Five wins out of six saw Town on top of the First Division, and in mid-September 31,000 turned out for the 0-0 home draw with star-studded Sunderland. That constituted a tenfold increased on gates from a year earlier. Town, once so poor, were now not poor at all.

Goals, however, plentiful in the Second Division (97), were scarce in the First (42). Taylor and Swann struggled to find the target in the higher league and, following their promising start, the team won only twice between September and February. Taylor was sold to Second Division Sheffield Wednesday for the surprisingly high fee of £3,250. Several players filled his shirt during the winter months, including Shields, Islip, Lunn and Wright, but with little success. The goals only really started flowing again after the arrival in March of Clem Stephenson. By then, Herbert Chapman was in charge of playing matters.

In defence, 34-year-old left-back and captain Fred Bullock's early form earned him an England cap in October for a 2-0 win over Ireland. Bullock became the first of numerous Town full-backs to be capped, a tradition which extended to 1966 when Ray Wilson helped England win the World Cup. Sadly Fred's football career was over six months later. He failed to recover from what would today be a simple cartilage operation. After his enforced retirement he became landlord of the Slubbers Arms pub in Halifax Road, but soon took his own life by drinking ammonia.

Despite the downturn in form, attendances held up at Leeds Road. Although the ground record of 47,527 was never under threat, the league record crowd was regularly broken. At Christmas, 32,430 saw a 0-1 defeat by Middlesbrough, and on Easter Tuesday 33,862 turned up for a relegation-tinged match with Sheffield United which Town won 1-0.

In the league, Huddersfield picked up strongly to finish well clear of the drop. In the FA Cup, there was to be no repeat of the previous season's heroics. In the third round (the equivalent of today's fifth round) Aston Villa were pulled out of the hat in a repeat of the 1920 final and won 2-0 at Villa Park in front of 60,000 spectators. Clem Stephenson was again Town's tormentor, in what would be one of his last games for the Birmingham club.

It was around this time that Huddersfield Town decided to seek an assistant manager for Ambrose Langley. It is not clear from the club minutes whether this move was instigated by the board or by the manager. Langley was perceived to be one of the 'old-guard' and had been a strong supporter of the move to Elland Road. He must have realised that, in the event of a dip in club form, his days at Leeds Road would be numbered. The man now appointed to be his assistant manager would, in the space of two months, take over from Langley. His name was Herbert Chapman.

Chapter 2

~ CHAPMAN AT THE HELM ~
(FEBRUARY 1921 – JUNE 1923)

Herbert Chapman was born on 19 January 1878 in the small mining community of Kiveton Park, between Sheffield and Worksop. He was one of seven children of John and Emma Chapman, six boys and one girl. His parents were churchgoers and from an early age young Herbert and his brothers and sisters attended Sunday School. In adult life Chapman was a regular worshipper and in his latter years was a pillar of St Mary's Parish Church in Hendon, north London.

John Chapman was a coal-miner and like many others of his generation and social class was unable to read and write. His sons might have been destined to follow him down the pit, but for the Education Act of 1870, which made school compulsory up to the age of twelve. Herbert had opportunities denied to his father, and after leaving school he continued his studies at Sheffield Technical College where he studied mining engineering.

Young Herbert's talents were not restricted to the classroom. He excelled at football and cricket with the Kiveton Park team, and was also captain and secretary of the school football team. A younger brother, Harry, played some 300 games for Sheffield Wednesday and was a star of their League Championship-winning teams in 1903 and 1904.

Sheffield, in the last years of the Victorian era, was a hotbed of football and Herbert played as an amateur for several local clubs. Football was fast becoming a professional sport and to a young man of working-class origins it would have provided another way of avoiding having to follow his father down the mine. Chapman, however, at his stage saw his future in management within the mining industry. He retained his amateur status even when playing for professional clubs. Though he later turned professional, he is quoted in *Herbert Chapman on Football* as saying: 'I should prefer to remain an amateur. I do not believe any man would choose to be a professional if the question of earning a living did not arise.'

In 1897, aged nineteen, Chapman left home and began a nomadic life that saw him playing football wherever he could find work. He played odd games for various clubs in the Lancashire League, but in May 1898 he signed for Grimsby Town in the Second Division. On his Mariners debut, inside-right Chapman scored two goals. Sadly, Manchester City scored seven, to take the gloss off his achievement. By January he had scored only two further goals in eleven games and was on the move again, this time to Southern League Swindon Town.

Descriptions of Chapman's playing style are hard to find, but the *Grimsby Gazette* described him as follows: 'If on the small side, he is nevertheless sturdily built and takes a lot of knocking off the ball.' In 1899 the *Swindon Advertiser* called him 'an effective tackler, creating openings for goal, but having a tendency to ramble'.

Chapman played a few games for Swindon's reserves but could not find work in the railway town so he was off again, this time to Southern League Sheppey United in Kent. Sheppey were a poor side and destined to finish bottom. In his short time there he was probably their best player, finishing as top scorer with six goals in ten games, but in March 1900 he was injured and moved back to the Sheffield area. This time he knuckled down to his mining studies, playing on an amateur basis for Worksop Town of the Midland League.

During 1901, possibly after envying the success of his brother Harry, Chapman turned professional and was signed by Southern League side Northampton Town. He held a regular place in the Cobblers team, top-scored with fourteen goals in 28 games, and performed well enough against Division One club Sheffield United in the FA Cup that the Blades signed him the following summer. However, Chapman, who had by now gained his diploma from the Institute of Mining Engineers, insisted on reverting to amateur status and taking up a mining job to give him practical experience in the industry.

His time at Bramall Lane was undoubtedly the pinnacle of Chapman's modest playing career. Managed by John Nicholson, the Blades were one of the top teams in the country – in the past five years they had won the FA Cup three times and the League championship once. Chapman played alongside United legends, such as Alf Common, later to become Britain's first £1,000 player, twenty-stone goalkeeper 'Fatty' Foulke, and tiny England wing-half Ernest Needham. Chapman later described Needham as 'the finest footballer I have ever seen and my hero as a boy'. But the hard lesson for Chapman was that after 22 games and two goals it was clear that he would never make the grade in top-flight football.

Next stop was Notts County, who faced an annual struggle to stay in Division One. Chapman failed to win a regular place and was dismissed by the *Nottingham Daily Express* as 'too clumsy'. A friendly with Northampton in March 1904 renewed old acquaintances and soon afterwards he returned to the County Ground as a player.

The team picture of Southern League Northampton for the 1904-05 season shows a clean-cut Chapman standing in the back row, by some way the shortest player of the six alongside him. Chapman has a cherubic, round face and looks somewhat podgy compared to many of his lean teammates. His chubby physique earned empathy on the terraces rather than scorn, and despite playing only sixteen games for the Cobblers that season he finished as leading scorer with eight goals. He had probably found his level, though the Southern League of his day was a top professional league, exempt from the maximum wage, and infinitely stronger than its modern equivalent, the Nationwide Conference.

At this point, registration problems complicated Chapman's career. Tottenham Hotspur, also of the Southern League, showed interest, but his registration was still held by Notts County. Tottenham had to pay County £70 for his release. He was a virtual ever-present in his first season at White Hart Lane, top scoring with eleven goals, but found himself relegated to the reserves the following season. By April 1907, now aged 29, he contemplating retirement from the professional game and considering a career in mining where his academic qualifications could finally be put to use.

It was whilst at Tottenham that Chapman got his first taste of the pre-FA Cup seaside training trips. A week in bracing seaside air had become popular, after the famous Blackburn Olympic, one of England's first professional clubs, started making pre-big match visits to Blackpool back in 1882. Spurs visited Leigh-on-Sea, in Essex, in 1906 and trained at the Southend Kursaal whilst enjoying hot seawater baths, which reputedly had a stimulating effect on the players.

A twist of fate now changed the direction of Herbert Chapman's career and led him down a path of football management rather than mine management. Northampton were seeking a new manager. Walter Bull, a friend of Chapman at Tottenham, was their first choice. The club asked Chapman to have a word, but when Bull decided to stay at Spurs for one more season he urged Chapman to apply instead. Chapman discussed the matter with his wife overnight and decided to pitch in for the job. He wrote to Northampton putting himself forward as a player-manager and was taken on.

Chapman's last Spurs game was a 2-0 Southern League home win over Queens Park Rangers. The *Tottenham Herald* commented: 'Although we can hardly say that he is in the first flight of footballers he is a most conscientious player and a gentleman both on and off the field.'

Northampton, for their part, had finished bottom of the Southern League two seasons running and in 1906-07 had won only five games out of 38 and conceded 88 goals. The only way was up. Chapman introduced a raft of new players and a new style of play and twelve months later the Cobblers would climb to eighth, equalling their best ever finish.

George Badenoch and Fred McDiarmid, old colleagues from Spurs arrived in the close season, as did David McCartney from Chelsea and Fred Lessons from Nottingham Forest. None involved any transfer fee, as in those days it was customary for players to be tied to their clubs for one season only, after which they were free to join any club they chose. Only the very top players commanded fees, and the British record at the time was the £1,000 paid by Middlesbrough to Sunderland for Alf Common in 1905.

However, in November 1907, after the Cobblers' promising start had fizzled out – leaving the team winless in seven games – Chapman persuaded his chairman, Pat Darnell, to spend £400 on Edwin Lloyd-Davies, the Welsh international full-back from Second Division Stoke. It was the first time Northampton had ever paid out a transfer fee, and was the first indication that Chapman could exert significant influence at the club. In *Northampton Town: The Official Centenary History*, Frank Grande points out, 'without a doubt part of the money, if not all, came from his [Darnell's] pocket.'

In those far off times most teams played to a standard system. Five forwards attacked the opponents' goal. Two wing-halves supported the forwards but also marked the opposition wingers. The centre-half was the 'pivot' of the team, linking defence to attack, almost like a playmaker in modern parlance. The two full-backs were the only permanent defenders, generally big, muscular types chosen for their ability to clear the ball with massive kicks upfield.

Within this system, any 'tactics' were normally left to the captain and players, especially during the course of a game. The secretary-manager was more involved with administration and was at the bidding of the directors, whilst the trainer's role was to get the players fit. Chapman was still a player at this time, so there was nothing unusual in his involvement in the team's on-field tactics. Ruminating on a home defeat by Norwich City, Chapman realised that his half-backs had pushed up too far behind the forwards and, as a result, Norwich had packed their penalty area and squeezed the space available for scoring chances to be created.

Chapman's solution was, in future, to encourage his half-backs and forwards to withdraw. This would open out the game and entice the opposing defenders forward, exposing gaps behind them which could be exploited by swift attacks. These tactics also gave the defence more solidity and less exposure to counter-attacks.

Chapman is also credited with introducing a 'long-ball' game. His full-backs were coached in the art of long but accurate passes out of defence, unlike the modern 'long-ball' game, which is more about hopeful punts upfield for the forwards to chase.

Chapman introduced special Cup training at Northampton. Although the club could not afford pre-match trips to a resort, he nevertheless made it a week out of the ordinary. The *Northampton Daily Reporter* said it included: 'a spin round the County Ground track twice, followed by skipping and ball-punching, with a short walk into the country at the finish'. The following day saw a trip to the countryside, followed by a visit to a Turkish bath in Bedford. The training paid off: the Cobblers beat Sutton Town 10-0, a record Cup win for the club that still stands.

One year into the job, Chapman could feel pleased with himself. The board were convinced he was the right man to take the Cobblers forward, and all thoughts of a career in the mines appear to have been abandoned. His playing days were drawing to a close, and that summer Chapman signed a dashing replacement, Albert Lewis, from Coventry City. Several clubs had hoped to sign the prolific Southern League star but, according to the official history of Northampton Town, 'Chapman invited him into his office, locked the door, hid the key and told the player: "You won't get out of here until you have signed".' Lewis did so, and would score 56 goals over the next two seasons, including a club record 31 goals as the Cobblers were transformed from perennial strugglers into champions of the Southern League.

Northampton were in the leading pack from the start and, but for a slight wobble in March, would have clinched the title sooner. They had the meanest defence, conceding only 45 goals in 40 games, and the second best attack, with 90 goals scored. Chapman was not with the team to celebrate their clinching of the championship. He was in Yorkshire with his ailing father and his pleasure at Northampton's success could not match the pain of his father's death a few days later.

Looking back at Herbert Chapman's first two seasons in football management, the key values and philosophies that would accompany him through his career at Leeds City, Huddersfield Town and Arsenal were already apparent. At each of these clubs Chapman would always strive to maintain control over footballing matters. Most clubs at that time were run by the chairmen and directors, who selected the team, directed affairs, bought and sold players, and at some clubs dictated the tactics, despite little or no knowledge of the sport.

As a general principle, the secretary-manager's role was purely administrative. It is unclear how Chapman persuaded directors to relinquish their traditional role, but he certainly achieved it wherever he managed. What is astonishing is that very few football clubs followed the example he set. Perhaps directors elsewhere feared the perceived threat to their traditional dominance, and continued to allow their manager little autonomy. It was only after 1945 that matters changed radically, with managers such as Matt Busby and Stan Cullis in the vanguard.

At Northampton it was Chapman who recognised the need for a quality defender like Lloyd-Davies and persuaded his chairman to put up the money. Later, at Huddersfield, he would do the same when recognising that Clem Stephenson held the key to Town's future. Similarly, the veteran Charlie Buchan, another player considered by many to be over the hill, would be his first signing at Arsenal.

At the club reception to celebrate winning the championship, Darnell spoke of the manager's 'tact, judgement and discretion' and his 'consideration' for the team. Earlier he had referred to Chapman as the players' 'friend at all times,' and assured them they would be 'treated as men by the club whether they won or lost'. This sounds more sincere than the weasel words of typical modern Premiership chairmen. At the County Ground there appears to have been mutual respect between Chapman and his directors, or at least his chairman, something that would resurface at both Huddersfield and Arsenal later in his career.

Respect also played a major part in Chapman's relationship with his players. Darnell's words confirm that Chapman saw the need to treat people fairly if you wanted to get the best out of them. Dick Parker, a Huddersfield Town director during Chapman's reign at Leeds Road, later described Chapman's style: 'He would always listen to a player's problems and offer help where he could. He never spoiled, nor allowed others to spoil, his players with too much praise but struck a subtle balance between encouragement and discipline'.

Chapman always looked after his players and ensured that their facilities were the best available. He sought improvements to the dressing-rooms and ensured that injured players were treated properly, as Fred McDiarmid discovered in 1907 when his injury necessitated a trip to a Sheffield specialist. After winning the championship in 1909, Chapman organised a tour of Germany, both to reward the players and raise the profile of the club.

This should not be taken to mean that Chapman was all sunshine and light. He brooked no indiscipline and demanded good behaviour on and off the pitch. Football was a hard game, and there were many teams who would physically abuse weaker opponents. It is claimed that Chapman gave short thrift to any player deliberately injuring an opponent and, although there is no evidence of players discarded by Northampton for unruly behaviour on the pitch, Ernie Islip at Huddersfield and Tommy Black at Arsenal were both later unceremoniously kicked out after incurring Chapman's wrath. While at Northampton he told the local Boys Brigade team: 'Never do anything on the field to an opponent that will later prevent your meeting him in the street or in church later and shaking hands with him.'

At the Championship reception he spoke with pride about the behaviour of his team on away trips. Hoteliers would comment about 'the nice, quiet, gentlemanly lot of fellows they were'. In 1925, in his first programme notes after arriving at Highbury, Chapman spelled out the values he sought in a player: 'to employ, without exception, the very best type of player to represent the club ... above all, he must be a gentleman both on and off the field.'

On the pitch his innovative tactics, especially the deeper positioning of players, had proved to be successful. In order to play the system well however, Chapman needed the right players in their best positions. He had seen at first hand how individual talent could be stifled by playing players out of position, and always sought the right man for the job. He was also keen to develop local young talent and in the summer of 1909 organised trials in Northampton for promising youngsters.

Finally, Chapman was keen to promote the game at large and to look after the paying public. Ground improvements were made to the County Ground in the form of extra terracing and carpeting in the stand for FA Cup-ties!

Chapman remained at Northampton for five years. Having won the Southern League in his second season, they finished fourth, second and third thereafter, by which time the Cobblers' tag of being the joke team in the league had been laid to rest. Northampton also acquired a strong Cup tradition. In 1909 they took Second Division Derby County to a replay, and a full house of almost 15,000 saw the first game at the County Ground. The following year the Cobblers caused a shock by winning 1-0 at First Division Sheffield Wednesday in a replay, before losing to another top-flight club, Nottingham Forest, after another replay.

The finest Cup result of Chapman's time at Northampton came in 1911 with a 1-1 draw at Newcastle, the FA Cup holders. Near the end, Fred 'Fanny' Walden even hit the Magpies' crossbar. Northampton, in debt to the tune of £4,000, sold their home rights to the replay. This netted them over £1,000 but upset many of their followers. A penalty ended their Cup hopes and Newcastle went on to reach their fifth Cup final in seven years. In 1912 the team enjoyed their longest run, reaching the third round, the equivalent of the modern fifth round, before losing to Fulham of Division Two.

Chapman's reputation grew year upon year, and in May 1912 he was offered the position of secretary-manager of Leeds City, then struggling in Division Two. His managerial apprenticeship was over. He had made Northampton Town one of the finest non-league sides in the country. Gate receipts had trebled in his time, and in 1912 a profit of some £1,000 was announced. Northampton, however, had its limitations. It was predominantly a rugby union town and the football club relied heavily on support from the surrounding county area. The club also had its financial constraints and could not afford to sign the kind of player required to take the club into the Football League. The signing of Lloyd-Davies in 1907 had almost bankrupted the club, and in Chapman's time there would be no further 'big' signings.

It is not known whether Herbert Chapman was under contract at Northampton, but he appears to have left the club with their good wishes. The *Northampton Independent* praised his achievements: 'As a team manager, Mr Chapman has been strikingly successful, and he unites with his keen business abilities a winning personality that makes him very popular. A fine judge of a player, a skilled diplomatist, he has secured many good players for Northampton at very little cost to the club, whilst his tact and cheery optimism has resulted in his getting the best out of the men at his command.'

At Leeds City he found himself pitched into a nightmarish situation, and it raises the question why he would sacrifice the relative security of Northampton for the can of worms facing him at Elland Road. The club – which had only been formed in 1904 and joined the Football League a year later – had finished next to bottom in Division Two in 1912 and therefore had to apply for re-election.

What is particularly surprising is that Chapman joined Leeds before the outcome of their application for re-election, and he was forced to campaign vigorously on their behalf. Fortunately, from his point of view, Leeds obtained 33 votes, which was enough. Fellow Division Two candidates Gainsborough Trinity obtained only nine, which was not. Their place in the Football League was taken by Lincoln City, with 27 votes.

A month before Chapman's arrival the club's dire financial plight had come to a head when the bank called in the club's £7,000 overdraft. Although chairman Norris Hepworth, of the famous local clothier, made a large cash injection, a receiver was appointed to run the club's affairs.

More trouble arose in October when Leeds incurred a fine for making illegal payments to three players signed by Chapman in the summer.

This may have been an administrative error or an under-the-table scam, but either way it is extraordinary that someone with Chapman's experience should have allowed it to happen. The Football League commission, 'while finding it necessary to admonish Mr Chapman and two of the players ... also recognised the straight-forwardness of Mr Chapman in reporting the matter ... which is greatly to his credit, and that of his club.' The League were to be less forgiving some years later.

On the field Chapman – with seven new players at his disposal – transformed the Leeds team, which finished sixth (one place behind Huddersfield). Elland Road crowds rose from an average 7,500 to 13,500, the second highest in the division, and the club was able to announce a profit of £400. Among his early innovations, Chapman introduced regular golf sessions for the players and team-talks.

According to Stephen Studd's *Herbert Chapman: Football Emperor*, the idea for team talks came to Chapman on a train returning from an away match, when an argument broke out between the players over a game of cards. Chapman's thinking was that players ought to put as much effort into improving their football as they put into their cards. Chapman describes this in *Herbert Chapman on Football*: 'I thought it would be a good idea to get the players together every week to discuss the good and the poor points of play the previous week. My first experiment in this was at Leeds. Each Saturday morning when we were at home, the men were instructed to attend one of the hotels in the centre of the city. A light lunch was followed by a talk amongst ourselves.' Studd adds: 'Chapman was asking his players to contribute to a joint effort, to become more involved with each other as a unit. It was an appeal to intelligence as well as physical skill, and it had the effect of boosting self-respect, fostering a sense of loyalty, and raising a player's status above that of a mere paid servant.'

What we now think of as normal was revolutionary at the time. In *Alive and Kicking*, former Everton captain TG Jones described the situation at Goodison Park in the late 1930s: 'We had no coaches or anything like that. We had a wonderful old chap as trainer, a fella called Harry Cooke, but he never discussed football very much with us. He was simply a man who looked after the gear and saw everything was all right. As regards coaching, it was done from player to player. We had no manager as such. The so-called manager, a man named Theo Kelly, was really a secretary and not a manager. The players used to manage themselves. Whenever we called a meeting – we didn't have them very often, to be quite honest – it was all discussed then, or if you were on the ball they'd all be telling you what to do.'

England international Tommy Lawton played either side of World War II. In *Alive and Kicking* he says: '"Oh, team talks?" They just said, "Well you know what to do, don't ya?" You'd say, "Yeah".'

Chapman and Leeds did even better in 1913-14, finishing fourth, just two points off promotion. Attendances were up, too, and Chapman was weaving his magic to good effect. He felt that the main reason for not gaining promotion was a lack of strength in depth, and remedied this by recruiting his former Tottenham colleague Jack Chaplin as assistant trainer, with responsibility for the reserve team. (Years later, at Huddersfield, Chapman made the reserves a top priority and reaped the rewards.)

The outbreak of war in 1914 skewed Leeds' progress. Gates slumped by more than half. Many supporters shunned the game, at Leeds and elsewhere, believing that sporting competition had no place in wartime. At Elland Road, the financial situation, always fragile, deteriorated further and the team finished fifteenth.

Chapman stayed on. Along with other Yorkshire and North Midlands clubs, Leeds played in a wartime regional league. When players started being conscripted, City were forced to use guest players from other clubs. One 'guest' attracted by Chapman was Aston Villa forward Clem Stephenson, an FA Cup winner with the Midland club in 1913.

In 1916 Chapman took a senior managerial job in a local ammunitions factory but continued to advise Leeds City on financial and other matters. He returned to Elland Road in the summer of 1918, but three months later resigned to take up a full-time managerial position at an oil refinery in Selby.

League soccer recommenced in September 1919 and within weeks Leeds City were embroiled in another crisis. Allegations were made of illegal payments to players during the War. When a joint FA/Football League inquiry demanded to inspect the club's books, the club refused to produce them. As already stated, Leeds City were expelled from the League and a ban imposed on the club's directors, plus Chapman and his wartime deputy George Cripps. Having been formally reprimanded for financial impropriety in 1912, Chapman can hardly complain of victimisation when accused of similar wrong-doing seven years later.

Chapman continued to work at the oil refinery, but had to endure the stain on his character. This he must have found hard, considering his high principles and church-going morals. Late in 1920 the Selby works closed down and Chapman was out of a job. There seemed little hope of work in football unless he could get the ban lifted.

In January 1921 Huddersfield Town were seeking to employ an assistant to Ambrose Langley, and Chapman's fine record at Northampton and nearby Leeds made him a strong candidate. They offered him the job and this encouraged him to clear his name with football's governing bodies. This he did, though again the circumstances are unclear.

At Huddersfield Town's board meeting on 1 February 1921 it was agreed that Herbert Chapman would be the new Assistant Manager at £10 per week, £1 more than Langley's wage! In addition, Chapman would receive bonuses at the discretion of the board. The minutes report his duties: 'To have control of players and discharge all such other duties as the board may direct. The whole of the duties to be carried out in conjunction with the present manager Mr A Langley.' If Langley had not got the message by now, he soon did when Chapman was invited to attend board meetings.

Chapman and Langley probably knew each other. Langley had played alongside Chapman's brother Harry at Sheffield Wednesday almost twenty years earlier. However, contemporary newspapers say little about the pair's relationship.

A string of bad results in February saw Town slip to nineteenth place in Division One and relegation looked an increasing threat. The pressure on Langley was growing, although with Chapman supposedly helping out with team matters, one wonders why the new man did not make greater impact.

Chapman discussed with the board the question of possible new signings and it was minuted that he identified a number of players, including Bullock of Bury, Puddefoot of West Ham, Wilson of Tottenham and Blair of Everton. According to the late Dick Parker, a Huddersfield Town director at the time, Chapman put a strong case to the board for the purchase of the Aston Villa star Clem Stephenson: 'You have talented, mostly young players – they need a general to lead them, Clem Stephenson is that man and I think we can get him.'

It was common knowledge that all was not well between Stephenson and Aston Villa. The player insisted on living in his native North East and only travelling to Birmingham on matchdays. When Villa, struggling in the League, went out of the FA Cup, several clubs were alerted to the situation. According to legend, Chapman, the master tactician, anticipated events by arranging to meet Stephenson at Leeds on his way home from Birmingham. Press reports of the time say that Chapman agreed that Stephenson could continue to live in his home village of Seaton Delaval in Northumberland and a deal was struck. Town chairman Joe Barlow was quoted as saying, 'we have gone for the best and got him'.

Villa, the FA Cup holders and one of England's top clubs, were happy to receive £4,000, close to the British record transfer fee of £4,600, for a 31-year-old player whose reluctance to move to the Midlands had put him at odds with the club's directors.

He had signed for Villa in 1910, as horse-racing fan Clem remembered it, 'the day Jenkinstown won the Grand National'. By 1912 he had established himself in the first team, where he stayed for the next nine years, until Huddersfield came calling.

In March 1912 the Aston Villa *News and Record* wrote 'Clem ... has made considerable headway in the football world, not only as a player but also in the good graces of the critical crowd who assemble week by week at Villa Park. It did not take good judges very long to see that Stephenson had football in him, and it is equally certain that his sojourn in the Midlands has developed his natural talents to a considerable degree. Possessing plenty of pace and a sound knowledge of the game, he has developed fine shooting power, and there can be no denying his unbounded enthusiasm and earnest desire to do his best for the club of his adoption. If Stephenson continues to improve as he has done during the present season, he will make a big name for himself. That he has gifts beyond the ordinary is unquestionable, and he seems to be a level-headed young man who is not likely to be spoiled by the voice of flattery. We have great hopes of Stephenson. He has the ability and the brains – the rest remains with himself.'

Contemporary reports describe Clem as a great dribbler, passer and schemer. *Athletic News* in February 1920 waxed lyrical: 'There is no inside left who accomplishes so much with so little show as Stephenson. He is a one-touch artist and avoids artistry. There is nothing theatrical about his footwork but it is effective to a high degree.'

Interestingly, photographs of Clem in his Town shirt show a man with a face older than his years and what would now bluntly be described as a beer belly. Yet in his youth he had been a renowned sprinter.

Players in Stephenson's mould are hard to find in the modern game, but were more common in the immediate post-1945 era and Raich Carter and Wilf Mannion come to mind. One recent player who might come into the same bracket is Paul Gascoigne. At his best in the early 1990s Gascoigne had superb dribbling skills and could play the killer pass to set up goals for his colleagues, a talent that Stephenson had in abundance. Gazza also possessed a strong physical challenge, something that many contemporary pen pictures of Stephenson seem to mention.

Stephenson had a hard upbringing in Northumberland and had been a miner before joining Aston Villa. With his knowledge of mining, Chapman admired the strength and fighting qualities of men who had spent time down the pit. Clem had played for junior teams such as New

Delaval Villa, West Stanley, a club disbanded after a mining disaster wiped out many of its players, and Blyth Spartans, before joining Villa. He had won two FA Cup winners medals, in 1913, and (against Town) in 1920, but had by that time never been capped his country. His only representative appearances had been for the Football League – in 1914 against the Scottish League (2-3) and the Southern League (2-1), and in 1919 against the Irish League (2-2).

Stephenson's arrival at Leeds Road caught the imagination of Town's supporters and 25,000 turned up for his home debut – a 1-0 win over Aston Villa! His presence rubbed off on those lacking confidence around him, to such an extent that Town won seven of the last ten games. A final position of seventeenth suggests a dice with death but, in fact, Town finished thirteen points clear of the relegated clubs.

Stephenson's family, represented by his grandson – also named Clem – believe that the great man moved his family to Huddersfield soon after signing for Town. His new club had removed whatever it was that had been a sticking point for Clem at Aston Villa. As Town would have been unable to afford a signing-on fee to Stephenson, an under-the-counter payment may have helped smooth the decision to move. If true, it is impossible to resist the conclusion that Chapman was once again getting his fingers dirty.

Three days after Stephenson's debut, the board heard that the transfer had been successfully completed and that a further signing – of Sam Wadsworth from Nelson for £1,600 – had also been finalised. At the same board meeting, the chairman reported that Ambrose Langley had informed him that he 'had not been comfortable for some time and if the directors thought that it would be in the interests of the club that he should cancel his agreement'. Langley expressed himself happy to have his contract paid up. It was decided to offer him £500. At the next board meeting a week later it was reported that Langley's resignation had been accepted and that he had left with a £550 pay-off. Chapman was immediately appointed secretary-manager. According to Stephen Studd in *Herbert Chapman: Football Emperor*, 'Langley left for Sheffield where he ran a pub.'

The signing of Sam Wadsworth was scarcely less crucial than that of Stephenson. The former Blackburn reserve left-winger had seen active service in the Western Front trenches. Shrapnel had shattered his left ankle. His army doctor persuaded a traumatised Sam that his ankle would heal and could become stronger than his right one. On his return home, Blackburn made it clear he was surplus to requirements and he joined Nelson, another Lancashire side, and it was while playing for them in the

Central League (possibly against Huddersfield), that he was spotted by Chapman. With Bullock's knee injury looking unlikely to mend, Sam was given his chance at left-back for the last six games of the season. Within a year he was selected for the England team and appeared in an FA Cup final for Huddersfield.

Following that international debut in 1922, the *Examiner* reported a promising display: 'Wadsworth was not only the surest, safest and most accomplished back on the field but he was incontestably the cleverest debutant of the season. This Darwen man is well built and strongly knit, his kick is strong and true, well timed and adroitly placed. He never failed as far as I saw and never made a mistake. His intuition of the run of the game is excellent and as he has shown he has the right temperament for the big occasion he is likely to win further honours.'

A few weeks later the same correspondent glowed about Sam's performance in his second international, a 0-1 loss to Scotland: 'Wadsworth must be put down as the discovery of the season, the legitimate successor of Jesse Pennington [a regular England full-back between 1907-20]; throughout he played with a coolness of a veteran and the confidence of a master.'

Wadsworth would remain a fixture in the left-back position until 1929, when he moved to Burnley at the age of 33, after almost 300 games for Town. A confident, composed defender who timed his tackles to perfection and always used the ball well, Sam was considered to be England's top left-back between 1923 and 1926. But with only three or four international games played per season, he won a measly nine caps. Cartoons of the time depict him with a large protruding nose and a thatch of blond hair. Sam appeared in the 1922 Cup final but would miss the 1928 final against his former club, Blackburn, after being injured in the semi-final against Sheffield United. Sam was very fond of his terrier dog and it used to accompany him to training, where it would race up and down the cinder track trying to keep pace with his master.

By April 1921, we find early evidence of Chapman exercising his influence over the directors. The board minutes record: 'it was agreed that in future any player approaching a Director upon any club business whatever he [the player] should be informed he must first put all requests or discuss any matters relating to the club's affairs with the manager.'

It is not recorded what incident prompted this, but it appears that Chapman was determined that players and directors knew who was in charge. Soon afterwards the minutes state: 'all players' agreements would in future contain a clause prohibiting them becoming a license holder for the sale of intoxicating drinks'. Whether players wanting to become publicans prompted this action is not known. However, later, in December 1924, Billy Watson's request to accept a position as manager of the Adega Billiard Hall in Huddersfield was refused by the board. At a meeting to discuss Chapman's recommendations for players' contracts for the following, 1921-22 season, an interesting issue arises. Watson, Cawthorne and Islip's terms were all subject to a clause that they 'must reside in Huddersfield as soon as a suitable house can be found'. Chapman had clearly insisted on the matter, and again the mind turns to Clem Stephenson, who had left Aston Villa because, amongst other reasons, he was determined to live in Northumberland. Today, his grandson and daughter-in-law believe Clem did move to the Huddersfield area soon after signing for Town; otherwise, we might suggest, Chapman would have faced obstacles in demanding that other players live locally.

At that same board meeting, in April 1921, Chapman reported that an invitation had been received from Olympique Paris for Huddersfield to compete in a four-team tournament in Paris in May. England were the undisputed kings of world football at this time and English club sides were in great demand on the Continent as Europe began to recover from the Great War. Chapman was instructed to negotiate a participation fee of £400, plus a percentage of the gate receipts, and a week later he reported back that the fee had been agreed and that Town would receive 10 per cent of the takings.

The importance of the occasion is that it marked Town's first official trip abroad. It must have been an adventure for the players and officials, who took 24 hours to reach the French capital by train and boat. Those players who had fought, not least Wadsworth, must have had mixed emotions, as it would have been their first crossing of the English Channel since the armistice. Town played the host club and another top Paris side, Red Star, as well as fellow English club, Second Division Clapton Orient. Town won all three games, enjoyed a couple of days' sightseeing, and returned home with a bronze lion trophy. Chapman henceforth became a firm advocate of foreign tours, both for the publicity and profits they generated and for the experience gained against different playing styles.

It needs reminding that all this rush of activity happened within three months of Chapman's appointment. He evidently swept through the club like a whirlwind, penetrating every aspect of its affairs.

On his return from Paris he now had to prepare for his first full season and set to work with his backroom staff. He had recruited his former Leeds City trainer, Jack Chaplin, from Bristol Rovers and now strengthened his team by appointing Walter Balmer – the former Everton and England full-back – as coach, and former Town and Sunderland forward

Jack Foster as reserve-team coach and scout. The hefty fee paid out for Clem Stephenson meant the club could not afford any other big signings and would have to rely on scouts unearthing new talent and the reserve and third teams producing top-quality young players. Chapman, understanding their importance, took a keen interest in the scouting and the progress of the junior sides. The directors seemed suitably impressed; at a May board meeting they agreed to Chapman receiving a bonus for the previous season of £65. A month later his salary was increased to £750 *per annum*, a 50 per cent increase, plus bonuses. Four months into the job, in other words, he had earned his first pay-rise.

Chapman's trainer, Jack Chaplin, had an interesting background. One of eight children, he was the grandson of the lodge-keeper of Glamis Castle – the ancestral home of the Earls of Strathmore and Kinghorne and the childhood home of the woman later to become the wife of King George VI and the mother of Queen Elizabeth II. According to Jack's grand-daughter, Pat Armer, Jack named all the houses he lived in 'Glamis'. A useful full-back, he had two playing spells with Dundee, his hometown club, and three years with Tottenham between 1905 and 1908. During his second period at Dundee he was selected to represent the Scottish League against the Irish League. In 1910 he was tempted back to England by First Division Manchester City, but a serious injury cut short his career after only fifteen games with City. Then came the defining moment of his football career: in 1913 he joined his former Tottenham colleague Herbert Chapman at Leeds City as assistant trainer.

The two men hit it off, and Jack progressed to first-team trainer and assistant manager before football ceased. During the War he became a sergeant in the Royal Army Medical Corps, based at Leeds, where he met and married Eva Wallwork. On the return to peacetime he became trainer at Bristol Rovers, and Chapman wrote a glowing reference: 'He comes from a footballing family, has the greatest ambition for success, and can undertake and is master of any department in connection with spotting of footballers and football training, and no doubt his influence and example upon young players has a great effect.'

Chaplin had two younger brothers who also played first-class football at full-back. Alex – or Sandy as he was known – was ten years younger and played over 250 games for Fulham between 1919 and 1926. Sandy's family actually lived in Craven Cottage for a time. George, six years younger than Jack, won a Scottish cap before the War with Dundee and went on to play over 200 games for Bradford City and Coventry. Less commendably, he was a central figure in the Coventry bribery scandal in 1920 which resulted in him being condemned by a Football League enquiry for inducing Bury players to throw a match which Coventry won to avoid relegation. George Chaplin was banned from football for life in 1923. Brother Jack, now aged 40, was about to enter the most satisfying chapter of his career. Chapman knew and trusted Chaplin from their years together and relied upon the Scot to prepare his men for each game they played.

Finances were helped by record season ticket sales. Over £1,100 was raised, much of this from three guinea (£3.15) season tickets for the central main stand. Ground improvements were also undertaken in the close season with the terrace opposite the main stand heightened with extra ash banking to accommodate 24,000 spectators. In 1946 this area was still unchanged from the 1920s and was described by visitors to Leeds Road's one and only international match as a 'steeply, sloping unterraced top half where fans stood on broken bricks and tightly folded newspapers to keep on an even keel'. The press box was relocated to the front of the main stand, offering a much-improved view. Chapman also arranged for the players' dressing room and recreation room to be refurbished and for the pitch to be re-turfed. The price of ground admission stayed unchanged at one shilling (5p), with boys paying sixpence (3p). The paddock was two shillings (10p), whilst the stand cost from 2s 6d (13p) for the wing sections to four shillings (20p) for the centre section. It cost eight pence (4p) to watch a reserve team game from the terraces.

Apart from a run of six straight wins in October and November, the first half of the 1921-22 season was uneventful. Chapman kept a settled side but the team found goals hard to come by. John Swann, a heavy scorer in Division Two, was not a success in the higher level, and Chapman sold him to the ex-Town boss Arthur Fairclough at Leeds United. Ernie Islip, a relative veteran at 29, moved to centre-forward but failed to score consistently.

At Christmas an 18-year-old North Easterner by the name of George Brown was given a first-team chance and scored twice on his debut at West Brom. He followed up with a goal in each of the next two games. Brown, a miner from Mickley in the Durham coalfields, had signed for £75 the previous summer after Chapman travelled to the North East to meet the boy and his family. In *Chapman on Football*, Herbert relates how: 'After speaking to his mother I set out to find him, having been told that he had gone to the pit with a barrow to fetch some coal. I met a lad wheeling a barrow in the village street. "Are you George Brown?" I asked.' He was, and when the youth heard that Herbert Chapman wanted him to play for Huddersfield, 'I remember how he dropped the barrow. In fact, he was so eager to be off that he would have left it in the

street if I had not insisted that he should take the coals to his mother.'
George – later nicknamed Bomber because of his right-footed bullet
shooting which was his speciality – would go on to become the club's
record all-time goalscorer and play for England.

For the moment, Brown was back in the reserves when Town's FA
Cup campaign commenced in January 1922. Islip netted one of the goals
in the first round as Town came from 0-2 down at Burnley's Turf Moor
to force a replay. Burnley were the reigning League champions and had
gone 30 games undefeated. Their unbeaten home record stretched back
to August 1920 and they were stunned when Billy Watson snatched a last-
minute equaliser to set up a replay on the Wednesday afternoon.

Afternoon Cup replays were the bane of factory managers' lives, prior
to the introduction of floodlights in the 1950s and 60s. Supporters were
desperate to see their heroes' progress on the Cup trail and would con-
jure up any excuse to skip an afternoon's work in the mill or factory and
get to the game.

But this was a new phenomenon in Huddersfield – it was the first ever
midweek Cup replay – and after the thrilling comeback at Turf Moor
thousands of Town fans were determined not to miss out. The *Examiner*
noted: 'It is a long time since so much public interest was displayed in
footballers as has been the case in the last few days. From Saturday until
today the points of the tussle at Turf Moor have been the chief theme in
the area. That being the case, little wonder that further applications for
permission to be absent from work today were made yesterday and that
several workshops were closed down since noon today.'

At one engineering firm, Messrs J Blakeborough of Woodhouse
Works, Brighouse, there were so many applications for the afternoon off
that the company warned would-be absentees that they faced a three-
week suspension if they deserted their posts. On a wet afternoon, over
35,000 Leeds Road spectators went home drenched but happy as Town
overcame deep mud to win 3-2. It is unknown whether Blakeborough's
carried out its threat.

A second round tie at Third Division Brighton was no cakewalk. The
south coast club had knocked out First Division Sheffield United, and
Town needed a further replay to progress. The pattern was repeated in
round three against First Division Blackburn, and with three Wednesday
afternoon replays in six weeks the mill owners and businessmen of the
town were heartily sick of football.

Over 45,000 watched Town dispose of Third Division Millwall in the
quarter-finals and set up a semi-final with Notts County from Division
Two at Turf Moor. Town prevailed 3-1, but bad luck might have cost

them the tie. Town's lucky mascot, a stuffed donkey, caught fire. Happily, the flames were doused and supporters were relieved with the news that the donkey would be fit for the final.

Chapman prepared his side for the Stamford Bridge final with Preston North End meticulously. This would be the last final before the opening of the new Wembley Stadium. Circumstance decreed that the two teams met in the League the Saturday before the final. Town had won only one league game in fourteen during the Cup run, and had slipped uncomfortably low in the table. Preston were no great shakes themselves in the League. As the teams kicked off for that dress rehearsal, Huddersfield had just 33 points and Preston 35 – with two further fixtures to complete after the final – and neither was safe. A Cup final victory could, therefore, have been undermined by relegation, in which case Huddersfield's triple-triumph would probably never have happened.

Huddersfield did more than just claim the psychological high ground by beating Preston 6-0; they also inched two points nearer safety. Preston had saved their best form for the Cup, beating top division Newcastle, Arsenal and Spurs to reach the final, but their away form was dreadful – they had gone thirteen away league games without scoring a goal!

Chapman took his players to Blackpool for almost two weeks before the final. On their way to London their train stopped at Preston, and into the adjoining carriage stepped their opponents.

Advertisements from the time say supporters would have paid £1 6s 6d (£1.32) for a return train fare to London, leaving Huddersfield at 5am and returning from London at midnight. Pathe News clips of the day show Huddersfield fans being transported from a London rail terminus, possibly St Pancras, to Chelsea in a open-topped motor charabanc or 'sharra' as it was colloquially called. This was an early form of the motor-bus with bench-seats that could accommodate approximately 30 passengers. For 42 shillings (£2.10) you could – in addition to your train fare – have a charabanc collect you from the station and return you to it after the match, a sight-seeing tour of the capital, plus breakfast, dinner and tea. The fans depicted on Pathe News are all dressed up in suits with collar and tie and wearing caps. They appear in happy mood and many have wooden rattles, of the kind which survived into the 1960s. The newsreel shows the charabanc passing the Cenotaph in Whitehall, at which point the supporters doffed their caps for the dead of the Great War – which had ended barely four years earlier.

Tickets for the final cost three shillings (15p) for the uncovered terrace, to anything from five shillings (25p) to one guinea (£1.05) for covered seats in the stand. Silent Pathe News clips of the game were filmed from high up on Chelsea's terracing, so it is hard to pick out much detail. But newspaper accounts described the final as a huge anti-climax, settled by a dubious penalty from Billy Smith – consolation for the man who had missed the 1920 final through suspension.

The match was a bad-tempered affair with constant fouling and bickering, which resulted in a subsequent reprimand for both clubs from the FA. The crucial goal came after 67 minutes when Preston defender Tom Hamilton toppled Billy Smith. Newsreels later shown in cinemas upheld Preston's complaint that the foul had been committed outside the penalty area. Smith picked himself up to score, despite the gamesmanship of Preston's bespectacled goalkeeper, JF Mitchell, who jumped up and down and gesticulated wildly as Billy ran up to take the kick. Mitchell's antics caused the FA to change the rules whereby, in future, goalkeepers had to remain motionless until the penalty-kick was taken. What is also noticeable on the old Pathe News clips, is the defensive formation of both teams, with two full-backs patrolling and no sign of a defensive centre-half.

Sixty years later in *Alive and Kicking*, Huddersfield fan John Lee reminisced about his day out: 'We'd never been to London before so we had the morning just looking round, before the match, with our mouths open. We'd never seen anything like it before. Then we caught a tram up to the Stamford Bridge Ground. And we were amazed at the size of it. It was a real eye-opener.'

The attendance of 53,710 was well below capacity – the 1921 final at Stamford Bridge had attracted 72,000 – and at the time this was attributed to high ticket prices. It cost three shillings (15p) to stand on the Chelsea terraces when it cost only one shilling to stand at Leeds Road. Another factor is that a Cup final staged at a club ground lacked the wider appeal of famous neutral venues – Crystal Palace and, later, Wembley.

Both finalists needed to keep an eye out for another football result that day. As was normal at that time, a full league programme went ahead alongside the Cup final, and the result of 21st-placed Bradford City's home game with Arsenal was crucial. Had City won this, their penultimate match, they would have closed to within one point of Huddersfield and Preston, in which case post-final celebrations would have been muted – on the part of manager and players, if not supporters.

To round off a cracking day, Bradford City lost 0-2. They would, in fact, lose their last five games, and join Manchester United in Division Two. That allowed Chapman and his players to celebrate without thought of having to prepare for Monday night's League game against Middlesbrough which might otherwise have proved vital.

Back in Huddersfield, a crowd of around 1,500 assembled outside the Ramsden Street headquarters of the *Huddersfield Examiner* to await the result, whilst at Leeds Road several thousand watched the reserves play Liverpool's. The crowd threw their hats or caps into the air when news of the result came through.

The players obviously stayed down south, for it was not until Monday afternoon that the team's train – bedecked with the club's colours – steamed into Huddersfield station. The size of the crowd to greet them was put at 30,000. Pathe News cameras were again in attendance, showing an open-topped Corporation bus decorated in blue and white bunting and bearing the legends 'Bravo Town' and 'A Victory well earned'. The bus was preceded by a marching band, and followed in procession by a motor bus and a charabanc.

The open-top bus conveyed the team to the Town Hall for an official reception. Captain Tommy Wilson, in a black bowler hat, thrust the trophy aloft amid unforgettable scenes, with Chapman alongside him clutching the base of the trophy under his arm. The FA Cup had come to the York-shire town for the first and only time.

The team even had its own Cup final song, 'Oh! It's Our Night Out Again Tonight' (words and music reproduced on pages 71-73), which was published in sheet music form by Northern Music, priced sixpence. The words and music were written by Tom B Newsome and the cover of the sheet music featured cameo photos of the FA Cup final team. The *Huddersfield Examiner* reported that it was first played by the band at the semi-final at Burnley.

Another song, 'Smile Awhile' – popular in the music halls of the era – was adopted as the supporters' song and was sung on the terraces and played by the band for over 40 years. The words changed from time to time, and it later became known as the 'Town Anthem'. According to long-serving Town fan Richard Monteith, his father taught him the words that were sung back in the 1920s:

There's a team that is dear to its followers,
They call them the bright blue and white
They're a team of renown, they're the pride of the town
And the game of football is their delight.

All the while upon the field of play
Thousands loudly cheer them on their way
Often you can hear them say
Who can beat the Town* today?

Then the bell will ring so merrily
Every goal will be a memory
So Town play up and bring the Cup
Back to Huddersfield.

*   Richard believes that in the early 1920s many used the expression 'the Babes' instead of 'Town'.

Extraordinary as it might seen, Huddersfield had a league game that same night, which as it happened was unimportant, but might so easily have been critical. Following a civic welcome, the players headed straight for Leeds Road to take on Middlesbrough. During play the Cup was perched proudly at the front of the directors' box. At half-time it was carried around the perimeter of the pitch by assistant secretary Harry Beever, to the delight of the 29,000 crowd.

The club arranged for each player to be presented with a gold watch (value £20) to commemorate their success, and additional Cup medals were purchased for trainer Jack Chaplin and goalkeeper Edwin Davis, who had played in every Cup-tie bar the final and semi-final.

The souvenir programme published for the Middlesbrough game gives a fascinating insight into life in Huddersfield in the 1920s. It cost tuppence (1p) and comprised twenty pages, largely filled with head and shoulder photographs of the Cup final heroes, plus advertisements. One page was devoted to Middlesbrough and their players' pen pictures, but coverage of the Cup final itself was restricted to one small paragraph: 'it was a great victory, and our boys played a great game. They are worthy of the highest honours; we are proud of you! Huddersfield Town's history is very short, but it has been romantic. Saturday crowned the work of all. Three cheers for the Town. Hip, Hip, Hurrah!'

The adverts were plentiful – The Hippodrome Music Hall (twice nightly shows 6.40 and 8.40), and The Picture House (continuous from 2.30 to 10.30) with musical selections played by the Grand Organist LH England, Mus. Bac. (Oxon). For those with less high-brow tastes, the 'Adega' was offering six full-sized billiards tables and the 'Best Draught Bass in town'.

Food establishments were well represented and Town's patrons were encouraged to 'Eat Gothard's tripe'. The club's 'official caterer', AC Thompson, offered 'Good Teas during or after the match in the Tea Room under the stand at moderate charges'. Supporters were also urged to call at LN Wilson's shop, 137 Leeds Road (Opposite the Gasworks) for all well-known brands of Cigarettes and Tobaccos.

The team had not yet exhausted its haul of trophies for the season. Ten days after the Cup final, Huddersfield (as winners) beat Liverpool (League champions) 1-0 at neutral Old Trafford in the FA Charity Shield. The FA, in view of the reprimand handed out to Town and Preston after the unruly Cup final, thenceforth temporarily abandoned the Champions v Cup winners format. For the next three years the Charity Shield would be contested by Professionals v Amateurs. In consequence, Huddersfield never contested the Shield again.

Huddersfield's success meant that the club was heavily in demand for overseas tours and, once the last domestic fixtures had been wrapped up, the club embarked on a trip to Copenhagen. The club's coffers benefited to the tune of over £1,000.

The board minutes from the 1921-22 season show ample evidence of Herbert Chapman's growing power and influence at the club. At the start of the season Chapman made recommendations regarding complimentary tickets, with local schools and the town's Rugby League side being amongst the beneficiaries.

More importantly, it was agreed by the board that team matters would not be discussed at directors' meetings. This was a radical change as, up to that point, the team had been selected by the directors and was recorded in the minutes. On 4 October 1921, however, it was minuted that, 'the selection of teams to be left to the manager and the directors, as far as possible, to be informed each week the team before it appears in the press.'

Chapman held strong views on this subject and later wrote this in *Herbert Chapman on Football*: 'Thirty years ago all directors joined in picking the team and no-one today seems to be bold enough to suggest that the system is out of date and should be scrapped. In my opinion the club manager ought to pick the team. I would go further and say that he is the only official qualified to do so. If I were a director I should take this view. If the manager was not prepared to accept this responsibility I would have no option but to decide that he was not worthy of the job. In all the jobs I have held I have accepted the responsibility of choosing the team, it is not one, in my opinion, which can be shared. In every case too I have been loyally supported by my directors and I recognise that this has largely contributed to the success I have achieved.'

As the new, 1922-23, season approached, Chapman sensed he was not far from having a side capable of challenging for the League title. During the previous season the club had made the Cup a top priority, once they had steered past the tough first round obstacle of Burnley, which coincided with their losing touch with the league leaders. Chapman was still on the look-out for players to strengthen his team, however, and top of his list were a goalkeeper and a centre-forward capable of scoring twenty goals or more a season. As Town's share of the £31,000 FA Cup receipts had yielded unexpected riches, Chapman was permitted to seek the players he wanted.

First stop was trainer Jack Chaplin's former club, Bristol Rovers, where his recommendations – David Steele and Joe Walter – were signed for a combined fee of £2,500. Steele was another former miner, from the Lanarkshire coalfields, who had earned a reputation as a hard and tireless wing-half. Within a year he would become Town's first Scottish international. Photographs of Steele give an impression of a cold-eyed assassin, which conforms to the image portrayed in many contemporary match reports.

Joe Walter was a nifty right-winger who would play in half Town's games over the next two years without ever really convincing anyone that he was the best available in that position.

The goalkeeping problem was resolved with the signing of First Division Oldham's Ted Taylor. Chapman hoped to keep Athletic in the dark about his interest in Taylor, in case they refused to release him. Oldham had another goalie that the wily Chapman knew they rated highly, so Chapman hatched a plan and travelled to Oldham in a taxi with Town director Dick Parker, who later related a version of the story: 'He [Chapman] turned to me in the taxi and said he would not negotiate for Taylor at all, would pretend he knew nothing about him, and would go all out for the other goalkeeper.'

The plan worked like a dream. Oldham's directors were adamant that their top man was not for sale, so after several hours of fruitless negotiations Chapman asked: 'All right then, what about this other chap, Taylor?' A deal was struck and Chapman got the man he wanted. The goalie that Taylor replaced, 37-year-old Sandy Mutch, joined Newcastle for £850 and was unlucky to miss United's 1924 Cup final victory over Aston Villa after twisting a knee a week before the game.

Contemporary photographs of Ted Taylor, with his slicked back hair and matinee idol looks, bear a slight resemblance to Rudolf Valentino or a young Peter O'Toole. He stood only 5ft 8½in, but was one of the outstanding goalkeepers of the era. He was 35 years old when he joined Town, for £1,950, but had played just nine games for his new club when he was called up for the first of his eight England caps. A brave goalkeeper in an age when the laws of the game offered the union of custodians little protection, he was an important part in the triple title-winning team, despite suffering a broken leg at Maine Road in October 1924.

It wasn't long before Chapman made another inspired signing. Charlie Wilson arrived at Leeds Road in November 1922. He had spent three seasons at Tottenham immediately after the War but could never command a regular place, despite scoring at a good rate. He had joined Spurs after being demobbed in 1918 and played six wartime games that season, although for some unknown reasons he shrouded himself in secrecy. In four of those games he played under the name of 'C Williams', being described as a 'colt from the midlands', and in another game hid behind the pseudonym of 'C Forshaw'. Only in the sixth game did he finally take the field as Charlie Wilson.

Chapman gambled £3,000 on the belief that bustling Wilson would score goals, and the player's 62 goals in 107 games were a major component in the first two championship wins. In fact he top-scored in each of his three seasons with the club. A cigarette card of the time portrays a player with a confident, large, gap-toothed grin. Wilson stood only 5ft 8in tall, and did not belong to the 'target man' school of centre-forwards. He was more suited to deft flicks to keep his fellow forwards on the move, not to mention an eye for a goal.

In addition to Sandy Mutch, three more of the 1922 Cup winning side departed from Leeds Road during the course of the next season. Full-back James Wood, veteran of some 150 games, signed for Blackpool. Wing-half Charlie Slade, another player from the pre-War days, joined Middlesbrough for £1,500, only to suffer relegation in 1924. The balding inside-forward Frank Mann, a regular goalscorer before the War, but less consistent afterwards, moved to Manchester United for £1,800 where, despite being the wrong side of 30, he helped United back to Division One in 1925.

Inconsistent home form, coupled with injuries to Stephenson and Smith, hampered Town's league form and a mid-table finish looked likely until a run of six straight wins in March catapulted them into the top three. Although Town finished third, they were seven points behind Liverpool, champions for the second successive season, and never really title contenders.

The 1923 FA Cup held the lure of a place in the first Wembley final, and Huddersfield fans' hopes were high after wins over Birmingham and Millwall. But Town were held to a home draw by Bolton in round three and went out in a Burnden Park replay in front of a massive crowd of 61,000. The Trotters went on to win the first Wembley final, beating Second Division West Ham United 2-0 for the first of three Wembley triumphs in seven years. An estimated 250,000 people turned up for the first final at the new stadium, gates were broken down and at the planned kick-off time the lush turf was covered by thousands of spectators. Under the watchful eye of King George V, the police slowly but surely cleared the pitch – the final later became known as the White Horse final in memory of the mounted policeman George Scorey, who on his grey steed was largely responsible for clearing spectators off the pitch. Incredibly, no one was seriously injured but as a result of the events that day future finals were made all-ticket with a capacity under 100,000.

## Chapter 3

~ TITLE BUDS SPROUTING ~

(JULY – DECEMBER 1923)

Having lost just one of the concluding twelve matches of the 1922-23 season and finished in the dizzy heights of third in Division One, manager Herbert Chapman was even more confident that his Huddersfield Town side would be able to make a sustained challenge for the League Championship in 1923-24.

The excellent finale to the previous campaign had coincided with the departure of long-serving forward Frank Mann to Manchester United, and a prolific spell of six goals in ten games by his replacement, George Brown. That sudden transformation had gone largely unnoticed outside of Yorkshire and few pundits mentioned 'the Babes' – an alternative nickname ascribed to them by some when they joined the Football League – as championship contenders. The press favourites were reigning champions Liverpool, going for a third successive title, the two North East giants Newcastle and Sunderland, and Bolton Wanderers, winners of the first Wembley FA Cup final the previous May. Neither of the newly promoted clubs, Notts County and West Ham, were expected to be in the title hunt.

In 1923 there was no Premier League, rather a national First and Second Division, and a Third Division divided into Northern and Southern Sections. All four divisions contained 22 clubs, who played 42 league games. There were two points for a win, and one for a draw. Two teams were promoted and relegated between the top two divisions, but only the champions went up from the regional Third Divisions.

Huddersfield by now had a good blend of experienced players who had served the club since the War (Tom Wilson, Billy Smith, Billy Watson), shrewd signings by Chapman in the past two years (Ted Taylor, Sam Wadsworth, Charlie Wilson, David Steele, Ned Barkas and Clem Stephenson), and promising youngsters (George Brown and Roy Goodall). Stephenson had assumed the team captaincy from Tommy Wilson.

The summer close season for footballers in the 1920s was a relaxing time. Earning the maximum summer wage of £6 meant they didn't have to work, there was no training, and unlike the spectators who had to slave six days a week in the mill or factory, their lives were a comparative paradise. John Harding, in *Alex James: Life of a Football Legend*, writes: 'They were truly a privileged caste, leading lives that would only become the norm for working people in the 1950s.

Harding continues: '*Thomson's Weekly News* encouraged footballers to write letters for publication during the close season, telling readers what they were up to. To the weary factory-hand or miner or out-of-work mill operative it must have seemed like paradise (albeit of a distinctly male kind).'

Golf was the most popular recreation, and it is known that Herbert Chapman negotiated a club membership at Outlane Golf Club. Clem Stephenson and Billy Smith enjoyed long lazy days at the racecourse and the inevitable betting that went on there. Other players enjoyed pottering about in their gardens, fishing, decorating or spent weeks away camping. Motoring was now popular and whilst some players may have desired a motor car, very few clubs allowed their players to drive because of the risk of injury. Whether Town had a no-driving policy at this time is not known, but by 1927 it is believed that players were permitted to have motor cars. That year, according to John Harding's *Alex James: Life of a Football Legend*, Alex Jackson was involved in a serious accident on a fog-shrouded moorland in his 'dashing new sports car' that left three Preston North End players in hospital.

The Town players reported back for training on 31 July. At this time it is believed that training was carried out daily at the Leeds Road ground, although in November of that year the board minutes on the subject of 'practice grounds' request that Chapman 'make enquiries regarding the British Dyes football ground, on spare ground at the back of the Leeds Road end of the ground'.

After two weeks of fitness training, which consisted of limbering up exercises, lapping the cinder track around the pitch, and some body work with medicine balls and weights, the players were ready for the traditional public trial matches. These took place at Leeds Road on successive Saturdays before the season commenced. In the first, over 3,200 watched the Stripes, the first team, draw 3-3 with the Reds, the reserve team. Admission fees to the terraces cost tuppence (1p) and produced receipts of £114, which the club donated to local charities.

In the second trial game, a smaller crowd of 2,016 watched the Stripes overwhelm the Reds 4-0, with all the goals – two each for Charlie Wilson and Billy Smith – coming in a nine-minute second-half spell. Outside-right George Richardson limped off and was rated doubtful for the start of the league season the following Saturday.

In the meantime, team morale was boosted by a number of cricket matches against teams from the Huddersfield area. The *Examiner* reported that the 'fame of Town's cricket team was growing. Their latest victory was a crushing one over the Borough Police Force. Town bowled the "Bobbies" out for 85 and scored 136 for 2 in reply, with George Cook, a summer signing from Rotherham County, scoring 80 not out and Sam Wadsworth hitting a useful 20 runs.'

Cook was 28 years old and a late developer. He had come into the spotlight after scoring heavily for Bishops Auckland in their FA Amateur Cup triumphs in 1921 and 1922. Cook's arrival at Huddersfield followed a season at Second Division Rotherham County, which had ended in a disreputable manner. A Football League inquiry concluded that the club had made illegal payments to Cook whilst he was an amateur, when they signed him from Bishop Auckland. The League wielded the big stick by fining County £50 and cancelling the player's registration. Cook would prove to be an extremely useful signing, but all contemporary photos seem to show him with what appears to be a permanent sneer.

Another team-building exercise employed by Chapman was to hire a charabanc and take the team off to the spa town of Harrogate, where they would enjoy lunch at a local hotel and spend the afternoon playing bowls.

Four days before the season started in earnest, Chapman organised a golf outing to Pannal, a famous Yorkshire golf course near Harrogate. Town chairman Joe Barlow made a speech praising the players' efforts on the field over the previous three seasons and welcoming new players. He commended their loyalty and team spirit and pointed out that although the club's supporters were badly affected by the slump in the textile industry the club could weather the storm by having success on the field.

One player missing from the training and team-building sessions was the craggy Scottish wing-half David Steele. Signed a year previously from Bristol Rovers, Steele had been a virtual ever-present at right-half, replacing Charlie Slade. His outstanding form had won him three Scottish international caps, including one in a 2-2 draw against England, when he opposed his club colleagues Taylor and Wadsworth. Steele had caught pneumonia during the summer and was so ill he spent weeks recuperating in a private nursing home, presumably paid for by the football club. It would be mid-October before he returned to first-team action, and almost Christmas before he displayed his best form.

The season opened against Middlesbrough on a bright August day. A healthy crowd of around 20,000 – 5,000 more than the previous season's average crowd of 14,885 – made their way towards the Leeds Road ground. The majority would have travelled on foot, with some on bicycle. In those times, public transport mostly took the form of trams. On matchdays there would be milling hordes of supporters all being directed by uniformed tramway inspectors to a continuous procession of trams on Route 4 down to the Leeds Road ground for a tuppenny fare (1p). On reaching the ground they would disembark to join the queues outside the turnstiles, and the trams would turn round on loop lines at the back of the main stand and return to town to pick up more supporters.

The trams – painted in an Indian red and cream livery – were powered by electric overhead wires and ran on tramlines set in the road. At their peak, in the mid-1920s, the operational tramlines extended over 38 miles of roads in and around Huddersfield, from Brighouse in the north to Honley in the south, and from Marsden in the west to Bradley in the east.

If, like many supporters, you lived in other parts of town, or in the outlying villages, it was a more difficult journey to get to the game. Alec Lodge in *Kicking and Screaming*, describes his journey: 'I lived in a village about four miles from Huddersfield, and of course in those days there was very little public transport, certainly no buses, and we had a tram service which was about two miles away and a train service about one and a half miles away. We walked to the railway station and then dismounted just up the road at a place called Deighton. I still remember the fare was tuppence, and then you came to the ground and there were hundreds of bicycles. As years have gone by, Leeds Road has been widened and the gardens have got less and less, but in the old days the housekeepers could fit probably 30 or 40 bicycles in the garden and charge for them, which was quite a lucrative thing. And needless to say there was no danger of them being stolen. You went into the ground and there were about four policemen outside and one at each corner of the field. And on the train we usually had a chap from the village who brought a basket containing four pigeons. He let one of the pigeons off at quarter-time with a little tag on the leg with the score, another at half-time, one at three-quarter-time and one at full-time. There was no wireless in the early 1920s and certainly no television.'

A 1-0 home win over Middlesbrough confirmed that Town's defence was solid enough and unlikely to concede too many goals, but the forward players presented insufficient threat for championship contenders. The previous season's leading scorer, Charlie Wilson, headed the winner but Taylor in goal was rarely troubled.

On the second Saturday of the campaign, Town surprisingly lost 0-2 at Middlesbrough's Ayresome Park. Sandwiched in between was a 3-1 win at Preston's Deepdale. Billy Smith wrecked the Preston right flank, scoring one and making another for Charlie Wilson, before Cook – making his debut for the injured Islip – set up Stephenson for a third goal.

A week later, Preston, already looking good bets for relegation, travelled to Leeds Road and were on the wrong end of a 4-0 thumping. Wilson netted two goals to take his tally to four in four games. With Ted Taylor bedridden with flu, Billy Cowell – a former England schoolboy international – deputised in goal but was idle for long stretches.

As the cricket season drew to a close, Yorkshire clinched the County Championship for the second successive season. They were defeated only once all season and their veteran bowler, Wilfred Rhodes, finished top of bowling averages for the ninth time in his career and achieved the double of 100 wickets and 1,000 runs for the fourteenth time. Rhodes, a native of the Kirkheaton district of Huddersfield, continued to play first-class cricket to the age of 53 and ended his career with 4,187 wickets, the most ever in English first-class cricket.

As will by now be clear, the football fixture schedules at that time were very different to today's. Nowadays, the fixture computer tries to arrange things so that by Christmas each team has played everyone once, after which the fixtures are reversed. But it was not always like that. In 1923-24, for example, it was still the custom for teams to face each other back to back, home and away, in successive matches.

Town's next games were against newly promoted Notts County. After a physical confrontation which ended 1-0 in County's favour at Meadow Lane, the teams reconvened a week later at Leeds Road. In winning the Second Division title, County's mean defence had conceded only 34 goals and their full-backs, Ashurst and Cope, were renowned for their application of the offside trap. Allied to this, County had established a reputation for not taking prisoners, and some of the ferocious collisions at Meadow Lane were fresh in Town's players' minds as they prepared for the return.

Midway through the first half of what was an exhibition that brought shame on both clubs, County's goalkeeper, Albert Iremonger, was left motionless following an off-the-ball incident with Town's Ernie Islip. Standing 6ft 5in, Iremonger was the tallest man in the Football League, at a time when the average footballer stood no more than 5ft 8in. Iremonger was no stranger to controversy, and Islip had a short fuse which lit easily. The *Huddersfield Examiner* describes them as 'two of the most hot-headed players in the league'. The paper does not report what actually happened, but says: 'when the dust had settled Islip was sent from the field.'

Within minutes, the abrasive Flint of County was also sent off, after jumping on Billy Smith's ankles in a career-threatening assault. In the end it was a marvel that only two men were dismissed, as the brutality and petulance continued unabated. According to newspaper reports, the Leeds Road crowd were unimpressed and 'called for some football', but to little or no avail. At the request of Huddersfield Town, a Commission which included Football League President J McKenna was appointed to enquire into, and deal with, matters arising out of the report by the referee of misconduct by players in this match.

The Commission's judgment was that Islip and Flint be suspended for one month, while Iremonger was severely censured and warned as to his future conduct. The Commission also declared that the first half of the game was unduly vigorous and not played in the true spirit of sport. Both teams were warned as to their future conduct. Huddersfield Town, who asked for the Commission of Enquiry, were ordered to pay the expenses of the enquiry. Moves were also put in train to change the fixture procedures to avoid clubs meeting each other in subsequent weeks.

Chapman was so incensed that any player could sully the good name of Huddersfield Town that he vowed never to select Islip again. A few weeks later Birmingham paid Town a fee in the region of £1,500 for the 31-year-old, who took his short temper to St Andrews.

Chapman, unlike some managers of the time, was determined that his team have a reputation for not only playing attractive, passing football, but also one of being sporting in defeat. He decided to persevere with George Cook in place of Islip, a decision that in time would pay off handsomely. (Interestingly, Chapman repeated his disciplinary clampdown in 1934 when, as manager of Arsenal, his team were the victims of an FA Cup shock at the hands of lowly Walsall. Tommy Black, an Arsenal reserve player in an under-strength Gunners team, committed a dreadful challenge on a Walsall player. On the Monday after the game, Black was told by Chapman that he would never wear an Arsenal shirt again.)

Following the Notts County debacle, Town embarked on a run of nine games without defeat, during which the goals started to flow. A virtually unchanged side recorded some fine results, albeit against teams from the nether regions of the table. Billy Smith and Clem Stephenson were in fine fettle, and the winning sequence peaked with a dazzling comeback for a 4-2 win at West Bromwich Albion in early October. A week later Albion should have been beaten a second time, but Sam Wadsworth's penalty miss meant a 0-0 draw.

Town's excellent away form prompted a fan to write to the *Examiner* under the *nom de plume* of 'Leeds Roader': 'I believe that the atmosphere generated by the Leeds Road crowd is not conducive to our getting that delightful and brilliant football which we read and hear of our team giving before other crowds. Compare the happenings at West Brom and Leeds Road on successive Saturdays. At WBA Billy Smith is accorded an ovation for a display of wonderful football. But on his own ground he is mercilessly barracked because he cannot overcome the tight marking.' Other letters talk of 'loud-mouthed coarse anathemas from the terraces and stands with vulgar and ignorant criticism hurled at opponents.'

Wadsworth and goalie Ted Taylor were missing from the following week's game against Birmingham as they were winning caps for England against Ireland in Belfast. Ireland shocked England, winning 2-1, and both Town players would be dropped for the next international. In those days, postponement of League matches because of international call-ups was not permitted, and in 1928 – on the occasion of Scotland's 5-1 victory over England at Wembley – Town had to fulfil a league fixture with five players absent on international duty.

Billy Cowell should have played at St Andrews, but failed to appear, and Len Boot – a new signing from York City – took over Taylor's duties in goal, where he had little to occupy him. The board minutes for 29 October record that 'Cowell apologised for his absence the previous week'. But whatever his explanation, Cowell had burned his boats with Chapman. He never featured in the first team again and within a year joined Hartlepools United.

Roy Goodall, a young full-back from Dronfield Woodhouse, deputised for Wadsworth. The 21-year-old Goodall had been at Leeds Road for two years and was perceived as a star of the future. He had given up accountancy studies to follow a football career. It was said that he was so determined to succeed in football that he would train by moonlight, and even volunteered to work as a farm labourer over the summer to develop his physique. Later that season, as will be described, Goodall would be censured by the club for misleading them about the cause of an injury – actually sustained during a motor-cycle accident.

Goodall was tallish, around 5ft 10in, and wore his hair short even by the standards of the time, with a quiff at the front. This was only his third first-team game, but he had already shown in the reserve team enough talent to convince the Town staff that he was a gem in the making.

Billy Smith's goal gave Town both points at St Andrews, and a week later Clem Stephenson's cool finish repeated the scoreline at Leeds Road, although in both games Birmingham's Dan Tremelling – a future England goalkeeper and a man who would play a crucial part in Town's destiny that season – offered defiant resistance.

That second win over Birmingham saw Town rise, for the first time that season, to the top of the league table. They were level on seventeen points with the still unbeaten Cardiff City.

Disappointingly, only 12,000 had been at Leeds Road to see Town go top. The main explanation given by the *Examiner* was that 19,000 spectators were at Fartown to see Huddersfield Rugby League team contest a Yorkshire Cup game with local rivals Halifax. The town's rugby and soccer clubs normally arranged their fixtures so that they were at home on alternate Saturdays, which meant that the townsfolk could follow both codes. It was not the custom for large numbers of supporters to follow their club to away fixtures, except for FA Cup-ties.

The only occasions when Huddersfield would stage concurrent soccer and rugby games was when dictated by the draw for cup-ties. The Saturday of Town's home game with Birmingham (27 October) was the first of several such clashes this season. In the modern day, the two clubs would have agreed to staggered kick-offs, or one or the other would have switched their game to the Sunday. Neither was possible in the 1920s. Sport on Sundays was frowned upon, if not prohibited, and the absence of floodlighting meant there were not enough daylight hours in winter to accommodate two major sporting events.

Huddersfield's Rugby League side had dominated the sport in the five years before the Great War, and were still a major force afterwards. Rugby had been played at a senior level in the town since 1895; some thirteen years before the Association Rules club had been formed, and there is no disputing the fact that prior to Town's League Championship successes the Rugby League side attracted a bigger support. Relations between the two codes were, however, generally cordial. Just a few weeks earlier the *Examiner* reported that several Town players had opened a new billiards saloon in St George's Square by playing games against the Rugby League team. Billiards was a popular sport of the time and goalkeeper Billy Mercer, who joined Town from Hull City in 1924, had a fearsome reputation at the sport and had even played the legendary Joe Davis.

In early November, Town paid a visit to Anfield. The trip was as daunting then as it would be in the 1970s and 80s; Liverpool had been League Champions in 1922 and 1923 and were largely invincible at home, where they had lost only six games in three seasons. In 1923-24, however, the champions had started poorly and had reverted to a more physical approach in an attempt to regain lost ground. The game was memorable for the attendance of the new Prime Minister, Stanley Baldwin, no doubt electioneering with a General Election only a month away, for this was his first ever football game. Ironically, the Conservative Premier had connections with Huddersfield; his grandfather, George MacDonald, had lived in Queen's Square in the mid-nineteenth century. But Baldwin couldn't claim the strong connections of future Labour Prime Minister Harold Wilson, who was born and bred in the Milnsbridge district and was an avid Huddersfield fan. At Anfield, Town grabbed an early lead through Stephenson but relentless Liverpool pressure paid off and Harry Chambers' equaliser knocked Town off the First Division summit. In the return a week later, Town won 3-1, thanks to a stunning three-goal burst in three minutes just after half-time. Chambers' consolation goal was the first conceded by Town in six home games. David Steele, playing his fifth game since recovering from pneumonia, was beginning to show some of his best form at right-half as he regained his stamina.

Athletic News's correspondent, 'Impressionist', believed 'an outstanding example of the ebb and flow of football power was vouchsafed at Huddersfield. Here one saw the glory of Liverpool dimmed and the might of Huddersfield Town manifest to a striking degree. If it were a policy to need to form a judgement of one side's merits by the standards of another's reputation, one could instinctively visualise the Yorkshire club as successors of Liverpool. Time may lend its proof to what must now be conjecture. After the first few minutes of the momentous duel at Leeds Road, they made the champions into a disorganised, confounded, bedraggled company, which is paying sterling testimony to some quality. Lucas and McKinlay covered up the repeated breeches made as far as was possible. Then came the inevitable breaking point and then the brilliance of Huddersfield appeared in its full majesty.'

Town's next two opponents would test their championship mettle to the full – double-headers with FA Cup holders Bolton Wanderers and Sunderland, both in the leading pack – could decide whether or not Town were championship impostors. The results were inconclusive. Both away games were lost; both home games were won.

Bolton had a hex over Town – the Lancashire club had lost only once in eleven meetings since the War – and, like, Liverpool repelled all boarders at home. Wanderers had lost only seven games at Burnden Park in three seasons. In mud and sleet, Huddersfield were always on the back foot, and Charlie Wilson's late goal when Town were three behind gave a gloss on the score they did not entirely deserve. In fact, Ted Taylor's defiance in goal was all Chapman could look back on with favour.

A week later, the same teams had to contend with winter's first icy conditions. One of the linesmen was seriously delayed by frozen roads, and a replacement had to be found. The *Examiner* reported that Herbert Chapman ended up running the line until the errant official arrived in time for the second half. It is hard to imagine modern managers agreeing to such partisan intervention, but the concept of the 'fourth official' is a very recent one.

Right-back Ned Barkas was dropped after the Burnden defeat. Roy Goodall was handed another opportunity and stuck manfully to his experienced and wily Welsh winger, Ted Vizard. Town finally nosed in front in the last ten minutes when Cook's lob earned two important points.

At Roker Park it was back to the mud, but again Town faltered. Charlie Buchan, the League's leading scorer and an England international, scored a last-minute winner when it seemed that Town had weathered the storm. They had even survived a twice-taken penalty, but Buchan's goal clinched Sunderland's seventh successive home win. (Buchan would in 1925 become Chapman's first signing as Arsenal manager and in retirement became a much-respected journalist. He edited the eponymously titled *Football Monthly*, a much cherished schoolboys' football magazine of the 1950s and 60s.)

The tables were turned at Leeds Road, when Sunderland were on the receiving end of a late winner. Charlie Wilson outshone England star Buchan and netted his second goal of the game to make it 3-2 with four minutes left. This was Town's first win over the Wearsiders in eight meetings and was reward for doggedness and composure in the face of some hefty challenges. In the visitors' dressing room afterwards, England fullback Warney Cresswell sustained serious cuts to his head when a teammate tried to open a skylight and it crashed onto him in the bath.

Despite the up-and-down results, Chapman seemed happy with the composition of his team. In fact, in ten matches between October and Boxing Day, the only change he made in his starting eleven was Goodall's inclusion for Barkas after the Bolton defeat. The right-wing problem seemed to have resolved itself, with Bristolian Joe Walter now a regular. In December, Chapman was happy to allow veteran winger George Richardson to move to Second Division Hull. Now 32, Richardson had lost some of the acceleration that had made him a professional sprinter, competing for prize money at fairs and galas earlier in his career. His speed had made him a key player in the 1920 Cup-winning team.

By coincidence, another George Richardson (but this one was called Ted) – a 21-year old outside-left – made his debut in January, deputising for Billy Smith. Ted would not repeat the impact as his namesake, and he would disappear after six first-team games.

Struggling Arsenal were next up for Chapman's boys, and on the last two Saturdays before Christmas the Gunners were put to the sword. Charlie Wilson scored hat-tricks in both games. He had struggled in the autumn and had scored only once in twelve games. December would be his golden month and his double hat-tricks made it nine goals in four games. Naturally left-footed, one of Wilson's three goals at Highbury came off his weaker right, and as an ex-Tottenham player his achievement would have been very sweet.

Following the 3-1 win at Highbury, Town hit Arsenal for six a week later, Clem Stephenson scoring two and creating three others. The Gunners, despite their high-profile chairman, Sir Henry Norris, and their impressive new Highbury ground in north London, had massively underperformed since taking their controversial place in Division One after the War. Manager Leslie Knighton had little power and was even forbidden by Norris to sign players under 5ft 8in tall! This season would see a desperate fight against relegation which Arsenal only just avoided.

Charlie Wilson's goal-flurry ended at his old stomping ground, White Hart Lane, on Christmas Day. A crowd of 44,000 went away happy after Spurs had defeated high-flying Huddersfield on a slippery, icy pitch. More problems came for Charlie the following day in the return at Leeds Road. He limped off the snowbound pitch after fifteen minutes with a leg injury that would sideline him for over a month. Town however, in front of their biggest crowd of the season, 28,600, came from behind to win with two goals, one of them a penalty, from Billy Smith.

Wilson was not the only player injured against Tottenham. Clem Stephenson suffered a thigh strain and missed the final game of the year, a 0-1 defeat at Blackburn. Rovers had lost only twice at Ewood Park all season, but Town felt hard done by when the referee failed to give handball in the Blackburn penalty area in the dying moments. It was an opportunity missed, as leaders Cardiff slipped up at Villa – only their second reverse of the season. After Cardiff had bounced back to win 1-0 at Middlesbrough on New Year's Day, the top positions looked like this:

	P	W	D	L	F	A	Pts
Cardiff	24	14	8	2	42	21	36
Bolton	26	11	11	4	46	20	33
Sunderland	24	13	5	6	44	31	31
Huddersfield	23	13	4	6	38	21	30

Bolton, the draw specialists, were undoubtedly the form team, having gone eight games unbeaten since their defeat at Leeds Road, but they had played more games. In those days the Football League operated a strange fixture policy. They drew up a fixture list with 36 fixed games for each club and then gave clubs discretion with their other six. Those six were normally arranged in pairs at Christmas, New Year and Easter, to suit local holidays. But if two clubs mutually agreed, they could play them at any other time. For instance, Huddersfield and Tottenham were allowed to arrange their games on agreed dates – Christmas Day and Boxing Day. In 1923-24, Bolton had decided to play two of their 'discretionary' fixtures on midweek evenings at the start of the season. This, added to the fact that Town had decided not to play on 1 January, whilst Bolton did, explained the variance in the number of games played, for there had been no postponements.

Huddersfield Town went into 1924 six points off the pace.

Huddersfield Town — Champions of the Football League, Division I, 1923-24

Back Row (from left to right) — Wilson, Smith (A.), Shaw, Taylor, Wadsworth, Cook, Chaplin (trainer), Watson.
Front Row — Steele, Johnston, Stephenson (captain), Brown, Smith (W.H.), Cawthorne.

These eleven players turned out only once together as a team, at Aston Villa in the penultimate game of 1923-24. It is an unusual picture in that the two reserves are included in civvies, while other more prominent players are missing

The cover of the FA Cup final preview publication in 1922. Town beat Preston 1-0

A cigarette card of the era, showing Clem Stephenson

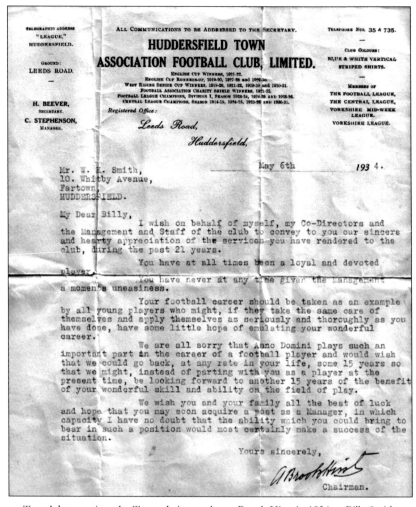

Top: A letter written by Town chairman Amos Brook Hirst in 1934 to Billy Smith.
Bottom: Clem Stephenson strikes the perfect pose against West Ham in April 1926

A card-school at Leeds Road in 1928. Left to right: unknown, Bob Kelly, Billy Smith, Hugh Turner, Sam Wadsworth, unknown

On the Scandinavian tour in May 1925. Alex Jackson (front, third right) has just signed from Aberdeen. Herbert Chapman (back, third right) will shortly join Arsenal

Action from a home game with Manchester United. Goalkeeper Ted Taylor looks to have the cross covered. The V-shirts were United's first-choice kit in the mid-1920s.

A posthumous caricature of Herbert Chapman drawn by Tom Webster of the *Daily Mail* in 1934

Huddersfield Town legend Billy Smith is wrapped up against the elements

FOREST OVERWHELMED.

Town Finish in True Championship Form.

WATCHING THE SCOREBOARD.

Huddersfield T. ... ... 3; Notts F, ... 0
Cook (2), Brown.

Never did a crowd keep such an anxious eye on the scoreboard as did the spectators at Leeds Road on Saturday. Everything depended on what appeared opposite the " B." to our programmes told us. The second half began a few minutes before the figures appeared telling the glad news that Birmingham were holding their own against Cardiff. Then there was nothing for it but to wait for the final score. It was an unusual sight when the match was over to see a large crowd hanging about the ground instead of rushing for the tram-cars. The little room at the end of the paddock, where the scores are received, became for once the centre of attraction. Through its windows we could see an anxious group waiting around the telephone. Then suddenly the door was flung open, and Mr. Chapman dashed out with his face one huge smile and shouting "We've won!" There was a tremendous cheer before the words had left his mouth. It was taken up inside the ground and out. The championship had come to Huddersfield for the first time.

The *Huddersfield Examiner* reports on Town clinching their first League Championship

Clowns entertain the crowd before an important game at Leeds Road

Copenhagen was a favourite destination for Town in their end-of-season tours. This photo was taken at the Tuborg Brewery on one trip, probably in the early 1930s

Young Billy Smith, probably taken
before the First World War

Town's hardman wing-half, Scottish
international David Steele

The team depart by charabanc for a day's golf at Harrogate in 1923. Most prefer large
caps, but a few choose a trilby. Tommy Wilson (front, second left) opts for a bowler hat

The sheet music for Huddersfield's 1922
FA Cup final song – 'Oh! It's Our Night
Out Again To-Night.' This was a popular
seller in the music shops of West
Yorkshire that year

"Oh! It's Our Night Out Again To-night."

I.

Bertie White till late at night had stayed out recently
To celebrate you see—each glorious victory
Won by the Town's great football team, and every Saturday
When wifie said 'come home to-night and take me out,' he'd say:

Chorus.
Oh ! it's our night out again to-night,
Oh ! it's our night out again to-night,
And you can bet, we'll make things hum,
Won't we have a beano, eh-by-gum,
For we'll all be sporting Blue and White
And we'll all be shouting with delight
Bravo Town—you'll want some taking down.
Oh ! it's our night out again to-night.

2.

On the sly with Miss McKie, Bert's wifie went one day
To see the " Townies " play—and somehow straight away
She got the football fever too, so when Bert (ill in bed)
Asked her to sit and read the football news to him, she said:
Chorus

3.

One day they, both went away,to see a tie re-played
And there they met their maid, in wifie's clothes arrayed.
" What's this mean Jane," snapped Bertie's wife ; said Jane
   " well ma'am you see
My bloke Bill Brown, who follows ' Town,' came round and
   said to me " :
Chorus

Team-picture from 1928-29, which was the last of Clem Stephenson's playing career.
Back: Brown, Raw, Evans, Dent, Redfern, Wilson, Turner, Naylor, Kelly, Taylor (trainer)
Sitting: Steele, Stephenson, Jackson, Cumming, Goodall, Wadsworth, Smailes
Inset: Smith, Spence

George Brown demonstrates his deadly shooting with a goal against West Ham.
The photograph captures the old Main Stand – burnt down in 1950 – in its full glory

Billiards was an extremely popular working men's sport, far more popular than snooker in those days. Here, cue-wizard Clem Stephenson takes aim

Wing-half Harry Cawthorne, an unsung hero, became a regular player in the third championship season

Left-half Billy Watson, an iron-man, made more appearances than any other player during the three title seasons

Alex Jackson (left) and Billy Smith indulge in some friendly wrestling during this photo-shoot from 1925-26. The footwear looks like rubber plimsolls

A singalong around the piano during a trip to Buxton some time after 1926. Jack Chaplin, by then manager, is in the bottom right in a dark suit

Five famous internationals after training: Billy Smith, Wadsworth, Stephenson, Tommy Wilson, Alex Jackson. The kit is typical – rolled neck sweater, shorts and plimsolls. In the background can be seen the original 'Cowshed', which was replaced in 1929

It is the start of 1924-25, and Town's forwards are on their marks: Joe Williams, George Brown, Charlie Wilson, Clem Stephenson, Billy Smith. The family 'paddock' is behind

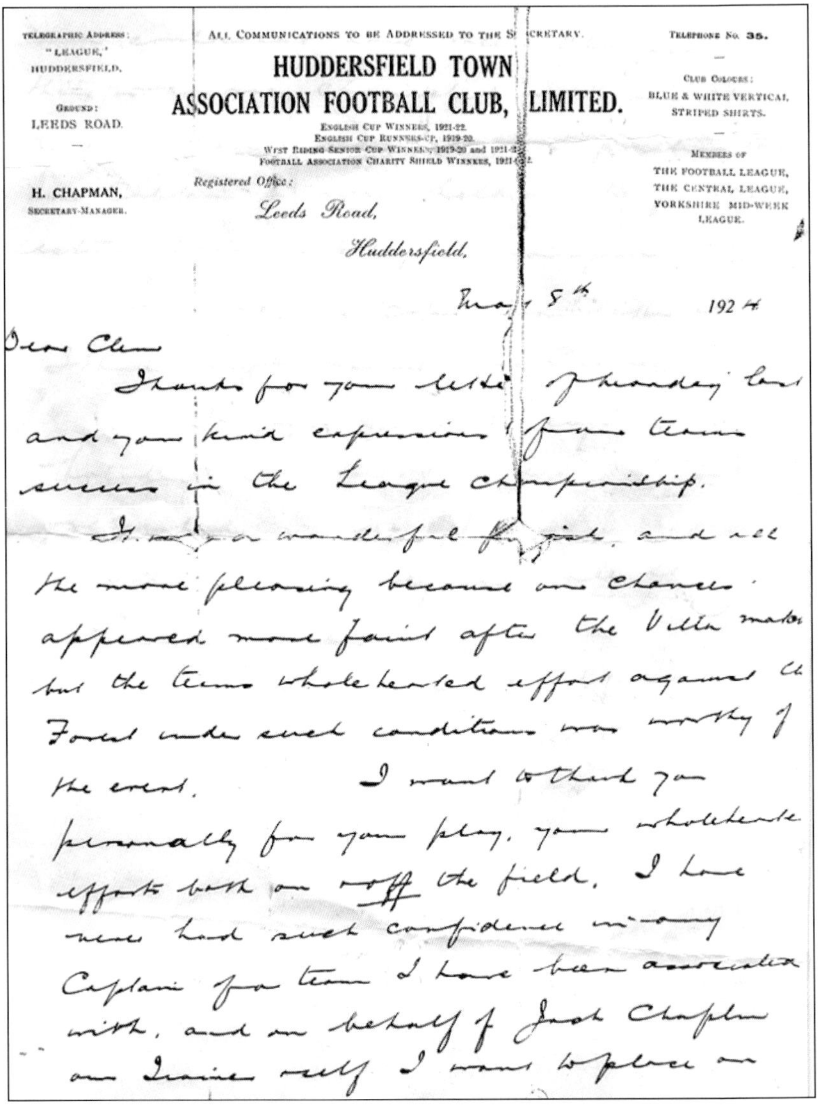

TELEGRAPHIC ADDRESS: "LEAGUE," HUDDERSFIELD.

GROUND: LEEDS ROAD.

H. CHAPMAN, SECRETARY-MANAGER.

ALL COMMUNICATIONS TO BE ADDRESSED TO THE SECRETARY.

HUDDERSFIELD TOWN ASSOCIATION FOOTBALL CLUB, LIMITED.

ENGLISH CUP WINNERS, 1921-22.
ENGLISH CUP RUNNERS-UP, 1919-20.
WEST RIDING SENIOR CUP WINNERS, 1919-20 and 1921-22.
FOOTBALL ASSOCIATION CHARITY SHIELD WINNERS, 1921-22.

TELEPHONE No. 35.

CLUB COLOURS: BLUE & WHITE VERTICAL STRIPED SHIRTS.

MEMBERS OF THE FOOTBALL LEAGUE, THE CENTRAL LEAGUE, YORKSHIRE MID-WEEK LEAGUE.

Registered Office: *Leeds Road, Huddersfield,*

May 8th 1924

Dear Clem

Thanks for your letter of Monday last and your kind expressions of our team success in the League Championship.

It was a wonderful final flourish, and all the more pleasing because our chances appeared more faint after the Villa match but the teams wholehearted effort against the Forest under such conditions was worthy of the event. I want to thank you personally for your play, your wholehearted efforts both on and off the field. I have never had such confidence in any Captain of a team I have been associated with, and on behalf of Jack Chaplin our Trainer and self I want to place on

Dear Clem, Thank you for your letter of Monday last and your kind expressions of our team's success in the League Championship. It was a wonderful final flourish, and all the more pleasing because our chances appeared more faint after the Villa match but the team's wholehearted effort against the Forest under such conditions was worthy of the event. I want to thank you personally for your play, your wholehearted efforts, both on and off the field. I have never had such confidence in any Captain of a team I have been associated with, and on behalf of Jack Chaplin our Trainer and self I want to place on record such assistance from you, for your help amongst the players, as without it Huddersfield Town could not have been champions, and there is no one connected with our club deserves more credit for our position than our Captain a man held in the greatest esteem by players, management and Directors. I am enclosing copy of a (over)

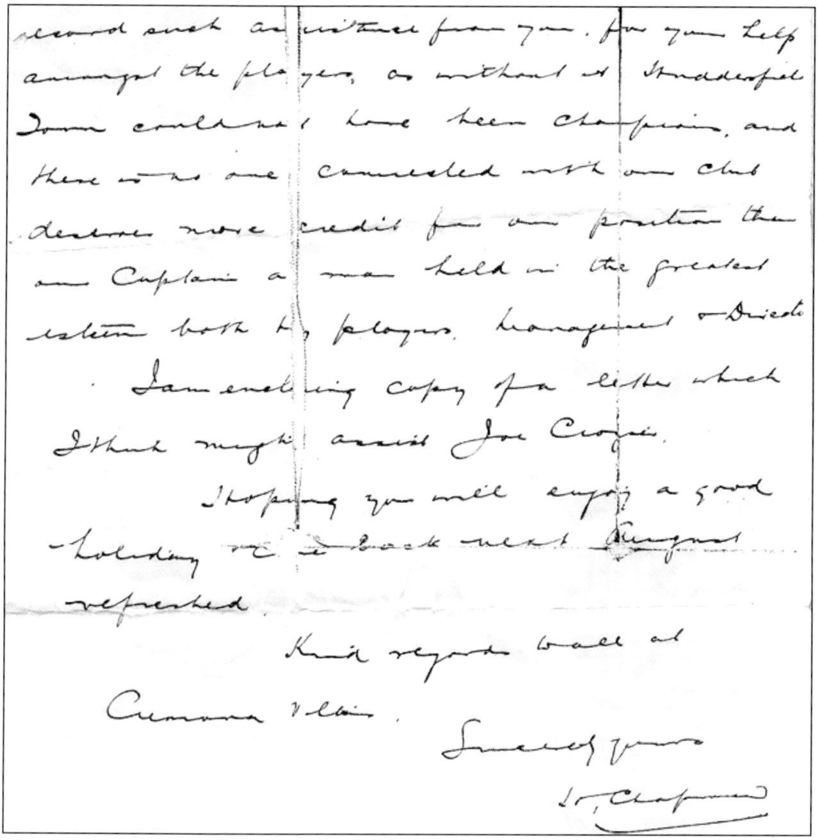

record such assistance from you. For your help amongst the players, as without it Huddersfield Town couldn't have been Champions, and there was no one connected with our club deserves more credit for our position than our Captain a man held in the greatest esteem both by players, Management & Directors.

I am enclosing copy of a letter which I think might assist Joe Crozier.

Hoping you will enjoy a good holiday & come back next August refreshed.

Kind regards to all at Cumona Villa.

Sincerely yours

H Chapman

(continued) letter which I think should assist Joe Crozier. Hoping you will enjoy a good holiday and come back next August refreshed. Kind regards to all at Cumona Villa. Sincerely yours, H Chapman

This photograph was taken during an end-of-season tour at an unknown venue

It is Blackpool in 1923, and the players are ready for a game of golf.
Herbert Chapman is in the front row in the bowler hat

Alex Jackson, the Gay Cavalier, scored 89 goals in 203 games for Huddersfield Town in five seasons

Sam Wadsworth, arguably the finest full-back of the era, played 312 games for Town in eight years

1922. Garrett and Haigh, the town's men's outfitters, display the FA Cup, the FA Charity Shield, and the West Riding County Cup. A near-lifesize cardboard figure of captain Tommy Wilson and photographs of each member of the team adorn the window

Town's first team, photographed before a home match in 1925-26.
Back: Jackson, Cawthorne, Goodall, Taylor, Tom Wilson, Wadsworth, Watson.
Front: Brown, Cook, Stephenson, Smith

Goal Scorers.—First Division.

	1923–4	1924–5	1925–6
G. Brown	8	20	34
C. Wilson	18	24	2
G. W. Cook	9	9	13
W. H. Smith	13	8	6
C. Stephenson	11	5	4
A. Jackson	—	—	16
J. J. Williams	—	—	6
W. Devlin	—	—	4
F. R. Goodall	—	—	2
S. Binks	—	—	1
J. Walter	—	1	—
H. Cawthorne	—	1	—
A. W. Smith	—	—	1
Pantling (Sheffield U.)	—	1	—
Wadsworth (Liverpool)	1	—	—
Raitt (Everton)	—	—	1
	60	**69**	**90**

Players' Appearances.—First Division.

	1923–4	1924–5	1925–6
E. Taylor	35	10	29
F. R. Goodall	14	38	28
S. J. Wadsworth	37	33	37
D. Steele	31	39	18
T. Wilson	41	40	40
W. Watson	42	41	39
A. Jackson	—	—	38
G. Brown	22	32	40
C. Wilson	31	38	4
C. Stephenson	40	29	35
W. H. Smith	39	41	27
J. J. Williams	—	35	23
E. Barkas	21	1	13
G. W. Cook	25	25	28
W. Mercer	—	27	12
G. E. Shaw	—	11	4
H. Cawthorne	16	2	23
G. Hobson	—	—	2
H. Raw	—	—	2
M. B. Spence	—	4	1
W. Devlin	—	—	4
A. W. Smith	—	1	1
H. Dennis	—	—	1
J. Walter	26	7	—

This celebratory publication went to press before the final game at Notts Co in 1926

FIRST DIVISION.

Season.	P.	W.	L.	D.	Goals F.	A.	Pts.
1923-4	42	23	8	11	60	33	57
1924-5	42	21	5	16	69	28	58
1925-6	41	23	7	11	90	56	57
	125	67	20	38	219	117	172

Town's Record—Three Seasons.

		1923-4	1924-5	1925-6	Total Goals F.	A.
Arsenal	H	6-1	4-0	2-2	12	3
	A	3-1	5-0	1-3	9	4
Aston Villa	H	1-0	4-1	5-1	10	2
	A	1-3	1-1	0-3	2	7
Birmingham	H	1-0	0-1	4-1	5	2
	A	1-0	1-0	3-1	5	1
Blackburn R.	H	1-0	0-0	3-1	4	1
	A	0-1	3-2	1-2	4	5
Bolton Wand.	H	1-0	0-0	3-0	4	0
	A	1-3	0-1	1-6	2	10
Burnley	H	1-0	2-0	2-1	5	1
	A	1-1	5-1	1-1	7	3
Cardiff City	H	2-0	0-0	1-1	3	1
	A	1-1	2-2	2-1	5	4
Chelsea	H	0-1	—	—	0	1
	A	1-0	—	—	1	0
Everton	H	2-0	3-0	2-0	7	0
	A	1-1	2-0	3-2	6	3
Leeds United	H	—	2-0	3-1	5	1
	A	—	1-1	4-0	5	1
Liverpool	H	3-1	1-1	0-0	4	2
	A	1-1	3-2	2-1	6	4
Manchester City	H	1-1	1-1	2-2	4	4
	A	1-1	1-1	5-1	7	3
Manchester U.	H	—	—	5-0	5	0
	A	—	—	1-1	1	1
Middlesbrough	H	1-0	—	—	1	0
	A	0-2	—	—	0	2
Newcastle U.	H	1-1	0-0	0-1	1	2
	A	1-0	3-1	2-0	6	1

Town's Record.—continued.

		1923-4	1924-5	1925-6	Total Goals F.	A.
Nottingham F.	H	3-0	3-0	—	6	0
	A	1-1	1-0	—	2	1
Notts. County	H	0-0	0-0	2-0	2	0
	A	0-1	1-1	—	1	2
Preston N.E.	H	4-0	1-0	—	5	0
	A	3-1	4-1	—	7	2
Sheffield U.	H	1-0	2-1	4-1	7	2
	A	1-0	1-1	3-2	5	3
Sunderland	H	3-2	4-0	1-1	8	3
	A	1-2	1-1	1-4	3	7
Tottenham H.	H	2-1	1-2	2-1	5	4
	A	0-1	2-1	5-5	7	7
West Brom. Albion	H	0-0	1-1	1-1	2	2
	A	4-2	0-1	2-2	6	5
West Ham U.	H	1-1	1-2	2-2	6	4
	A	3-2	0-0	3-2	6	4
Bury	H	—	1-1	2-1	3	2
	A	—	2-4	0-0	2	4
Leicester City	H	—	—	3-0	3	0
	A	—	—	0-2	0	2

The following is our record at the end of each Season since being elected to the League:—

English League.—First Division.

Season.	Points.	
1925-26	—	Champions.
1924-25	58	Champions.
1923-24	57	Champions
1922-23	53	
1921-22	39	
1920-21	39	

Second Division.

1919-20	64	Gained promotion with Tottenham Hotspur. War Period.
1915-19		
1914-15	42	
1913-14	34	
1912-13	43	
1911-12	32	
1910-11	34	

This page from the Triple Championship publication lists results and the club's history

Some say this 1928 team was the best, though it failed to win a trophy. Back: Redfern, Goodall, Mercer, Wilson, Brown, Meads. Front: Jackson, Kelly, Stephenson, Smith, Barkas

Billy Smith, wearing Huddersfield Town's 1922 FA Cup final shirt

George Brown, scorer of 159 Town goals, wearing his England jersey

Town players relax playing cards. It is likely that the photo was taken in a hotel, possibly in Blackpool during FA Cup preparations. Tommy Wilson (standing centre), keeps an eye on Stephenson (sitting, second left), Wadsworth (sitting, fourth left), and Jackson (right)

Billy Smith tees off. Golf was an important game for the players. Herbert Chapman regularly organised golf outings and arranged for the club to pay membership fees

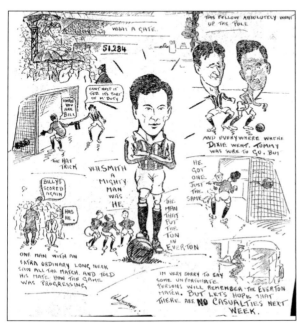

This 1928 cartoon celebrates Billy Smith's hat-trick in Town's 4-1 home win over Everton, watched by a record 51,000 crowd

The 1925-26 champions. Back: Cawthorne, Moralee, Goodall, Mercer, Wilson, Taylor
(trainer), Wadsworth. Front: Slicer, Devlin, Brown, Stephenson, Smith, Watson.
The eleven kitted players only played one game together, at home to Leicester on
2 October 1926. This photograph was probably taken before that match

Five Town players perch on the horse and roller used on the Leeds Road
pitch up until the 1930s. From left: Williams, Jackson, Cawthorne, Shaw,
Goodall. The name of the horse is unrecorded

A chimney at the Leeds Road end belches out smoke as the players take a break from training. From left: Evans, Jackson, Wadsworth, Wilson, Smith, Goodall, Kelly, Brown

The advertisement that would change everything. It appeared in *Athletic News* on 11 May 1925, and soon afterwards Herbert Chapman had got the job

ARSENAL FOOTBALL CLUB
is open to receive applications for
the position of
TEAM MANAGER.
He must be fully experienced and possess the highest qualifications for the post, both as to ability and personal character.
Gentlemen whose sole ability to build up a good side depends on the payment of heavy and exhorbitant transfer fees need not apply.
Applications (which will be treated as strictly confidential), stating fullest possible particulars, including salary expected, to be made in writing to Chairman, 24, Sheen-road, Richmond, Surrey.

The club's board minutes from 1 February 1921, the meeting at which Herbert Chapman was appointed.

'. . . of the unemployed in Huddersfield was discussed. The matter was left over untill [sic] later. Bedlington AFC. Letter read from Bedlington AFC re centre half. Resolved the manager go on Saturday to Shildon and watch this player. R Watson. Letter read from R Watson re players. The manager was instructed to write Mr Watson asking him to go and see Carlisle United play and watch the right wing and if satisfied with them to ask them their lowest figure. Accounts passed for payment as follows: Boro Police £14-7-0 Collector of Customs £16-2-9 Barker and Sons £21-15-11 JH Taylor and Co £4-11-10 Resolved that Mr H Chapman be appointed out of candidates applying at a salary of £10 per week and bonus on results at discretion of Board to be Assistant Manager and to have control of players (over)

& discharge all such other duties
as Board may direct- the whole
of the duties to be carried out-
in conjunction with the Present-
Manager Mr A. Langley

Team v Blackburn Rovers at Huddsfld
selected as follows
Mutch Wood Bullock Slade
Wilson Watson Richardson
Mann Wright Islip Smith WH
Res Rodgerson

Res Team v Blackburn Res Away
Davis Goodall Cawthorne
Brough Linley McKay Fawcett-
Smith W Barkas Johnstone
Kennedy Res Lunn

Joseph Barlow
Feby 8th 1921.

Present- Directors Meeting held Feb 8 1921
Messrs J. Barlow (Chairman)
N. Robinson & C. Mitchell D. Parker
R. Mitchell J.H. Raynor Directors
A. Langley & H. Chapman Managers

(continued) and discharge all such duties as Board may direct the whole of the duties to
be carried out in conjunction with the present manager Mr A Langley.
Team v Blackburn Rovers at Huddersfield selected as follows: Mutch Wood Bullock
Slade Wilson Watson Richardson Mann Wright Islip Smith WH Res Rodgerson.
Res Ream v Blackburn Res Away Davis Goodall Cawthorne Brough Linley McKay
Fawcett Smith W Barkas Johnstone Kennedy Res Lunn.

Joseph Barlow
Feb 8th 1921

A rare action photo from the era. The opponents are Sheffield United and George Brown
shoots for goal as Charlie Wilson jumps clear. The 'Terrace' is in the background

Below: Two images of Newcastle United (in their change strip) at Leeds Road on
24 October 1925. This was the game that ended Town's 27-match unbeaten run

Stephenson's left-foot shot can find no route past nine Newcastle United defenders

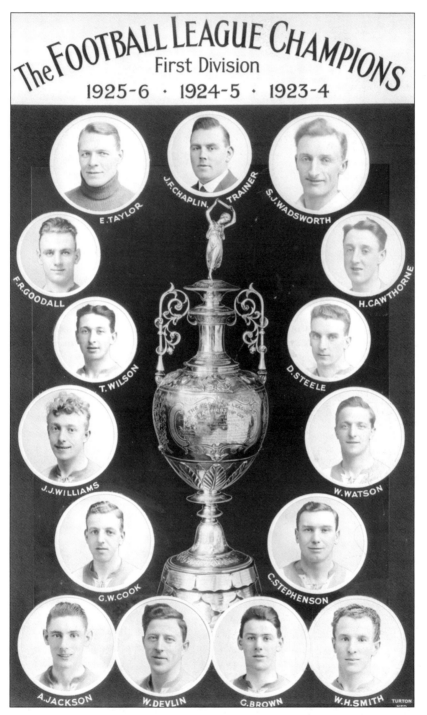

A page from the Special publication produced to commemorate Huddersfield
winning their third League Championship in 1926

Clem Stephenson, architect of so much of Huddersfield's success. But he won just one England cap

Tommy Wilson, who also won just one cap. That was in the nightmare 1-5 Wembley thrashing by Scotland

Another charabanc trip. Sam Wadsworth looks almost asleep near the back, whilst Billy Watson (standing at the rear) looks like a country squire. Several players are smoking pipes and one at the front has a cigarette. The hazards of smoking were not then known

Huddersfield's programmes for the Championship period are now like gold-dust and change hands for staggeringly high prices. This programme is from the 1921-22 season and at the time cost tuppence (1p)

informing him that the Directors would give a Cup (not to exceed £10) to be competed for annually by the School Houses.

Supsequent Cup Match. It was decided to write Mr A.E. Fogg of Bolton, asking him if possible, to officiate as Referee in this game.

Mr Potter was asked to retire & after a long discussion as to his position with the Club it was resolved that Mr Hirst & Mr Dawson interview him at once, with a view to terminating his agreement.

Mr Hirst & Mr Dawson reported that Mr Potter would be willing to terminate his agreement at once if the Club paid him £400.

Resolved unanimously that Mr Potter be paid £400 to immediately terminate his agreement with the Club.

It was agreed that the next meeting be held on Friday, August 20th, at Mr Dawson's office

A Brook Hirst
23rd Aug 1926.

Minutes of Directors Meeting held at Mr Dawson's Office. Friday. August 20th. Present :- Messrs A Brook Hirst (Chairman) W Dawson, J. Mitchell. J Barlow, A Robinson. J Hayner. S. Parker & the Secretary.

It was decided that the Annual Outing should take place on Tuesday. Aug 24th

Above: The board minutes that give clues to the sacking of Cecil Potter (see page 155)

The dream forward line from 1927-28 onwards: Alex Jackson, Bob Kelly, George Brown, Clem Stephenson, Billy Smith. All five were full internationals

Previous page (bottom): A promotional photograph taken in the late 1920s, with the players modelling fashionable raincoats and headwear

Cecil Potter, who succeeded Chapman and led Town to the Championship, but who left Leeds Road under a cloud

Between 1920 and 1927, Town lost eight successive games at Burnden Park, and also struggled to beat Bolton at home

Leapfrogging at Leeds Road. The jumpers are Langham, Tommy Wilson and Wadsworth. Those making a back are Watson, Brown and Stephenson

On a windy putting green, Stephenson sinks his putt, while Billy Smith holds the flag

Chapter 4

~ RACE FOR THE TITLE ~

(JANUARY –MAY 1924)

In those far-off days the FA Cup held far more allure than it does now. The competition had originated in 1872, some sixteen years before the Football League. To win the Cup was indisputably a bigger prize than the League Championship. For the supporters, the Cup final offered a day or weekend in London, a treat beyond the reach of most people in the days before mass transportation systems and motorways. There were no European competitions on offer, just the glory for the fans and a bit more money in the coffers for the successful club.

Some correspondents, even then, were reluctant to downgrade the League Championship. 'Tityrus' in *Athletic News* wrote: 'While the tournament for the Association Cup is gripping the multitude and causing either great joy or intense sorrow the competitions of the Football League may be lost sight of by those who are only seekers for sensationalism. But to the clubs and their legions of followers there is no test so stern, so prolonged and so important as that which determines position in the various divisions. The championship of the First Division may not appeal to the public at large in the same way that a triumph in the Cup does. The Cup has a lustre of its own. There is no reason to minimise any such success. Yet in intrinsic merit the premiership of the strongest group of League clubs stands alone. Luck plays a prominent part in the Cup-ties and has often decided the issue. But rarely does good fortune decide the League championship in a programme which is generally seven times as long as the struggle for The Cup. The feature of League football is consistency, and to maintain a high standard week in and week out the club needs to escape the ills that flesh is heir to and the accidents that so often overtake players in such a robust game.'

The League tested the club's consistency over a 42-game programme played in all weathers on a variety of surfaces. The Cup offered the opportunity for shock results and the dream of a trip to Crystal Palace or, latterly, Wembley Stadium. The fact that 250,000 tried to get in for the first Wembley final in 1923, however, testifies to its vast allure.

For Huddersfield Town in the early weeks of 1924, the FA Cup provided some respite from the pressure of league action. The first round draw paired Town at home to Birmingham, whom they had defeated the previous season at the same stage.

Up until 1925-26, the first round was the equivalent of today's third round. The First and Second Division clubs were exempt until this stage, and the first round was traditionally pencilled in for the first or second Saturday in January.

An early goal from Billy Johnston, Town's reserve inside-forward, deputising for the injured George Cook, was enough to clinch Town's third 1-0 victory of the season over Birmingham. Scotsman Johnston had been signed in November 1920 from Selby Town: perhaps he had come to Chapman's attention during his time working in Selby. Johnston made eight appearances in 1923-24, but was sold to Stockport County in the summer.

Billy Smith returned to the side against Birmingham, having being excused from the Blackburn away game owing to the sudden death of his father. According to the *Huddersfield Examiner*, his father was killed in a 'traffic accident', but no details are known. City's Ernie Islip returned to his old club and was Blues' best forward, but they rarely looked like causing an upset.

Town's performances were, not surprisingly, attracting the interest of the England team selectors. There was no England manager in those days. An FA committee picked the team, an anachronism that persisted until the 1960s, when Alf Ramsey became the first autonomous England manager. The selection committee system continued unchanged after World War II, when Walter Winterbottom had become the first full-time England coach. He wrote about his experiences with the selectors in *Alive and Kicking*:

'I didn't have the full responsibility of picking my own teams, and I shall never forget the first meeting of a selection committee. We met in a hotel in Sheffield, and we had eight selectors plus a chairman. The way things were done was 'Nominations for goalkeeper?' and we had five goalkeepers nominated and then, through a process of reducing that number, we gradually got down to the last two and it was a vote then amongst nine people and if it was four and four then the chairman would decide which goalkeeper it was. Remember, in those days selecting a national team was really a means of giving recognition for high skill. It wasn't really looking at building a team to play on and win anything. It wasn't until we got into World Cup football that people began to realise we had to produce a team that might have a chance of winning the World Cup, and that meant playing the same players together as often as you possibly could.'

The selectors themselves were FA committee members who might or might not have played the game. More usually they were administrators. They would come to meetings armed with the opinions of their club managers and often without having seen the candidates play. The selectors used a combination of club form and trial matches to help them pick team. Trials tended to be between select teams from the North and South or England and the Rest. When the teams for a North v South trial match at Leeds were announced, Sam Wadsworth and Clem Stephenson found themselves in the North's team, with centre-half Tommy Wilson named as a reserve. Stephenson's call up was reward for some dazzling performances but many wondered why he had not been selected before. *Athletic News* applauded his selection: 'He is, among moderns, one of the finest schemers who has never received an England jersey. He was an inter-league player against the Scottish team, ten years ago. But the FA have found him at last.'

The *Huddersfield Examiner* believed Ted Taylor had been omitted because the selectors 'knew all about him'. The *Sporting Chronicle* said of Wadsworth, 'There cannot be any doubt on the score of England's left back. Samuel Wadsworth has made the position his own. He is just the same unruffled, calculating defender, a splendid combination of trenchant and adroit methods.' The same writer suggested that Taylor should play in goal for England and if a new centre-forward had to be found to replace Birmingham's Joe Bradford, then Charlie Wilson of Huddersfield was the man.

Stephenson inspired the North to a 5-1 win, scoring a goal and winning rave reviews from the press correspondents, from whom his long awaited first cap was predicted. Billy Smith was also in great club form and vying with Stephenson as the player of the season, but on the day his performance did not impress the selectors.

Meanwhile, struggling Chelsea had come to Leeds Road and wrecked Town's unbeaten home record. Charlie Wilson's absence was felt, and young George Brown was struggling to find goals and form. Additionally, Joe Walter was rested with Cook moved unsuccessfully to the right wing. Despite much huffing and puffing from Town, the Pensioners held out and grabbed a winner with virtually the last kick of the game to record only their third victory in 23 games.

A distinctly unamused Chapman made several changes for the return at Stamford Bridge, including the introduction of reserves Barkas and Harry Cawthorne. Knowing perfectly well that a second defeat to Chelsea might prove critical in the title race, Chapman was determined not to lose and adopted a tighter formation geared to a counter-attacking style. His tactics, whilst not winning many admirers amongst the London press corps, were perfectly designed to secure a one-goal win, which is exactly what happened. The correspondent of the London *Evening Standard* wrote: 'For a team to make only one serious shot at goal and win a match may not be a record but is certainly a rarity. Huddersfield indicated that they are all out for the Cup and don't care very much, at the moment, for league honours. I understand they came to London by train but they gave such a lackadaisical exhibition that a caustic critic behind me was quite justified in his belief that they must have walked.' How wrong the critics proved to be, thinking that Chapman only had eyes for Wembley in the FA Cup!

In the week that Stanley Baldwin resigned as Prime Minister, Town approached their second round FA Cup-tie with Second Division Manchester United with proper professionalism. Herbert Chapman took his players to Blackpool, where his team had prepared for the successful 1922 Cup campaign and where the manager had a set routine. The team arrived at the hotel – the Queens Hydro on the South Shore, which was popular with the players – on the Monday evening and they spent Tuesday morning having invigorating Turkish and tonic baths.

It was golf on Tuesday afternoon, followed by a billiards tournament in the evening, usually handicapped to ensure that Stephenson didn't win every time – 'his prowess with the cue is remarkable'. Wednesday was more golf, with a trip to the theatre in the evening. On Thursday a light training session at Blackpool's Bloomfield Road ground, more golf and a walk in the 'bracing air'. Friday, the eve of the game, would have been spent 'quietly in the fresh air'.

The time spent at the seaside helped bond the players further and also, importantly, kept them away from the Cup hullabaloo back in Yorkshire. If the team was preparing for a home Cup-tie, Chapman liked to get them back to Leeds on the Friday night, where they often stayed at the Queens Hotel and then made the short journey to Huddersfield after lunch on the Saturday.

Very few fans attended away matches in the 1920s, for a number of reasons. There was little spare money around for relatively expensive train journeys to other far-off towns and cities, and many men would have to work on a Saturday morning and found it impossible to find the time to go away. The FA Cup, however, was a different matter, and the mill and factory owners of Huddersfield must have been generous to their workers on the Saturday of the Cup-tie at Old Trafford. Over 20,000 supporters made the trip across the Pennines to see their heroes at Old Trafford, mainly by bus and rail. Many thousands walked the five miles from Manchester's Victoria railway station to the ground because of an over-loaded tram service, and many went without food because of over-crowded cafes and restaurants.

Old Trafford in 1924 was a vastly different stadium to what it presents today. Ground 'capacities' were really a licence to squeeze in as many as possible. They were, in any case, fairly arbitrary in those days. The foot-ball annals of the day reckoned that Old Trafford – only opened fourteen years previously – could accommodate 80,000, although the ground record at the time stood at 72,000, for a Cup semi-final the previous sea-son. Three sides of Old Trafford were open terracing, but the facilities in the one grandstand caused one writer to describe the ground as 'a won-der to behold'. It had billiard and massage rooms, a gymnasium, plunge-bath, and attendants to lead patrons to their five-shilling tip-up seats from the tearooms.

Huddersfield's excellent FA Cup record since the Great War, not to mention their current league form, was sure to attract Manchester folk out in their tens of thousands. United prepared for the expected arrival of huge crowds by employing 'crowd packers', whose function was to patrol the perimeter of the pitch and ensure an even spread of spectators and avoid bottle-necks on the terraces. Across the country spectators were packed like sardines in scenes that would have horrified Lord Justice Taylor of Hillsborough fame. Thankfully no one was seriously injured in the 66,000 Old Trafford crowd, an attendance that was rarely bettered at the ground until the modern era.

In 1928 Town would return to Old Trafford for an FA Cup semi-final with Sheffield United. Over 69,000 were present on that occasion to see a 2-2 draw. Pathe News clips of the occasion show hundreds of specta-tors on the pitch with police horses clearing them off before the game could commence. During the match itself, many of those present are shown perched on the perimeter of the pitch inside the terracing. Viewed in this light, it is a mystery how in excess of 76,000 spectators crammed into Old Trafford to watch the 1939 FA Cup semi-final between Wolves and Grimsby Town, when the ground record was set.

Back in 1924, a swirling wind made good football difficult, but Town, with Steele and Charlie Wilson back in the eleven, acquitted themselves well. It was Wilson who was once again the hero, with two good goals to see Town through 3-0.

Athletic News was one of several newspapers which predicted that Town could progress a long way in the Cup: 'Their men of experience in every line are not too experienced, and they possess just that tincture of dash in front of goal that clinches many an argument.'

An unconvincing 1-0 win at Newcastle – who rested several key play-ers ahead of an FA Cup replay – followed next for Town, but a 1-1 home draw with mid-table West Ham, in their first season in the top division, a week later proved to be an unexpected setback for the title aspirants. Goals were an increasing source of concern for manager Chapman; in the last six league games Town had scored only four, and three of those had come from Stephenson's boot. Former Scottish schoolboy interna-tional Billy Johnston had failed to adequately replace Cook, and Chapman toyed with the idea of recalling George Brown after the Mickley-born leader had impressed in the reserves.

The problems in the goalscoring department were highlighted in the FA Cup third round tie at Burnley, when Huddersfield suffered only their fourth defeat in 26 FA Cup-ties since the Great War. The home side raised their game in front of a record 54,775 Turf Moor crowd, and once they had gone ahead in the 22nd minute Town rarely looked capable of retrieving the situation. A massive following of Huddersfield supporters evacuated Turf Moor disheartened by their team's Cup exit, only to find entrepreneurial Burnley fans in the streets selling funeral cards telling of Town's demise. The loyal devotees, however, did have the consolation of an exciting period of league football to look forward to in the coming weeks.

On the following Wednesday afternoon, Huddersfield played out a second successive 1-1 home draw, this time against Newcastle United. Clem Stephenson – at last selected for the England team for the game with Wales at Blackburn a week later – was on target again. Freezing weather and the impossible task for most supporters of getting an after-noon off work kept the attendance down to 6,000. Chapman introduced George Shaw, a full-back signed the previous week from Doncaster Rovers for £1,500, in place of the rested Barkas. Many observers ques-tioned Chapman's wisdom in signing yet another full-back when the club already boasted England international Wadsworth, the prodigious Goodall, not to mention Barkas, who would have walked into any other First Division side. Within weeks of Shaw's arrival, Town's board minutes reported: 'should any club enquire if we were prepared to transfer Barkas we should ask a fee of £3,000.'

On 29 February a blizzard engulfed Huddersfield and the surround-ing areas and many believed that the following day's big match with league leaders Cardiff would be a victim of the weather. In the days before Radio 5 Live and local radio, communication between football clubs and supporters was pretty antediluvian. Curiously, Leeds Road escaped the worst of the snowfalls and the game went ahead, whilst thousands who lived outside of the town boundaries stayed at home, either believing the match was sure to be called off, or because they themselves were snowed into their rural communities. In truth, in those days before undersoil heating very few matches were postponed because of inclement weather. Players were expected to turn out come rain or shine, ice or fog, and play through the severest storm. The modern footballer, used to playing on pitches prepared by lawn scientists and drained by state-of-the-art drainage systems, would blanch at the surfaces common to footballers in the 1920s.

Players' long service with their club was rewarded with benefits. After five years the player was normally awarded a sum in recognition of his loyalty. He could choose a particular league fixture as his benefit game, and he would be paid the sum agreed out of the gate receipts. If the receipts were less than the benefit agreed, the club would normally make up the difference.

In 1926, for example, Stephenson and Wadsworth were each awarded £650 by the club for five years' service, but Harry Cawthorne was only offered £450 after seven. In addition to receiving money from the club, the players were permitted to take a collection at their designated benefit match, when supporters could show their appreciation of the player by making a donation.

Long-serving Billy Watson had chosen the Cardiff game in March 1924 as his benefit match. Four attendants carried an open blanket slowly around the pitch, with the crowd invited to lob coins into the blanket. Needless to say, lobbing coins from a great height ran the risk of missing the blanket and striking those manning it or, worse, landing a crashing blow on the heads of children, who often took up position at the foot of the terracing so that they would not have to try to peer over the heads of adults in front of them. It remains an oddity that coin throwing was tolerated for so long when the risk of serious injury was so high. Those readers old enough to remember pre-decimal currency, will not need reminding of the size and weight of pennies, half-crowns and florins, and threepenny bits were like miniatures slabs of lead. Those coins missing the blanket, and mercifully any human target, would be snatched up from the running track by a further attendant.

The money collected would be presented to the beneficiary and generally amounted to a few weeks' wages. Watson chose the Cardiff game for his benefit because one of the biggest crowds of the season was expected, but he had no way of anticipating the blizzards. The weather kept the crowd down to 18,000 instead of the expected 30,000, and Watson's takings were sharply reduced in consequence.

To face Cardiff, Herbert Chapman decided that the time was right to promote George Brown, and the bustling centre-forward yielded two first-half goals. These were enough to beat a disappointing Cardiff and close the gap to three points. The victory would ultimately be crucial to the destiny of the title. The form of the two clubs over the next month would diverge. Beginning with Cardiff, Town would win five games in a row, while their rivals picked up only two out of twelve points. Sunderland, too, were coming up hard on the rails. The leading positions after Huddersfield's 2-0 win over Cardiff looked like this:

	P	W	D	L	F	A	Pts
Cardiff	30	17	9	4	51	27	43
Sunderland	31	17	8	6	53	34	42
Huddersfield	30	17	6	7	45	24	40
Bolton	33	13	13	7	54	27	39

A week after the Cardiff win, George Brown netted the winner as fifth-placed Sheffield United were beaten at Bramall Lane. Charlie Wilson scored the solitary goal in a tight return game at Leeds Road, when the local reporter in the *Examiner* described the crowd 'gasping at some of the skills displayed by Stephenson and Smith'. Stephenson's long-awaited England debut against Wales at Blackburn had ended in a disappointing 1-2 defeat, following which the press called for wholesale changes to the England team, despite generally complimenting Clem. The *Sporting Chronicle* correspondent wrote: 'Although Clem Stephenson never spared himself and made many judicious passes I cannot say that he was a pronounced success. At least this can be said of him without disparagement.' Another report of the match said 'he was most noticeable for what he did and tried to accomplish'.

Those of Clem's descendants who still live in Huddersfield retain the mementos from his brief England career. His one and only England shirt is still in immaculate condition and treasured by his grandson, Clem. The shirt is cream and looks too large for someone of Stephenson's relatively small physique, which suggests that it might have been a standard one-size issue. The kindest description of the material is that it is rough, like an army shirt, and heavy and a bit like serge. It must have been comfortingly warm on a cold day, but excruciatingly hot on those occasions when the sun blazed down. The shirt has a pleat in the back and two tails like a nightshirt. Unlike his Huddersfield shirt, and other club jerseys of the time, the England shirt has a collar, almost like that found on a dress-shirt. There are buttons on the sleeve; four buttons up to the collared neck and, oddly, two holes at the neck, as though a stud was to be used. There is no maker's name inside, and no number on the back, but there is a Three-Lion badge on the front.

Grandson Clem also possesses Stephenson's England cap, a maroon velvet cap with a rose on the front and the opponents' name (Wales) on a small peak. Unlike the England caps of the 1950s onwards, which were closer to a traditional schoolboys cap, these FA caps share more in common with a Jewish skullcap.

Another Stephenson family heirloom consists of the blue and white ribbons, snaffled by Clem from the handles of the FA Cup in 1922. His family are not able to supply details of how they were obtained, but 80 years on they look as good as new.

According to *The History of the Football Association* by Geoffrey Green, Clem Stephenson would have received a fee of £6 for his solitary international appearance. Stephenson was also named in the 100 great League footballers in 1988, on the occasion of the Football League's centenary celebrations.

Talent in the Stephenson family was not restricted to footballer Clem. His wife was an accomplished violinist who performed under her maiden name of Miss Violet Smith. She was invited to play at a special benefit concert for Watson and Billy Smith, the two recipients of club benefits that season. The two players would share the proceeds of the concert, minus any costs.

Back on the pitch, a midweek trip to West Ham proved to be no pushover and Town twice had to come from behind to win 3-2. Charlie Wilson poached two goals to sink the Hammers and sneak Town back to the top of the league for the first time since October.

The last Saturday in March was a free one for Town, so they travelled to York for a friendly game with City, a match organised as part of the deal that took Len Boot to Leeds Road. Huddersfield were far too strong for the Midland League outfit and ran out 8-1 winners. This time Charlie Wilson netted five. In addition to selling Boot for £300, York had recently sold youngster Joe Hulme to Blackburn for a similar sum. Hulme went on to become a big success at Highbury, after Herbert Chapman signed him for Arsenal, winning three League championship medals and nine England caps, not to mention appearing against Town for Preston in the 1938 Cup final.

When Aston Villa visited Leeds Road on 5 April, it was the first of eight games for Huddersfield that month that would decide the destination of the league crown. Town's own Cup commitments, coupled with league postponements on the day of the fourth and fifth rounds, meant that they had games in hand over their rivals. On paper, Huddersfield's run-in did not look too taxing. But Chapman knew those vital matches had to be won if the title was coming to Huddersfield and the glut of fixtures would stretch his team to the limit in the next month. Villa, fresh from reaching the FA Cup final by virtue of beating Burnley 3-0 in the semi-final, were beaten by a first-half Smith penalty after Charlie Wilson was sent tumbling in the penalty area. In other games, Sunderland won to stay top, but Cardiff and Bolton both drew, leaving the situation at the top of the table as follows:

	P	W	D	L	F	A	Pts
Sunderland	37	21	8	8	66	43	50
Bolton	39	17	14	8	64	30	48
Huddersfield	34	21	6	7	51	26	48
Cardiff	35	17	11	7	52	32	45

Bolton, with just three games to play, could only gain 54 points, which surely would not be enough. Town, on the other hand, had what every club wants – their destiny in their own hands. Thirteen points from their last eight games would make them certain of the title. Having won their last five, this did not look such a tall order. Those critics who had written off Town's chances were now being forced to eat their words, as the team extended their unbeaten run to nine games. Excitement was beginning to intensify in the town and in that night's *Leeds Sports Post* – a Saturday evening sports paper, 'Aire Man' put it succinctly: 'Town's bid for the championship has caught the imagination and sympathy of all West Riding Socker [sic] supporters.'

April 12th was the date of the annual England v Scotland game, the first international at the new Empire Stadium at Wembley. Hitherto, England internationals had been played at club grounds, such as Villa Park, Goodison Park, Bramall Lane and Highbury. Wembley's official opening for the previous year's FA Cup final between Bolton Wanderers and West Ham United had been close to catastrophic. An estimated 250,000 fans had turned up for what was not an all-ticket match. After an enquiry, the authorities took action to ensure that there would be no repetition of the chaos. The forthcoming international and FA Cup final would provide a stern test for the Football Association, the stadium and their officials.

Ted Taylor in goal, winning his sixth cap, and Sam Wadsworth, winning his fifth, were both in the England team, but Clem Stephenson was dropped following the Wales defeat in March, despite his consistently excellent club performances. Club form, by all accounts, counted for little in the eyes of the England selectors, and Clem was one of several scapegoats for the Welsh defeat.

Four days before their Wembley date, Taylor and Wadsworth – along with the rest of the Town first team – had to fulfil a West Riding Cup-tie against Bradford. A potentially volatile club v country row, which would have been inevitable today, was not even mentioned. The West Riding FA's rules were clear: every club had to put out its strongest team in the competition. The teams drew 1-1, and fortunately Town's two England men came through unscathed.

Until 1960, clubs whose players were selected for internationals were not permitted to postpone their own matches. Therefore, successful clubs were handicapped in proportion to the number of their players who were called up. However, there were far fewer international matches in that era, with England typically playing Scotland, Wales and Ireland in the Home International Championship, and maybe having an end of season tour on the Continent.

Len Boot and Roy Goodall deputised for the two England men as Town struggled in heavy rain against Manchester City. George Brown put Huddersfield ahead midway through the second period but City equalised with a controversial goal from Roberts, who was seen to handle the ball before netting. The linesman flagged for the infringement but was not heeded by the referee and the game ended 1-1. Elsewhere, Sunderland went down at Arsenal but Cardiff's second win in a week took them up to 49 points, level with Town, and a point behind the Wearsiders.

Down at Wembley, England and Scotland drew 1-1. Fears of crowd problems were dissipated by the miserably wet weather, which kept the gate down to under 50,000. The England selectors came under fire from journalists for the team's poor record (they had failed to win any of their three Home Internationals), with few pundits understanding the rejection of Clem Stephenson, let alone the non-selection of Tommy Wilson, widely thought to be as good as any England centre-half. It was hardly surprising that the team looked like strangers against Scotland. The selectors had once again picked in-form players and made seven changes from the team that lost to Wales.

Town now travelled to Cardiff's Ninian Park for a vital 'four-pointer' on the Monday. With the clocks having gone forward, the extended evening daylight allowed a 5.30 kick-off, which permitted many factory workers to attend straight from work. A vociferous home crowd created a vibrant atmosphere for what was billed locally as the title decider. By the final whistle Town were more pleased than their hosts with a point apiece from a 0-0 draw. As the re-arranged games began to unravel, Town and Cardiff were now at the top of the pile, level on 50 points but with Huddersfield having the advantage of two games in hand. With Town's reserves top of the Central League and the Yorkshire Midweek League, Huddersfield seemed to be carrying all before it.

Sunderland, however, were not mathematically out of contention. On Good Friday, Huddersfield dropped another point, this time at Turf Moor, while Sunderland beat West Brom to leapfrog over both Town and Cardiff, who had a blank day. The games were fast running out for Sunderland, though, and their challenge fell away limply when they took only one point from their last three fixtures. On Easter Saturday, whilst Town drew at Manchester City's brand new Maine Road stadium, Cardiff won at Burnley to leave all three leaders on 52 points.

On Bank Holiday Monday, Cardiff beat Middlesbrough 1-0 to go top again, whilst Town were resting. Twenty-four hours later Huddersfield pulled level again by sneaking a 1-0 home win against Burnley, in what was probably the worst home performance of the season. The nerve ends were exposed for all to see, and Charlie Wilson hobbled off with a knee injury following a clash with Burnley's Hill. That night the top of the league table looked like this, Bolton having completed their fixtures:

	P	W	D	L	F	A	Pts
Huddersfield	39	22	10	7	55	29	54
Cardiff	40	21	12	7	59	34	54
Sunderland	41	22	9	10	70	49	53
Bolton	42	18	14	10	68	34	50

Despite the recent dropped points, Huddersfield could see the finishing line in sight. The advantage was definitely with Town, by virtue of their game in hand, but it was away at Aston Villa, the FA Cup finalists, who had lost only once at home all season. Town's other games were home and away fixtures with lowly Nottingham Forest, whilst Cardiff faced a double header with Birmingham.

Charlie Wilson's injury meant he would miss all three games, and with Billy Smith also on the treatment table, Herbert Chapman drafted in George Cook, who had not featured since January. He also recalled Walter on the right-wing with Eddie Richardson switching to the left in place of Smith.

Joe Walter would be remembered not so much as an outstanding footballer, but for his longevity. He struggled to win a place after the arrival of Joe Williams in the summer of 1924, and left Town in 1925 to return to the West Country. Walter returned to league football with Blackburn Rovers after a year with Taunton United, but never really hit the heights. He did, however, reach the ripe old age of 100. By 1994, when Leeds Road closed, he was the sole survivor of Huddersfield's immortal team. He was a guest of the club at a special celebration and received a wonderful reception from the crowd. He died before he could be a celebrity guest again, this time at the opening of the McAlpine Stadium later that year.

Interviewed for *Alive and Kicking* shortly before his death, Joe Walter was effusive about his manager at Huddersfield Town: 'Herbert Chapman was wonderful. I shall never forget him. And Jack Chaplin was a good trainer. We had a good trainer and a good manager and nothing whatever to grumble about. Herbert Chapman used to look after us, you know, tell us to behave ourselves. No messing about. No ladies! He used to tell us to cut the smoking out. He wouldn't allow us any cigarettes if he could help it, but we could have a drink at night. We always had a glass of sherry before we went to bed. Herbert Chapman had a lovely manner with him of getting you to play. You were just going out on the field and he always had a glycerine tablet to give you. I always remember that. First we put it in our mouth, get it on the field and throw it away. Going out on the field he'd just pat you on the back. He said, "Best of luck, Joe, do your best." He knew we knew what to do with the ball. He just left it to us: "Try to get the ball and always make use of it." He used to say, "Get up the wing and get the ball over, get it well over, out of the goalkeeper's reach." I used to go up that wing and nobody could catch me. I could move then.'

With Walter in the side, Town dropped a point at Forest's City Ground when a mistake by Tom Wilson induced pandemonium in Town's defence which Forest exploited. At Ninian Park, Cardiff were far too strong for Birmingham, but could do no better than win 2-0. The Welsh side missed a host of chances and, with goal average emerging as a potential deciding issue, those misses were to prove crucial.

Town's game in hand was staged at Villa Park on the Wednesday night, following Aston Villa's defeat in the FA Cup final. Two late Newcastle goals had sunk them. Villa fans were a fickle lot and only 14,000 now turned up to see their final home game. As often happens in the modern game, a side beaten in a big game bounced back to win what was, for them, an insignificant match. The Villa players, who must have been devastated by losing at Wembley, pulled themselves together to became only the second side to score three goals against Town that season. The muddy surface was a great leveller and Town were swept away by Villa's darting forwards, the home side winning 3-1. Huddersfield's vital game in hand had been squandered and suddenly the pendulum had swung in Cardiff's favour.

On the day of reckoning, Cardiff travelled to St Andrews and Town entertained Nottingham Forest. Huddersfield supporters, probably resigned to Cardiff winning the trophy, did not turn out at Leeds Road in great numbers – 19,000 was just above the average for the season. Those who stayed away would probably rue the fact for the rest of their lives, for they had turned their backs on the day when Huddersfield Town became Champions of England.

There is a postscript to this wonderful season in the form of a letter written by Herbert Chapman to Clem Stephenson, dated 8 May 1924 (see pages 78-79).

'Dear Clem,

Thanks for your letter of Monday last and your kind expressions of our team's success in the League Championship.

It was a wonderful final flourish, and all the more pleasing because our chances appeared more faint after the Villa match but the team's wholehearted effort against the Forest under such conditions was worthy of the event. I want to thank you personally for your play, your wholehearted efforts both on and off the field. I have never had such confidence in any Captain of a team I have been associated with, and on behalf of Jack Chaplin our Trainer and myself I want to place on record such assistance from you, for your help amongst the players, as without it Huddersfield Town could not have been champions, and there is no one connected with our club who deserves more credit for our position than our Captain, a man held in the greatest esteem both by players, management and Directors.

I am enclosing copy of a letter which I think should assist Joe Crozier. Hoping you will enjoy a good holiday and come back next August refreshed.

Kind regards to all at Cumona Villa.

Sincerely yours

H Chapman'

This is a touching letter written by a man who sounds genuinely appreciative of his captain's efforts. It demonstrates a close relationship between manager and captain. It also illustrates Chapman's man-management skills by the way he praises Stephenson saying 'I have never had such confidence in any Captain'. Stephenson obviously cherished the letter and it has been handed down to his grandson, who has had it framed in glass, and today beams with pleasure at reading it.

Chapter 5

~ STUTTERING CHAMPIONS ~

(JUNE – DECEMBER 1924)

Hardly had the cheers died down from the championship success than work began to improve the pitch and undertake other minor ground improvements. When the *Examiner*'s reporter visited the ground in early August he reported: 'The Leeds Road ground is looking wonderfully spick and span just now, and the turf on the playing area is in better condition than for many seasons past. In fact frequenters of the ground ever since it was constructed state that the turf has never looked so well, and it is knitted together much better than usual.'

A new half-time scoreboard – double the size of the old one – was erected on the Bradley Mills end of the ground. There were improvements to the running track to assist the players in their lapping, the ground's heating system was upgraded from coke to gas, and a new drying room installed. Most noticeably, however, the roof on the main stand had been extended to provide more covered standing room. With an entrance fee of 1s 6d (7½p), it would cost an extra sixpence to stand under cover as opposed to the open terrace.

A fresh loudspeaker system was installed and the *Examiner* reported that the half-time entertainment at Leeds Road would be changing. The music-playing bands, a great tradition at the ground, would be replaced by wireless concerts transmitted over the new speakers. In the match report for the second home game, against Sheffield United, however, it was admitted that there were 'hiccups from the new system and it sounded like a steam organ suffering severe spasms'. As soon as the gremlins were sorted out, standards improved. An early programme of half-time entertainment included excerpts from Verdi's Il Trovatore, a march by the Coldstream Guards, and advertisements read by an announcer proclaiming 'certain unnoticed qualities in beef juices'. By October, however, the board minutes stated that, 'the secretary had arranged with the Mirfield Band for the remainder of the season to play at first team matches'. One can only assume the gremlins reoccurred, or the fans lobbied the club for the return of the popular band.

Alec Lodge remembers that brass band: 'The band was from Mirfield. It used to walk round the field, play at each corner and at Christmas particularly; it was really fascinating because they used to play carols and the people used to sing carols. The mascot at that time was a fellow dressed like Charlie Chaplin and his main thing was that he had a bowler hat that he used to knock off. He used to go round the field, supposed to be picking this up, and his foot just caught it and kicked it a yard forward, and he'd go round the field to tremendous cheers. But people respected him and clapped him as he went past.'

The Charlie Chaplin lookalike was Jack Richards, an excellent mimic of the legendary Hollywood comic. Richards barely missed a game at Leeds Road between the early 1920s and World War II. According to Ian Thomas in *Leeds Road: Home of My Dreams*, he was 'chased off by the constabulary' the first time he went on to the pitch, but he soon became Town's official mascot and used to perform with the club's black cat. Jack was at Wembley to see Town play in 1928 and 1930 and caused a sensation by firing a starting pistol into the air.

In *Huddersfield Town 75 Years On*, George Binns explains what happened with the band: 'A large sheet of cloth was carried around on the cinder track. The exciting part was the art of throwing pennies from way up the terraces in an effort to hit the sheet dead centre. It was often a hazardous task for the bandsmen whose duty it was to carry the sheet round that day. On the terraces supporters of both sides would mix together, although away followings were far smaller in those days than now. There would be lots of banter and good-natured chat but no aggro. Fans would criticise their own players as well as their opponents and the referee without any outward show of aggression.'

Herbert Chapman added only one player to his staff that summer, right-winger Joe Williams, whose cost, according to the *Examiner*, was 'dirt cheap' at under £2,000, from Rotherham County. Joe Walter had not been retained and Chapman saw his speedy, tousle-headed replacement as the man to create more chances for his goalscorers. Williams, who impressed in his early months at the club, gave the forward line better balance, by making the team more potent down the right flank. At just 5ft 3in, Williams was the smallest player in the League and was nicknamed, for obvious reasons, 'Tiny'. However, Tiny could upset physically bigger opponents with his bravery as well as his pace.

One player whose signing eluded Chapman was Burnley's England international Bob Kelly. The board minutes of 12 May 1924 reported that Kelly was Chapman's top target, but Burnley were not prepared to sell. Kelly was one of the top inside-forwards of his time. He would finally join Town, but only via Sunderland and after Chapman had departed for Arsenal, thereby completing Town's famous all-star forward line. As a result of several factors, not least higher crowds at home and away, the club's finances were in a much healthier state. If Burnley had been willing to sell Kelly, the large fee is unlikely to have been a problem for Town. The club's accounts for the year to May 1924 showed a handsome profit of £4,850 on gate receipts of £34,000. The modern day equivalent of that profit would be £200,000.

Before the new season got under way, there was a celebration dinner held in the club's honour at Huddersfield Town Hall. The guests numbered 180, among them Football League President J McKenna and six members of the League Management Committee, Huddersfield's Mayor and Mayoress, as well as local MP Mr J Hudson. All were entertained, said the *Examiner,* 'in a convivial atmosphere'. The board minutes reported that Messrs Whiteley provided the catering and the meal cost 8s 6d a head (42p) – which at that time would have purchased quite a meal.

Charles Sutcliffe, a senior League committee member who would later succeed McKenna as League President, made an after-dinner speech: 'The secret of the success of the club was that there was a united band of directors determined to carry the club to the highest position it could occupy, a whole-hearted team of players who were loyal to the club, and who were ambitious in their aims and purposes; a manager who was modest but enthusiastic, always seeking to render the best he could for the club; a trainer who served as only the man behind the scenes could serve; and a reserve strength which was always urging the first team to put its best foot forward. With such a combination victory was sure to come.'

Chairman Joe Barlow replied, and predicted another trophy in twelve months' time and said the club had the best manager in England and the best trainer in England. Clem Stephenson and Chapman said a few words before the Mayor presented league championship medals to fourteen players, plus Jack Chaplin and Chapman. The Football League only permitted the champions twelve medals, but the board minutes confirm that two additional medals were purchased by the club for Roy Goodall and Harry Cawthorne at a cost of approximately £3 each. The Birmingham firm of Vaughton's manufactured the solid gold medals. The club gave souvenir gifts to twelve players, and Barlow explained that each player had a choice of a souvenir, up to a value of £20, and the Mayor presented these. There were however two exceptions. Gifts were not to be presented to Tommy Wilson and Ted Taylor as both players had 'Picked such big things that they would not come into the Town Hall'. Clem Stephenson chose a silver tea service, which was inscribed with suitable wording. A programme of music rounded off a memorable evening, including a performance by the Lindley Male Voice Quartet.

Ten days later, the new League campaign kicked off with a trip to Newcastle to face the FA Cup holders. Williams made his debut and Roy Goodall came in at right-back. Some 47,000 Geordie fans, the biggest crowd of the day, watched their team outclassed 1-3. Ex-Town custodian Sandy Mutch, recovered from the injury which had forced him to miss the Cup final, could do nothing to stop the course of events. The result was the first of Town's four victories in a row. It extended to a run of ten unbeaten games, Huddersfield's best ever start to a season.

Goodall could count himself lucky to be in the side. During the summer he had been in trouble, as the board minutes of May 1924 report: 'The Secretary reported on Goodall's accident whilst riding a motorcycle. It was decided that a letter should be sent to him pointing out that the directors deprecated his attitude in misleading the management as to the cause of his injury and warned that any future injury from motorcycling would result in the loss of his wages.'

For the 1924-25 season, the Football League reverted to a more standard fixture list. Up until 1914-15 a system devised in 1898 by a Mr WF Fletcher of Birmingham had been used to compile the League's fixtures. After the Great War, Charles Sutcliffe, a driving force within the League's administration, introduced his own formula, which for unknown reasons saw clubs play each other home and away on successive Saturdays.

The Sutcliffe system had never been popular with clubs. One obvious reason was that meeting the same opponents two weeks running invited grudges and feuds to be carried over into the second game – a situation Town had recently experienced against Notts County. At the 1924 Annual General Meeting, clubs voted to revert to the Fletcher method. Sutcliffe, however, was loathed to give up his role and came up with a hybrid system that, although similar to the Fletcher system, was sufficiently different to avoid infringement of copyright. In consequence, he was able to retain the role of fixture 'fixer'. After Charles Sutcliffe's death in 1939, his son Harold took over the compilation of the League's fixtures. He reckoned that it took him 150 hours to complete, starting in March and ending in July. Since Harold's death in 1967, the fixtures have been computerised.

The new fixture arrangements still allowed for home and away midweek games between the same clubs early in the season, when light evenings allowed games to kick-off at 5.30 or 6pm. Huddersfield faced Nottingham Forest during the first two midweeks of September and won both games.

The early signs were that Town's defence would once again be hard to penetrate. Only two goals were conceded in the first six games. But having scored six goals in their first two games, the forwards scored only three in the next four. The only injury to report was Clem Stephenson who was given a rough time by Sheffield United defenders in the 2-1 home win and left the pitch with strained ligaments. He missed eight games, but George Cook was a capable deputy and, on Clem's return to the side in October, Cook retained his place at the expense of Charlie Wilson, who was dropped after some lacklustre performances.

Since Bradford City were relegated in 1922, Huddersfield had for two seasons been West Riding's sole representative in the top flight. But while Town were winning Division One, Leeds United were winning Division Two under the managership of former-Town boss Arthur Fairclough. Fairclough's involvement, plus that of ex-Town players Jimmy Baker and Jack Swann, ensured that interest in the first meeting between two clubs which almost amalgamated was enormous. Over 41,000, a ground record, squeezed into Elland Road. In a cup-tie atmosphere, with the touchline almost hidden under the weight of spectators, Town won a physical contest which, at times, threatened to get out of hand.

There had been a change in the laws of the game in 1924. For the first time, goals could be scored direct from a corner-kick, but no one had yet done so. On 11 October, at home to Arsenal, Billy Smith wrote himself into the record books by becoming the first League player to exploit the new rule when his inswinging corner entered the net just inside the near post. This was opposite to the more common approach, whereby a high swinging corner veers back towards the angle of the far post. Arsenal were thrashed 4-0, so could have had no complaints.

Huddersfield's success, however, began to have unwelcome consequences. Tommy Wilson and Wadsworth were selected for the Football League XI to play the Irish League in Belfast on the day of the Arsenal game. Town had little choice but to release them, and reserves Harry Cawthorne and Marshall Spence stepped in to replace them and played well. These inter-league matches were a valuable source of income for the Football League. For many years, however, clubs had been increasingly reluctant to release players for Saturday games, in addition to Home Internationals, and by 1929 the inter-league fixtures would be switched to midweek dates.

At Maine Road on 18 October, Ted Taylor suffered a serious injury. He dived at the feet of a Manchester City forward and, after a melee in the goalmouth, failed to get to his feet. According to the *Sporting Chronicle*: 'Mr Sharpe, the referee expressed the opinion that Wadsworth had accidentally kicked his colleague as he went to his assistance. A medical examination showed that the muscle behind the left knee had been badly injured and it is feared that Taylor would not be able to play for two or three weeks.' With no substitutes, Billy Watson wrapped himself in Taylor's green woollen polo-necked jersey, and played as if to keep it for ever. Chapman bravely ordered his team to continue attacking, which was applauded by the Maine Road crowd. Taylor's injury, however, proved to be more serious than expected and a lengthy absence was predicted.

They say bad things happen in threes, and this was never truer than Huddersfield's results over the next three Saturdays. No side can go 27 games undefeated without a little bit of luck, and Town had enjoyed their share, but it all dissolved when three games in a row were lost. First, Birmingham City, 'a set of bustling, big booted spoilers,' defended like dervishes and snatched the points with a goal that Town's stand-in keeper Len Boot should have saved.

With another General Election looming, Town had invited all three election candidates to attend the Birmingham game. Ex-Town player Ernie Islip was given a warm reception and the 'most exciting thing of the first half was when he retired with torn knickers'. Islip later incurred the wrath of the Huddersfield crowd with some strong challenges on Williams. Will Watch in the *Sports Post* commented: 'It was the Town's bad day, which was bound to come sooner or later. The wonder is, of course, not that they were doing badly today but that they had played so consistently well over such a long period.'

Then West Bromwich, 'a wonderfully, virile team', one of Town's strongest challengers for the title, beat them by a solitary goal. Finally Tottenham, a team languishing in the lower reaches of the table, were handed a late winner by Boot, when the maverick deputy rushed out to a through ball. The odds had been stacked against him reaching it and he was left stranded. In the space of three weeks Town had slipped from the top spot to ninth in the League.

The lack of goals was worrying supporters, and one, 'Friendly Critic', had his letter published in the *Examiner*: 'I suggest they drop Brown and bring Tommy Wilson from the half backs to centre forward, allowing Spence to come to centre-half. I feel sure this will bring some of the goals of which we are badly in need.'

Other fans felt that Charlie Wilson should be recalled, and Chapman did recall him in place of George Brown for the Spurs game. Charlie's rest seemed to have rejuvenated him, for he netted ten goals in the next nine games, including four in the 5-1 win at Burnley on Christmas Day.

Following his heroics between the posts at Maine Road, Billy Watson was dropped after 90 consecutive appearances and reserve Norman Smith, after some outstanding displays for the reserves, made his one and only appearance of the season. Not a lot is known about Norman Smith, other than the fact that he came from Mickley, the same Durham mining village as George Brown.

Watson's loss of form was temporary – he was recalled a week later – and would miss only a further two games in the next two seasons. Billy was a tough, no-nonsense Yorkshireman. Contemporary photographs show a man with immensely broad shoulders and thick legs like tree trunks. Now approaching his 30th birthday, the loyal servant had been at Leeds Road since 1912, becoming a regular during the wartime games in the ersatz leagues. For one who made so many appearances – over 400, including wartime games – it is surprising that he was never selected for England or for an inter-league game, nor even appeared in an international trial match. His position was left-half and his main job, prior to the change in the offside law, was to stop the right-wingers, many of whom were small, fast and skilful, and this he did to excellent effect.

The excitement of Town's first ever win at Liverpool's Anfield fortress was tempered by another defeat, a week later, at Bolton. It was the sixth defeat in a row at Burnden Park, but it could have been avoided if Boot had not committed another costly blunder.

The *Examiner* reported on a speech made by Herbert Chapman to Highfield Young Peoples Society on the subject of 'The troubles of a Football Manager'. 'He impressed his audience with his comments about the emphasis that the club put on the need for good character in the players they engaged. He told of the care that was taken to look after the welfare of young players who came as strangers to the club. Chapman described how the club were always on the look out for fresh talent. They had four scouts who went to games all over the country each Saturday and reported back to Chapman. Chapman amused his audience with his stories of the difficulties he had had inducing young players to join Town. He appealed to the audience to support the team; especially the young ladies whose presence he said would raise the tone of the football spectator generally. Bad language, barracking and gambling were the three great evils of the game.'

The weather that winter in the West Riding was dreadful. The contemporary match reports described poor conditions due to weather every week from around mid-November through to the beginning of March. On 22 November, for the home game with Notts County, 'drizzling rain and poor visibility keep the crowd down' – there were only 12,300 there for the 0-0 draw. Three weeks later, the *Examiner* reported 'the worst fog for many years over most parts of England and Wales but Town's game at Cardiff went ahead'.

Christmas was a particularly miserable time with heavy rainfall across the West Riding. The match report on the home game against Newcastle is graphic: 'rain fell pitilessly for an hour before the kick-off, and the ground was practically under water at the start. The stand was packed with spectators but on the whole of the uncovered bank opposite not more than 30-40 braved the downpour. Every step the players took sent up a shower of muddy water, and the early exchanges were accompanied by shouts of laughter from the spectators under cover, as the players slid hopelessly in the splosh.'

The game was understandably riddled with mistakes but Town adapted better than the Magpies, with the exception of Town's right-winger: 'Williams was right out of his element in the aquatic display and at half-time required special attention to invigorate his frozen limbs.'

The return match with Leeds at the end of January also suffered from rain, but that did not deter a large contingent of 2,000 United supporters who made the short trip to Huddersfield. The *Examiner* noted that heavy rain in the morning kept the crowd low and when the teams kicked off there only seemed to be around 8,000 in the ground. Large areas of the pitch were under water and by half-time the players' had to change into clean kit, but within minutes it was dirty again. A week later, for the home game with Aston Villa, spring-like good weather had arrived too late to help a sodden pitch. And by the time Manchester City visited on 21 February, the match report confirmed the worst: 'Damage done by the wet winter was plain for all to see. There was barely a blade of grass between the two penalty areas.'

The poor conditions were not restricted to Leeds Road. In mid-February, Town played at Highbury, where 'hailstorm and rain before the kick-off turns the pitch into a quagmire'. Two weeks later at St Andrews the start was delayed 24 minutes because of a rainstorm. The game was in doubt and then threatened by 'a haze descending on the pitch making visibility poor. Dale's miskick in the mud lets in Brown for a soft goal. The haze gets worse and the game finishes in semi darkness. The mud makes any football impossible.'

On 24 January, Britain witnessed a partial eclipse of the sun. In West Yorkshire the eclipse was expected to start just before 3pm and reach its nadir at 3.45. The sun would not be seen again that day as sunset was at 4.30pm in Huddersfield. The *Examiner* pointed out that this, however, was a theoretical sunset: 'In Huddersfield we are not accustomed to see much of the sun even on sunny days in winter for half an hour or so before it actually sinks below the horizon, for it becomes lost with the smoke cloud.' Some local rugby games kicked off early to avoid even poorer light than usual, but the Football League Management Committee said games should start at the usual time (which at that time of year was normally 2.45pm). Town reserves were at home that day and the *Examiner* reported that the light was so poor that the referee did not see a blatant penalty.

Alec Lodge recalls in *Alive and Kicking*: 'Sometimes I went to games with my mother and the big attraction for her was when it became dusk. There were no floodlights, of course, and it became dusk about four o'clock in the winter, and she used to watch all the men lighting their cigarettes and pipes. It was just like a monstrous Christmas tree, and it was so fascinating for her to watch all the lights on the other side of the field.'

In the same book, Harold Riley reminisces: 'The crowds actually looked very much more uniform. Men tended to dress in similar ways and everyone wore a cap or a hat. You could smell the body odours and the tobacco.' Deodorant for men was not even a gleam in someone's eye at that time and there were no replica shirts. Men would wear a collar and tie, a suit or jacket and trousers and a raincoat.

Despite the dreadful playing conditions, Town were virtually invincible after the blip in November. Following the Bolton defeat the club had signed a new goalkeeper, Billy Mercer, a £2,000 buy from Hull City, and Len Boot's Town career was over. He left to join Fulham the following summer and, although he later played for Bradford City and Nottingham Forest, he was never a regular first-choice goalkeeper.

The 36-year old Mercer, on the other hand, would be first choice for the rest of this momentous season, and then spend the next three years vying with, first, Ted Taylor and, later, Hugh Turner for the Town goalkeeping jersey. It was astonishing that Mercer was playing first-class football at all – in the War with the Royal Engineers he had been blinded by gas – but he went on to make over 200 appearances for Hull before arriving at Leeds Road. In fact, Mercer was a good all-round sportsman – once topping Hull Cricket Club's batting averages – and, as a prominent local billiards and snooker player, he took on the great Joe Davis, fifteen times world snooker champion between 1927-46. One presumes Mercer lost, but surviving photographs portray a man older than he was. In fact he looks as if he is in his fifties.

Protected by what was undoubtedly the best defence in Britain, Billy Mercer would only finish on the losing side once in his first 27 league games. His arrival seems to have given the defence an added confidence, and he kept a clean sheet in his first three games, the third of which helped secure a 4-0 home win over Sunderland, the joint league leaders at the start of the day.

George Cook had replaced the temporarily ineffective George Brown in the attack in early November, and had played well alongside Charlie Wilson as the goals started once more to flow. The pundits recognised that Town were not going to give up their title without a major fight. Cook scored twice as Town recovered from a 0-2 deficit at Ninian Park to gain a point, but the December goalscoring plaudits went to Charlie Wilson, whose four goals on Christmas Day helped Town to a 5-1 win at Turf Moor and erased those bad Cup memories on the ground a year earlier. Over 30,000 watched the return with the Clarets on Boxing Day, which Town won 2-0, and 24 hours later Town's rain-affected draw with Newcastle left the top of Division One looking like this:

	P	W	D	L	F	A	Pts
West Brom	23	14	4	5	36	17	32
Huddersfield	23	11	8	4	36	15	30
Bolton	22	10	8	4	40	24	28
Birmingham	23	11	6	6	26	26	28

George Brown's time in the reserves was coming to an end and, once back in the first team, he would not look back. He was to become one of the most prolific scorers in Football League history and, as an *hors d'ouevres*, served up fifteen goals in the last seventeen games of the season. It later came to light that another unnamed Yorkshire club had made strong overtures to try to sign Brown during his weeks in the wilderness, but George had preferred to stay and fight for his place. Huddersfield Town fans would be glad he did.

Chapter 6

~ Champions in Style ~

It was that time of year when the FA Cup comes round. Huddersfield enjoyed what many neutrals considered to be the plum tie of the first round, but which their own followers viewed as the draw from hell, away at Bolton Wanderers, their bogey side. The Wanderers were having another excellent season and were virtually invincible at Burnden Park, where they had now chalked up eight wins in a row. There was no evidence however of Herbert Chapman throwing in the towel. His preparations, as usual at Blackpool, began ten days before the big game, and the side travelled from and back to the seaside resort for their League game at Bramall Lane seven days before the clash.

The *Examiner* revealed that Huddersfield's mascot, a donkey, was preparing to travel to Bolton. The Town had never lost a game when the donkey was in attendance. Their opponents' mascot was a small pony with 'trotters' on its back. The donkey was reported to be 'quietly training at Scapegoat Hill, ready for the fray'. Bolton's team were training at Cleveleys near Blackpool.

There was massive interest in the Cup-tie, locally and nationally. The *Huddersfield Examiner* reported that all grandstand tickets could have been sold twice over, and although the tie was not all-ticket, Burnden Park's capacity, estimated to be around 55,000, could be reached. The local railway company announced special trains to Bolton for 4s 9d, leaving Huddersfield between 10.40am and 12.05. On Saturday, a station official described the first train as 'one of the most crowded football trains I have ever known'. Not everyone could afford a train fare, however; the newspaper revealed how three young men who worked in a carpet factory arrived in Bolton at 6am after leaving Huddersfield on foot at midnight on Friday. Over Blackstone Edge, the cold was so intense that icicles formed on their clothing.

At the kick-off there were estimated to be 8–10,000 Town supporters in a crowd of just over 50,000. On a pitch so muddy, the referee had to toss his coin three times before it would fall flat. Bolton took the game to Town and after 22 minutes the home side led 2-0. Town's full-backs, normally so solid, came in for sharp criticism. Wadsworth, captain of the

England national side, looked unfit, whilst his partner Goodall 'became rattled by the laughter of the crowd at some of his earlier mistakes, and lost his nerve'. The *Leeds Mercury* summed it up: 'To those who have studied Huddersfield in their brightest moments their incapacity was amazing.' The final score was 3-0 to Wanderers and Town's only consolation was a cheque for £1,389 18s 5d, being their one-third share of the receipts from the large crowd.

That day marked the first occasion in which the *Huddersfield Examiner* published a regular Saturday night edition, but the news from the other side of the Pennines was bad. An oft-used cliché was trotted out in its first edition: 'Town will be able to concentrate on retaining the league.' Saturday's *Examiner*, like its sister daily, was a broadsheet, like most provincial newspapers of the period. It was available in various editions throughout the afternoon and early evening, contained eight pages, and covered all local sport. To cater for Huddersfield Town fans, there was a match report on the day's game on the back page, along with that day's results and league tables. Inside was a column of news from Leeds Road, describing 'goings-on' in the previous week. There was usually an excellent topical sporting cartoon and a crossword puzzle for football fans compiled by a reader.

The Cup defeat prompted Chapman to make changes against West Ham. Once again Charlie Wilson was the scapegoat, with Syd Binks, a tall athletically-built centre-forward, getting a call-up after starring for the reserves, but Binks would find himself out of his depth. Williams was out with an injured knee and Joe Walter played his first game of the season after injury. The Hammers came to Leeds Road and took advantage of the Cup hangover to record a surprise away win, only their second of the season. Wadsworth had another poor game, after which the England man felt the sharpness of Chapman's axe. George Shaw replaced Wadsworth, and Cook also was dropped, allowing the patient George Brown to step in at inside-right.

The response was remarkable. Huddersfield went on a seventeen-game unbeaten run that ensured Town won a second League Championship, but only after surviving a nerve-racking race for the line with West Bromwich Albion and Huddersfield's old foes, Bolton Wanderers. Albion had been League champions in 1919-20, but that side had been broken up and replaced by some exciting young talent, including a gifted forward line of Tommy Glidden, Joe Carter, George Jones, Charlie Wilson and ex-Town winger Jack Byers. Albion enjoyed a reputation for fast-flowing football at home and a tight, holding game away from the Hawthorns.

Town went top on 7 February as a result of their third successive win, 4-1 over Aston Villa, thanks to a George Brown hat-trick. It could not have been tighter at the top of the table:

	P	W	D	L	F	A	Pts
Huddersfield	28	14	9	5	47	21	37
West Brom	27	16	4	7	41	24	36
Bolton	27	14	8	5	48	25	36

Bolton slipped up in February, losing crucial games at Sunderland and Preston, but Albion won three in a row to go into their 7 March top-of-the-table clash with Huddersfield level on 42 points.

Charlie Wilson had been recalled after just two games on the sidelines and celebrated with a hat-trick in the 5-0 victory at Highbury, his second successive three-goal haul at Arsenal. Wilson, in fact, should have scored a fourth goal, but a barking dog in the crowd caused him to fall over the ball when clean through on goal. 'Caius' in the *Examiner* described Town's display: 'No side in the league could have stood against the subtlety, strategy and the sledge-hammer quality of the attack to which Arsenal were subjected'.

Wadsworth was also back in favour, but his five-game absence had generated much speculation about his future. Among the stories circulating was one from 'reliable sources', insisting that he had played his final game for the club and would be transferred. The rumours grew to such an extent that Wadsworth had to inform the press that he was far from unhappy and did not want a transfer. Less than a month after returning to first-team duty, Sam was back to his best and selected to captain England at Hampden Park in early April.

The title clash with Albion proved to be a damp squib, with defences on top and although Town led until the last ten minutes a draw was a fair result. Ten days later Bolton came to town and also earned a draw. It ended 0-0 but could easily have been 5-5, and in the context of the table both results were more positive for Town than for their opponents. In between those two draws Huddersfield recorded one of their best results of the season, becoming only the second team to lower Spurs' colours at White Hart Lane. George Brown's late winner was his tenth goal in eight games and the London press recognised that they had just seen the best team in England.

In the meantime, West Brom had failed to capitalise on their game in hand and, having drawn three and lost one of their four games in March, they still trailed Town by one point:

	P	W	D	L	F	A	Pts
Huddersfield	34	17	12	5	57	24	46
West Brom	34	19	7	8	51	30	45
Bolton	34	17	9	8	61	30	43

With eight games to go, Town were now the favourites to retain their title, but faced a challenging Easter programme with a double-header against high-flying Bury and a menacing-looking trip to Sunderland. West Brom leapfrogged over Town when they beat Sheffield United in mid-week whilst Town rested.

A 2-0 win over struggling Everton, boasting their boy prodigy Dixie Dean, who would become the greatest goalscorer England has ever seen, coincided with the England v Scotland annual joust at Hampden Park. Wadsworth captained England but there was no place for Tommy Wilson, who had been playing some of the best football of his career and had shone in an international trial earlier in the season.

The *Sporting Life* defended Wadsworth against press criticism: 'There is likely to be much adverse criticism of Wadsworth's selection, seeing that, not so long since he was left out of his own club side, and yet he is a fine player for big football, and it is in his favour that he has once more found his best form, and his speed, his power of quick recovery, and his positioning should be of immense service.'

Whilst Wilson was keeping Dixie Dean in check, England's defence was given a testing time by a Scottish attack that included the flying Aberdeen right-winger Alex Jackson and Airdrie's dynamic centre-forward Hughie Gallacher. Gallacher scored both goals in the 2-0 win, taking his international haul to five goals in four games. Both Scots would move south of the border within a few months, Jackson to Huddersfield and Gallacher to Newcastle, where they would become true giants of the English game.

Although Tommy Wilson was judged undeserving of an England cap by the selectors, he was highly thought of in football circles. The experienced Bolton referee JT (Jack) Howcroft, renowned for the bow-tie he wore whilst officiating, spoke eloquently about Tommy, as well as Town as a whole, at a Huddersfield Town Supporters Association meeting: 'If all footballers were of the type of Tommy Wilson and others at Leeds Road then the task of referees would be easy'.

Howcroft was a top referee for almost twenty years in an era when not all of them were up to scratch. Chapman was a big admirer, and later wrote in *Herbert Chapman on Football*: 'The secret of Jack Howcroft's popularity, as soon as he appeared on the field the players knew that every foul would be penalised and they would soon be in trouble unless they obeyed the rules. They also knew they would get every opportunity to play the game in the best sense, something that all footballers hoped for.' In *League Football and the Men who Made It*, Simon Inglis describes some of the 'not so' honest officials: 'In 1919 three referees were struck off the list for having lied about their ages. Six years later, the League demanded proof of each referee's date of birth, and discovered that twelve of the seventy-six had been lying. One man was so keen to remain on the list that he took his younger brother's identity!'

In 1924 eight referees and linesmen were sacked for fiddling expenses. The clubs, however, were more worried about biased officials, which has never been easy to prove, or officials turning up late, a problem usually blamed on unpunctual trains. The League's Referee Committee was strict on morals, too. In the 1920s one linesman was forced to resign when it was discovered that he was a publican. Another was sacked for betting on a football match, another after being found guilty of stealing a vehicle in order to reach a match on time. Linesman S Young of Newcastle was struck off the list for being 'hopelessly drunk in the street' outside Roker Park after a match in which he had run the line.

Referees in the 1920s customarily wore dark blazers, some adorned by referee association badges, and long shorts. Under their blazers, most referees wore an open-necked shirt, but contemporary photographs show Howcroft with his trademark dickie bow.

At this time Town, like most teams, played a straight 2-3-5 formation, the defence consisting of two full-backs who adopted a fairly central role, with the midfield consisting of three half-backs. The centre-half's role was essentially that of a central midfield man or pivot, a term in use until the 1970s, operating from box to box, supporting both attack and defence when required. That is not to say that the centre-half did not defend and often his role was to man-mark the centre-forward. However, that was not his only, or indeed his main, role. Whilst defending, the centre-half would often shackle the centre-forward, and the wing-halves, generally mobile and athletic players, would attach themselves to the wingers. At the back, the full-backs were often large and cumbersome players whose main tool was a hefty boot up the pitch. Undoubtedly some of Town's success was down to Chapman's use of more skilful, less unwieldy full-backs, like Wadsworth and Goodall. Wilson was undoubtedly one of the best 'pivots' in the English game, and yet would adapt to the new offside rule which was introduced in the summer of 1925.

Around this time an evil rumour spread around the town that Tommy had burnt to death. The truth was that a wax model of Wilson, created in 1922 after the Cup win, had caught fire whilst in storage at Blackpool's Madame Tussaud's waxwork museum.

Huddersfield's tough Easter programme yielded five points out of six, and with Albion securing only three points and Bolton four, the pendulum swung again in Town's direction. They now led Albion by a single point, but had a crucial game in hand. A week after Easter, though, a tired-looking Town could only draw 0-0 with the FA Cup finalists, Cardiff City, at Leeds Road, and Albion pulled level on 54 points by defeating Nottingham Forest. With three games to go, Bolton were still mathematically in the hunt on 50 points but it was in effect a two-horse race.

The penultimate Saturday of the season turned out to be its defining day. Huddersfield travelled to already-relegated Preston and won 4-1, whilst Albion could only draw at home to Bury. As Town had a hugely superior goal average, they now needed only one point from their final two games to clinch the league title.

On the Wednesday night the team travelled to Notts County, with the game kicking off at 6pm. Amazingly, that day's *Examiner* spared barely a word about the game. A single paragraph informed readers that Town would field an unchanged side. There was no mention of the fact that they required one point for a memorable second championship. However, the paper did draw attention to Town's reserves' home game with Bury which, if won, would secure the Central League title.

Despite injuries to several players, Chapman put out a full-strength side at Meadow Lane. Goalkeeper Billy Mercer was hurt early on during some heavy Notts artillery, which Town just about survived. Charlie Wilson's goal just after half-time settled the nerves but with fifteen minutes left County equalised and proceeded to bombard the panicky Town defence for the rest of the game. In a desperate finale, with injured Roy Goodall a passenger on the wing, and captain Clem Stephenson trying to provide defensive cover in the right-back position, Huddersfield's players were reduced to kicking the ball wildly into touch or upfield.

But Town were not to be denied. The final whistle signalled a second championship triumph. Back at Leeds Road, the reserves beat Bury 2-1 to clinch their own title, and it was reported that 'between 2–3,000 supporters cheered the team as they left the field'. The news of the result at Meadow Lane was relayed to them and generated another mighty roar.

There were reports of 'informal' celebrations on the train back from Nottingham, and when the steam engine pulling the victorious team pulled into Sheffield station *en route* to Huddersfield the players found a congratulatory telegram from Huddersfield's Lord Mayor, Law Taylor, awaiting them.

The following morning, the football club found itself the rare focus of an editorial in the *Examiner*. In brief, it suggested that the fame brought to the town by the football club would soon eclipse that brought to the town by the woollen industry. The editorial went on to note that there were no Huddersfield-born players in the team – 'in accordance with traditions of modern football' – and that many find it hard to understand how a Town crowd can cheer on players bought from various clubs around the country. Finally, it pompously stated: 'A minority of supporters view football as an art form, scorn the applause of the mob and appreciate the game like theatre-goers appreciate drama. To such people it does not matter that the players come from far afield much as it matters little to music lovers that Paderewski was born in Poland. May the numbers of such spectators increase.'

As the town prepared to honour their heroes at the final game, at home to Liverpool, 'Old Player' had his letter published in the *Examiner*. He 'urged all local people to go to Leeds Road', that Saturday, 'and hail the champions. All local cricketers should postpone their matches and support Town in their final game.'

The Liverpool match was overshadowed by the excitement of Town's followers, as League President J McKenna presented the Championship trophy after the game. Throughout the match the magnificent trophy, bedecked in blue and white ribbons, had stood gleaming in the sun, alongside the Central League trophy, at the front of the directors' box. The team had emerged onto the pitch between two lines of Mirfield Military bandsmen, playing 'See, the Conquering Hero Comes', a popular tune of the time from Handel's 'Judas Maccabaeus'. The players looked sheepish, almost embarrassed by all the fuss, and wide-eyed in the face of the blue and white bunting colouring all corners of the stand. Confetti and streamers filled the air, and the crowd's roar was something to behold.

During the half-time interval, long-serving members of the Leeds Road staff, H Dodson and W Furness, carried the trophies around the pitch, trailed by the band to a cacophony of applause. Five minutes before the end of the game a crowd started to gather in front of the main stand, but they had no malicious intent. On the final whistle they parted to allow the players to ascend to the directors' box, and by the time chairman Joe Barlow started to speak the throng covered almost a third of the pitch.

Barlow's speech was short and sweet: 'the feat of winning the Football League and the Central League in the same season was unique'. After presenting the trophies to Clem Stephenson and the reserve-team captain,

Marshall Spence, President McKenna described Town's players as gentlemen on and off the field. He added that club unity was one of the key factors in the club's success. The two captains replied on behalf of their teammates, whereupon the first team was carried off on the fans' shoulders. 'Tremendous enthusiasm prevailed everywhere.'

A national celebrity, Tom Swift, famous for walking huge distances to football matches, had turned up at Leeds Road just a week after walking from Sheffield to London for the FA Cup final – won, incidentally, by Sheffield United who overcame Cardiff City 1-0. Swift had walked an incredible 9,760 miles in five seasons to watch football games.

The tens of thousands of exuberant Huddersfield Town supporters who applauded their heroes on that sunny day in May 1925 were oblivious to the fact that when the new season started – just over three months later – the great Herbert Chapman would no longer be with the club.

## Chapter 7

~ All Change ~

(May 1925 – January 1926)

A week after the memorable day that saw Huddersfield Town lift the Football League Championship trophy for the second time, the club announced, via the *Huddersfield Examiner*, that it had made a new signing. Aberdeen's 19-year-old winger, Alex Jackson, had first come to the attention of Huddersfield and other leading English clubs after helping Scotland win all three Home Internationals that spring. He was not widely known to most football followers in England at the time, but Jackson would, before the decade had ended, become one of the foremost players in the country.

Chapman had realised that he had to continue to strengthen the Town squad to maintain standards. The club's board minutes of 3 April 1925 reported: 'Mr Chapman had identified the positions that needed strengthening as outside right, inside left and left half back.'

The expressed weakness at outside-right comes as no surprise. Joe Walter had temporarily solved the problem position, but then got injured and returned to Somerset, whilst Joe 'Tiny' Williams had started well but fizzled out on the heavier pitches. The two other positions earmarked for strengthening are puzzling, for Town's inside-left was Clem Stephenson, and although Clem had been less influential than in the previous season he was still seen as the vital cog in the machine. Similarly, Watson at left-half had missed only one game all season and was thought to be a key player by supporters and the press. Was his abortive attempt to become manager of the Adega Billiard Hall still held against him?

A further board meeting took place three days later, by which time Alex Jackson had been identified as a target and 'the secretary and Mr Mitchell [a director] were given the task' of attempting to buy the player.

In *Herbert Chapman: Football Emperor*, Stephen Studd asserts that the transfer details were thrashed out after Chapman watched Jackson when Aberdeen played Queen's Park at Hampden Park. According to Aberdeen's fixture list, this would have been the weekend of 11-12 April 1925, one week after Jackson had turned on the style on the same ground for his country against England, and five days after Town's board agreed to pursue him. Events, in other words, moved very quickly.

It is unclear whether Chapman had seen Jackson play against England, but if he hadn't then full-back Sam Wadsworth certainly had – at close quarters too – and England's captain would surely have enthused about Jackson's form in the international.

Studd describes how Chapman agreed a fee with the Aberdeen chairman after the Queen's Park game, then returned to Huddersfield. Both Sunderland and Liverpool also coveted Jackson's signature and, fearing that their target was slipping from their grasp, made last-ditch efforts to muscle in. Liverpool officials even arrived in Glasgow, where Jackson was still staying. It appears that, irrespective of the verbal deal with Chapman, Aberdeen officials gave Liverpool permission to speak to the player and for a while it looked like Jackson would be headed for Anfield.

Herbert Chapman, 200 miles away in Yorkshire, somehow learned about Liverpool's snatch-and-grab intentions. At 10 o'clock that night, as Jackson was walking past Glasgow's Sauchiehall Street station, he was approached by a stranger – later identified by Jackson as a private detective – and escorted to a 'secret' boarding house to await Chapman's arrival. The next morning the great man arrived in Glasgow and accompanied Jackson to meet his parent's family in Renton, where Chapman 'magnetised the old people with the charm of his personality'.

Jackson later described that visit in an article in the *Examiner*: 'It was at my father's house that I signed for Huddersfield at a fee of £2,500, after Chapman and my father agreed terms. When the paperwork was concluded, the manager said, "and now Mr Jackson, you and I will go along the street and celebrate this happy day with a glass of the wine of your country. The boy can have a lemonade".' Neither for the first time nor the last, Chapman had outwitted his opponents and got his man. Sadly, Chapman was not to get the opportunity to manage his expensive signing.

Chapman later explained his strategy with regard to new players. In *Herbert Chapman on Football* he wrote: Before signing a player I want to know the circumstances for the player wanting to leave his club. He may have an adequate reason for wishing to leave but these are matters that I want to enquire into. Indeed the first enquiries I make when contemplating the engagement of a player is, how did he behave, what sort of life does he lead and if the answers are unsatisfactory I do not pursue the matter further. Today there is only room for the decent fellow in the dressing room.'

Alex Jackson had an unusual background. Born in Renton, near Glasgow, he played briefly for Dumbarton before heading across the Atlantic to play for Bethlehem Iron Works in Pennsylvania, where he had a brother playing. In 1924, after just one season in America, he returned and signed for Aberdeen. He dazzled in the Scottish League and earned a place in the Scotland team as well as the attention of English scouts.

Standing 5ft 9½in, Jackson was tall for a winger in those days (Williams was only 5ft 3in and Walter 5ft 5in) but he possessed many of the qualities that make a great player – speed, balance, close control and quickness of thought. In an age when ball-control was not as highly developed as in the modern era, Jackson could 'kill' a ball deftly and run fast with the ball at his feet. Harold Whitaker, aged 91, remembers Jackson: 'Alex Jackson was my hero – he was the fastest footballer I ever saw. He would push the ball past the defender and beat him for speed. He had a powerful shot and scored some fantastic goals.' No less important, he had the attribute you needed from a top-class winger – he was an excellent crosser of the ball. In six seasons at Huddersfield, Jackson would become a legend in the game. He then disappeared from the scene almost as quickly as he had arrived.

One of Jackson's party-pieces was to keep the ball in the air by keepie-uppies on his head. The man who bought him describes this in *Herbert Chapman on Football*: 'When I engaged Jackson I was told he was able to bounce the ball on his head while walking from one goal to the other without letting it fall to the ground. I was assured he could do that at least once out of three attempts. I never put it to the test but I do not doubt his ability to perform the trick for, from what I have seen, the boys in Scotland seem to spend their time playing with a ball and any sort of ball is good enough for their purpose.'

If the dates are accurate, then Jackson's signing was kept secret for almost a month, until the season had finished both north and south of the border, a situation that would be inconceivable with today's media-hungry football circus. In the meantime, there is more than a strong possibility that Arsenal made their first approach for Herbert Chapman to become their manager.

Arsenal in the period prior to Chapman were not a major force in English football, despite the ambitions and influence of their autocratic chairman, Sir Henry Norris. Norris had used that influence to move the club from its roots in Woolwich, south London, to their new ground at Highbury in north London in 1913. After the War his persuasive political tactics and behind-the-scene lobbying thrust Arsenal, some say unfairly, into the newly enlarged First Division. He appointed Leslie Knighton, ironically a former assistant secretary of Huddersfield, as his manager but success was elusive and in six seasons the Gunners' highest league position was ninth and on two occasions they only just avoided relegation.

Knighton was rarely allowed to manage without interference from above, and Norris imposed severe restrictions on the buying of players, preferring cheap purchases and homegrown youngsters. He placed a ceiling of £1,000 on transfers at a time when any half-decent player would cost £3,000 and even forbade Knighton to buy any players under five feet eight inches! In *Arsenal: A Complete Record*, Fred Ollier notes that 'during the 1924-25 season Knighton displeased Norris by challenging his authority with demands to buy key players'. A final position of twentieth and a first round defeat in the FA Cup convinced Norris that Knighton was not up to the job. On Monday, 11 May an advertisement appeared in *Athletic News*, the weekly newspaper that was indispensable for all football folk (supporters, players and managers).

ARSENAL FOOTBALL CLUB
is open to receive applications for the position of
TEAM MANAGER
He must be fully experienced and possess the highest
qualifications for the post, both as to ability and
personal character.
Gentlemen whose sole ability to build up a good
side depends on the payment of heavy and exorbitant [sic]
transfer fees need not apply.

The wording of the advert seems to indicate that Norris, famous for his yearly endeavours at the Football League's Annual General Meeting to have a ceiling placed on transfer fees, appeared to be looking for yet another compliant manager. The *Examiner* said this when reporting Knighton's departure: 'He has not had a free hand. He has had to work to the orders of the directors.'

The last sentence of the advertisement would surely have deterred many prospective candidates, but Herbert Chapman, whose track record with transfers was a mixture of big signings and bargain basement buys, would have been confident in his ability to persuade the Arsenal directors, and Norris in particular, to take a different approach and 'invest' in new players to bring success to Highbury. Chapman had done the same at Huddersfield with Clem Stephenson, Steele, Taylor, and latterly Alex Jackson.

Some sources believe that the advertisement was a formality and that Arsenal had already made a private approach to Chapman. Others insist that Chapman made the first move by replying to the advertisement. News of his departure to Highbury was broken by the *Huddersfield*

Examiner on 10 June, six days after Town had returned from a three-week tour of Scandinavia.

The unanswered question is: was Chapman approached by Arsenal or the other way around? Either way, he obviously saw the Arsenal job as a major challenge. He had been successful with relatively small provincial sides – Northampton, Leeds and Huddersfield – but Arsenal's massive potential could hardly be ignored. In the season just finished the Gunners' average attendance of just under 30,000 was the biggest in the Football League. Conversely, nothing could alter the inescapable fact that Huddersfield remained very much a hot-bed of Rugby League. Despite the soccer team winning three major trophies in four seasons, crowds at Leeds Road averaged under 18,000. One assumes that this inscrutable man knew deep down that his work was done at Huddersfield and that Arsenal offered a new challenge. Chapman wanted and deserved a bigger stage for his immense talents.

London football at the time was desperate for success. It is hard to believe that in 1925 no London club had *ever* won the Football League Championship, despite the large crowds and the subsequent financial clout that the capital's three Division One clubs could exert. Tottenham had won the FA Cup in 1901 and 1921, and Chelsea had finished third in 1920, but Arsenal – potentially the biggest of the three – had never come close to winning anything.

In 1924, 'Tityrus' writing in *Athletic News* put forward one theory to explain this lack of success for London clubs: 'The plea which is most often heard is a reflection on the loyalty of the players, who, it is urged, have more freedom than in provincial centres and more liberty in a city where there are more temptations. It is said that players cannot be watched in London like they can be in Burnley or Sunderland, and the insinuation is that these young professionals do not live in a way to obtain the best results.' Tityrus's theory was that, unlike the bigger provincial clubs, London clubs lacked a 'home crowd', a partisan crowd that supports only their home team and cheers them on irrespective of the fluctuating highs and lows of form. An example given in support of this theory was the sporting way that Huddersfield's players had been applauded at Highbury on a couple of occasions, something unlikely to be seen at grounds like Bolton, Burnley and Sunderland, where passionate partisanship was taken for granted.

Arsenal were offering an unusually high salary for a manager – £2,000 *per annum*, believed to be double the wages that Chapman was paid by Town. Even if Huddersfield's directors did offer to match Arsenal's attractive package – which is debatable – Chapman's mind was made up.

The first reference to Chapman's resignation in the club's minutes appears on 16 June, when it was decided to advertise for a secretary-manager. The advert would appear for three days in the *Sporting Chronicle* and one issue of *Athletic News*, with 'replies addressed to the Chairman no later than Friday 26 June'. On 2 July 1925 the minutes reported that former Derby County manager Cecil Potter be offered the position with a two-year contract at a salary of £600 *per annum*. The same minutes reported that 200 guineas (£210) be paid to Chapman, 'in appreciation of his services'.

The parting was reluctantly accepted but clearly amicable. This was further demonstrated by Chapman's appearance at Huddersfield's Annual General Meeting at the end of June, where he presented the report of the club's financial affairs. A few days previously he had entertained the club's stewards to a farewell dinner at which he was presented with a gift of a gold pencil. At the AGM, chairman Joe Barlow complimented Chapman for his efforts for the club.

The way that the media covered the sport in those distant times was vastly different to the present day. There was little speculation, and newspapers reported facts rather than gossip and rumour. From the announcement of Chapman's resignation to the date of his successor's appointment, the whole subject barely merited a line in the *Huddersfield Examiner*. It is hard to imagine a similar state of affairs applying in today's news-hungry media world. Today, after the resignation, every newspaper would have its list of contenders, the bookmakers would be offering odds on the identity of the replacement, and every move of the directors of the club concerned would be monitored in an attempt to identify the new manager.

Life in Huddersfield, however, seemed to go on perfectly normally in the summer of 1925.

On 3 July the local newspaper reported that Herbert Chapman would formally leave Huddersfield Town the following day, but that he had already been involved with Arsenal's signing of veteran England star Charlie Buchan, in a deal that was reminiscent of the acquisition of Clem Stephenson back in 1921. On the same day, the *Examiner* also reported that rumours were rife that Chapman's replacement at Leeds Road was to be Cecil Potter.

Thirty-six year old Potter, with his steel-framed glasses and three-piece suit, was a studious-looking man with more the look of a schoolteacher than a football manager. He had left Derby in June after narrowly failing to take the team to promotion for the second successive season. Although press reports of the time indicate that he resigned his post, it is probable that he was eased out by a Derby County board that had set their sights on George Jobey as the man who could take them back to Division One. According to contemporary reports, Potter had intended to turn his back on football to run a dairy business in his home county of Sussex before he received communication from Huddersfield offering him the manager's position. One presumes he applied for the job, although the minutes do not confirm this.

Although born in Sussex, Cecil Bertram Potter – the son of a Congregational minister – was raised in Suffolk. He started playing for his local club, Melton, before joining Ipswich Town, then a Southern Amateur League side, in 1910. He made his name with Norwich City as a forward, making 131 appearances and scoring 31 goals before the Great War. After 'guesting' for Hull City and Tottenham during the conflict, he signed full-time for the Tigers in 1919. A year later he was offered the player-manager's job at Hartlepools United, and helped guide them into the Football League in 1921.

After leading Hartlepools to fourth place in their first season, the pipe-smoking Potter was lured away by Second Division Derby County. In his first season at the Baseball Ground the Rams finished fourteenth and reached the FA Cup semi-final. A place in the inaugural Wembley final was denied after losing 2-5 to West Ham. In 1923-24, Derby missed out on promotion on goal average, and finished third again the following season, but this time there could be no complaints of bad luck. County seemed to have one foot in Division One, but failed to win any of their last six games.

Taking over from a footballing colossus is invariably a poisoned chalice and whoever took over from the now-legendary Chapman faced a Herculean task. Comparisons would inevitably be made with his predecessor at every possible opportunity and the strain would inevitably be great. Nothing less than another League Championship would be good enough to satisfy Town's followers and directors. After all, the manager might have gone, but the players had not. In the event, not even a third title would be good enough!

Potter's first public engagement as manager of Huddersfield Town came when he met the Shareholders and Supporters Association in Northumberland Street Methodist School in early August. The *Examiner* reported that 'he was given a warm welcome. He asked supporters to show the same loyalty to the club as they had shown in the past.' On the eve of the new season it was reported that Potter had 'created a good impression with his tactful and courteous manner', and was 'confident about the season ahead'.

Certain London newspapers were dismissive of Huddersfield's championship prospects without Herbert Chapman at the helm, and the consensus in Fleet Street was that Town would not win a third league title. The argument that Huddersfield would find Chapman's absence an insuperable handicap was persuasive, but the other reason put forward – 'because it has never been done before' – was a feeble line of reasoning.

But Potter, and every other manager in the country, had a further key issue to deal with. The biggest change to the laws of Association Football since the introduction of the penalty kick in 1891 had just taken place. The offside rule had been radically altered.

Football's offside law had invited controversy and raised tempers for years. Commentators, players and spectators had complained about the dearth of goals, the huge number of stoppages for offside, and the negative tactics employed by the many clubs who followed the lead of the so-called 'father of offside' – Newcastle's Bill McCracken. The previous season, Tottenham and England forward Jimmy Seed had written in his *Leeds Sports Post* column, 'if steps are not taken to lessen our troubles, we shall surely qualify for the lunatic asylum. Everybody keeps telling us forwards to think and keep behind the ball – we would be able to handle it but our critics don't have to play against these negative defences every week. One FA official mentioned that in a recent Division One game he saw 57 infringements for offside. If each stoppage took twenty seconds, then nineteen minutes of play were lost. That kind of thing is making the "powers" seriously consider some alteration to the offside law.'

The contentious change in the law – which remains in place to this day – reduced from three to two the number of players required to be between an opposing attacker and goal when the team in possession plays the ball forward. This was a radical decision for the FA to take; a year previously they would not even countenance a trial game to experiment with the proposed new law. Prior to the law change, clubs would employ an offside trap by pushing their two full-backs as far upfield as the halfway line. A forward would either run into the 'trap' and be adjudged offside, or spring the trap, in which case he would have two men immediately chasing him down. The law changes handed the initiative back to forwards by halving the difficulty of springing the 'trap'.

Far from being overawed by the inevitable changes in tactics and team formations, Town quickly adapted their methods of play to suit the demands of the new law. Tommy Wilson's role was initially modified to incorporate more defensive duties, but ultimately the wearer of the No 5 shirt became a 'stopper' centre-half, playing deeper than previously, with the sole purpose of marking the opposing centre-forward.

Many thinkers about the game feared that the amended laws would produce a flood of goals as forwards were presented with more opportunities to score. But others felt the risk was worthwhile if it speeded up the game and made it more attractive for the spectators. On the opening day of the season Aston Villa beat Burnley 10-0 and the 44 League games yielded 160 goals, compared to 91 on the same day the previous year. The critics roared their disgust, but their verdict was premature. *Athletic News* spoke with common sense when it wrote: 'It is too early to speak definitely of the result of the change, but it promises, from the opening displays, to bring greater continuity of play, plenty of good fast-moving football uninterrupted by the dismal screech of "Off-side!" that often had rendered the game annoying rather than entertaining.'

Huddersfield kicked off the season with a 1-1 home draw with West Bromwich Albion, and Alex Jackson made an eye-catching start. Ted Taylor, now fully recovered from what turned out to be a broken leg, resumed in goal, but Billy Smith was absent. Two weeks previously he had been reported as having a 'severe chill on his stomach' but it seems that he had gone down with something more serious, as he did not appear in the first team until the last Saturday in October. Several board minutes from August and September refer to Smith's absence, and at one stage Potter was instructed to 'travel north' to see Smith, if the player had not reported for training within the week. 'Tiny' Williams, displaced by Alex Jackson on the right flank, took Smith's place against West Brom and scored. On the evidence of Town's first game, the impact of the new law change was positive; there were only three stoppages for offside in the whole match.

Town's players professed mixed views about the new law. The *Huddersfield Examiner* quoted Sam Wadsworth as saying that 'defenders would have to be quicker to cope'. Clem Stephenson thought 'forwards would score more goals until defenders got used to the new law'.

One of the unanticipated effects of the law change was that the game speeded up. Players had to be faster and, as a result, incurred more injuries. Town were victims in the first two games. First, Roy Goodall badly injured his ankle in the West Brom game, then a week later Charlie Wilson suffered a bad knock in a rough game at Bramall Lane against the FA Cup holders. Watson and Stephenson also suffered minor knocks in a match played in 'a fine drizzle of sooty water and a cold and clammy atmosphere'.

Leslie Unsworth in the *Examiner* had tipped Bury, Bolton, Sheffield United, Sunderland and West Bromwich as the major rivals to Town's hat-trick challenge. Bury would go on to have the best league season of their 118-year history, but Town were too good for them in match three and won 2-1.

Huddersfield's undefeated run, which stretched back to January, was only seriously under threat once in an unbeaten ten-game start to the season. That was at White Hart Lane, when Spurs, the league leaders, and Town fought out a exhilarating 5-5 draw, with George Brown netting the equaliser four minutes from time. The game, played in torrential rain throughout, making the slippery pitch hazardous for defenders, highlighted the uncertainties engendered by the new offside law. Jimmy Seed, the architect of Tottenham's 5-3 lead, was brutally fouled by Wadsworth. The incident sparked Spurs' late collapse and Wadsworth receiving a barrage of abuse from the home crowd.

A week later the goal glut became a virtual torrent, as 59 goals were scored in eleven First Division games. Bury lead the way with a 7-4 win over Sheffield United, whilst Blackburn Rovers and Manchester United each scored six. At Leeds Road, it was a relatively tranquil 2-2 draw with Manchester City. Freak scores abounded but – with the exception of the 5-5 draw at White Hart Lane – Huddersfield seemed to be one of the clubs least affected. This might have had something to do with Town's high-quality defenders, and Tommy Wilson quickly settling into his new deeper role.

A 4-0 win at Elland Road on 17 October extended Huddersfield's unbeaten start to ten, including this, their fourth win in five away games. When added to the seventeen unbeaten games at the end of 1924-25, Town's sequence of 27 unbeaten games was only three short of Burnley's all-time record of 30, established three years previously. That record would stand for almost 45 years until Don Revie's Leeds came along in 1968-69. Town, in other words, had stamped themselves as one of the all-time great English sides. Equally clearly – since they do not hold the record – their first defeat was just around the corner.

Huddersfield Town's wages book for the 1925-26 season makes fascinating reading. The average weekly wage-bill for the 30-strong professional playing staff was £199. Sixteen first-team players 'enjoyed' the League's maximum wage of £8 a week, reserves were normally on £6, with newer teenage recruits on £5. The manager's £600 *per annum* salary equated to eleven guineas (£11.55) per week, whilst trainer Jack Chaplin was paid £7 10s (£7.50), with other training and coaching staff on £4-5 per week.

Once the playing season was completed, players reverted to summer wages. For first-teamers, this was £6 per week, with reserves on £4-5. From their basic wage, the club secretary deducted 9d (4p) as a health insurance contribution (presumably a forerunner of National Insurance stamps) and 7d (3p) as an unemployment insurance contribution.

There are several ways of putting these wages into perspective. The modern day purchasing power of a player's basic wages of £8 is £314 – a figure below today's average national wage. The footballers of the 1920s, however, were probably better off than their counterparts of the late 1950s. Before the abolition of the maximum wage in 1961, their £20 a week would have a purchasing power today of only £265. Many players in the 1950s had to take second jobs to supplement their football earnings, which in the 1920s was quite unusual. The other remarkable fact is that the player's maximum wage stayed at £8 until 1938!

A Town first-team player in 1926 earning £400 *per annum* was well paid compared to manual workers in the mills and factories of Huddersfield at the time. Skilled workers would earn approximately £180 *per annum*, whilst their unskilled colleagues would receive £126. In other parts of the region, miners earned just over £100 a year, with two thirds of their take-home pay going in rent, fuel and food. A schoolteacher in Huddersfield at that time would have earned approximately £200. Footballers' earnings were more on a par with factory managers, who could expect to earn around £480 *per annum*.

Incidentally, in Huddersfield in 1926, a modern three-bedroomed house in Woodhouse Avenue, Fartown, with a bathroom and a WC, would have cost £600.

At the time, many other sportsmen earned more than footballers, with professional golfers and tennis players well rewarded for exhibition matches and sponsoring equipment. Even County cricketers would earn £10-15 a match, making footballers the poor relations.

In the decades before the abolition of the maximum wage, the players often complained that the clubs were reaping huge profits through the turnstiles at the expense of the very people whose talents lured the fans. In 1926 Huddersfield's average attendance of 19,000 would have generated an annual turnover of approximately £40,000. Players' wages would have accounted for around £12,000, a wages/turnover ratio of 30 per cent. According to Deloitte and Touche's Annual Review of Football Finance for 2003, the current wages/turnover ratio amongst Football League Clubs is 73 per cent. Whilst it is impossible to carry comparisons too far – for example, today clubs keep all their gate revenue, but didn't in 1926 – it would appear that in football finance terms players were poorly paid in an era when the Players Union could exert little power.

But back to the action. Huddersfield's winning run, and Cecil Potter's honeymoon, came to an abrupt end a week after beating Leeds 4-0, when

Newcastle won 1-0 at Leeds Road. With the top of the table very congested, a subsequent draw at Old Trafford and a 0-3 defeat at Villa Park pushed Town down to seventh place. Smith and Goodall returned from injury for the Villa game, but Cook continued to deputise ably for Charlie Wilson. Potter had rested the inconsistent Ted Taylor and recalled Billy Mercer in goal.

The *Examiner* reflected on the end of the long winning run: 'The attempt to beat the Burnley record, coupled with their third championship effort, has been a great strain on the players, and has caused matches to be exceptionally strenuous. Now that Town have been beaten there will be less inducement for their opponents to regard their fixtures as being in the nature of cup-ties.' This was a reference to Town's status as undisputably the top team in the country. Every opposing team raised their game and were out to claim Town's 'scalp'.

Newspaper match reports of the time frequently refer to Town being subjected to physical tactics by opponents. Back in October, against struggling Burnley, Town finished the game with nine men after Steele was incapacitated and Wadsworth dislocated an elbow. Wadsworth also suffered concussion and was left 'sleeping' in the dressing room at half-time. He recovered his senses during the second half and decided to re-enter the fray. Town's 'bulldog' display carried them to victory.

On the following Monday, the *Examiner* reported a serious road accident involving football supporters near Deighton. One man was killed and eight injured when a Ford lorry that had been converted into a fourteen-seat charabanc struck a tramway standard on the way home from the game. A coach driver under the influence of alcohol was later charged with drunken driving.

The nature of Huddersfield's second defeat of the season, at Aston Villa, caused consternation. Match reports describe 'six or seven Town men off-colour'. Tommy Wilson had been found wanting for the first time since the offside law was changed. Villa's prolific centre-forward, Len Capewell, took advantage to score a second-half hat-trick – taking his season's tally to eighteen goals. Ted Taylor had been due to return to first-team action but 'became indisposed' on the evening beforehand. Within days Taylor had been sent to Babbacombe in Devon for two weeks' recuperation – for 'a holiday and a change of air'. The board minutes reported that 'it was agreed to send Taylor £20 for his stay in Devon'.

Potter experimented with Alex Jackson at centre-forward, with Brown switching to inside-right to displace Cook. The flying Scot scored four goals in four games in his unaccustomed position but few were impressed with his performances and Jackson was soon back on the right wing with Cook restored.

Town's admirable record of ensuring that – no matter the weather – the game would go on, did not survive the deluge that preceded the home game with Liverpool in November. A submerged pitch meant that the game was called off shortly before kick-off. The fixture was re-arranged for a working Wednesday afternoon later in the month. Then, on a bitterly cold afternoon, factory and mill workers saw little incentive to leave their comparatively warm places of work to watch football. The attendance of 7,285 was the smallest at Leeds Road for a first-team game for almost two years.

Ten days later, on 5 December, a crowd of three times that number turned out for the return of Herbert Chapman with his new Arsenal team. Chapman had quickly persuaded Henry Norris of the benefits of a more expansive transfer policy, and the signing of Buchan was hailed as a masterstroke. The old England international had scored twelve goals already, and the revitalised Gunners were ahead of Town in second place in the table. The weather was still icily cold and a frozen surface threatened another postponement. In an effort to thaw the pitch, fiery braziers were placed upon it, an action that would have repercussions later in the season when barely a blade of grass was left. Buchan was the star of the show at Leeds Road. Arsenal twice took the lead; Buchan scored their second but Jackson equalised for Town.

The Bolton bogey continued with a 1-6 drubbing. Wanderers' awesome home record of seventeen successive wins had been broken earlier in the season, but Bolton were far too good on the day. The only mitigating factors were the absence of Billy Watson and the serious eye injury suffered by David Steele before half-time. When the ball struck him in the face he was temporarily blinded in both eyes and could not return for the second half. Haemorrhaging was feared, but by the time Steele had returned to Huddersfield his sight had returned. Such was the pain, however, that he was retained in Huddersfield Infirmary for several days. The previously ever-present Steele was soon back on his feet, but before he could regain his first-team place he suffered knee ligament damage that curtailed his season completely.

Manager Potter rang the changes after Bolton. Ted Taylor, Watson and Charlie Wilson returned to the side, but the injury jinx seemed to have struck again when Alex Jackson suffered facial lacerations when toppling into the terraces during another rough-house contest with Notts County; fortunately his cuts were superficial. Wilson's return was to be short-lived – he was the first high-profile casualty of the Potter reign and by March he was on his way to Second Division Stoke City to help them in their (failed) fight against relegation.

The wretched weather continued over Christmas, and Town's game at Roker Park on Christmas Day was postponed. On Boxing Day morning the top of the league table was intriguing:

	P	W	D	L	F	A	Pts
Arsenal	22	13	4	5	51	32	30
Sunderland	22	12	4	6	53	39	28
Huddersfield	19	9	7	3	38	31	25

That day, Arsenal lost heavily at Notts County, while Town and Sunderland fought out a 1-1 draw at Leeds Road. Sunderland were generally regarded as the title favourites at this time. The virtually unknown Scot, Dave Halliday, signed to replace Charlie Buchan, was scoring goals at an astonishing rate – by Christmas he had bagged 24 and topped the division's scoring charts. In early December, Sunderland had paid a British record fee of £7,000 for Burnley's England international inside-forward Bob Kelly. Kelly was hoped to provide the missing link that would reinforce Sunderland's position at the top of the league and help them to their first League title since 1913. Their home form was exemplary – they would beat Town 4-1 in the rearranged game at the end of January – but their inconsistent away results ultimately let them down.

Arsenal, too, were becalmed. Whilst the Gunners were losing three league games in a row in late January and early February, Huddersfield won at Cardiff (2-1) and Maine Road (5-1) to top the table for the first time that season, squeezing ahead of Arsenal on goal average, and with two games in hand.

Against Manchester City, Roy Goodall successfully converted his second penalty in the space of a few weeks. He had taken over penalty duties following the departure of Charlie Wilson and would retain that responsibility for the next few years. In that era, the general approach to penalty kicks was to entrust the task to a player who could kick the ball with immense power, direction being neither here nor there. It was therefore common to find full-backs, often the strongest players in the team, taking such kicks. Most of Goodall's 21 goals for Town in a fourteen-year career came from the penalty spot and one story illustrates his professionalism. The team were playing a friendly at Llandudno against the local amateur team in 1926 and were awarded a penalty near the end with the score standing at 15-4 in Town's favour. Goodall refused to let any other player take the kick, insisting that he needed the practice.

The Maine Road victory came seven days after Huddersfield had slumped out of the FA Cup at the second hurdle on the same ground, and constituted Town's first ever win at either Maine Road or Manchester City's previous home, at Hyde Road. The 0-4 Cup thrashing had been a major shock, especially as Manchester City were in the lower reaches of Division One (and would ultimately be relegated) and their leaky defence had conceded 71 goals in 27 league games. They were, however, saving their best form for the FA Cup and would go on to reach (but lose) the final, scoring 30 goals in the process.

A huge crowd had been expected for that Cup-tie, with City talking of up to 90,000 spectators and employing special packers to maximise Maine Road's capacity. Huddersfield's supporters were excited by the occasion, too, and it was reported that five special trains would carry them to Manchester – the cost was 3s 5d (17p). Tramway authorities laid on special trams from Manchester's Victoria station to the ground. The *Examiner* related how supporters poured into Manchester from early morning and 'surged along Market Street to be met by those battalions of street hawkers who believe that football fans are not happy without "Cup and colours", a mascot or two, plenty of fruit and a varied assortment of chewing gum and peppermint.'

The invasion by Town fans grew in numbers until 'by one o'clock an inhabitant of Huddersfield only had to shut his eyes for his ears to convince him that he was back in his native town.' Boarding a tramcar, however, even so long before the match, was a feat requiring a 'combination of cunning and strength, for the local authorities seemed to have given up all attempts to subdue the crowd in queues'.

Maine Road's record crowd of 76,166 had been set two years previously against Cardiff. It remained intact, but only just. The official crowd of 74,799 caused unbearable stress in some parts of the stadium and five people were treated for injuries after a wall collapsed. 'At 2.15 a triple row of spectators was formed in front of the concrete wall that bounded the playing field, in spite of all police efforts to keep the ground clear.'

Town's players arrived by taxi and looked confident as they disembarked at the ground. As the teams trotted onto the pitch 'there was little difference in the volume of cheering that greeted each of the teams', as they faced 'a battery of camera and kinematograph machines'.

Huddersfield, in their red change-strip shirts, were let down for once by the defence, with Wadsworth strangely ill at ease against the tricky Austin on City's right wing. Town were under pressure from the first whistle and barely escaped from their own half in a one-sided first period. By the end of the match, many Town supporters had already slunk away, as they had done at Bolton and Burnley in the previous two seasons. Lancashire was definitely the graveyard for Town's Cup dreams.

Leading scorer George Brown was, however, firing on all cylinders. Although he failed to net at Maine Road in the Cup, he was the star seven days later, scoring a second-half hat-trick to take his season's tally to 23. That was some way behind the aforementioned Halliday of Sunderland, who had now reached 30, and Blackburn's Ted Harper with 29. Brown had now scored in seven successive games through December and January, and had set his sights on Sammy Taylor's club record of 35 League goals set in 1919-20.

Chapter 8

~ RECORD BREAKERS ~

(FEBRUARY – MAY 1926)

With their FA Cup hopes dashed for another season, Huddersfield Town had only the hat-trick of League Championships to concentrate on. The manager and team now demonstrated their determination by reeling off a run of seven wins in eight games. The effect was similar to that of a 10,000-metre runner putting in a 50-second lap four laps from home. Town's main challengers were left breathless and almost incapable of a response.

Against Everton, in their first home game for a month, Huddersfield put on a super show to win 3-0 on a pitch cleared of snow and ice, but which 'preserved a farmyard appearance by reason of a girdle of hay-cocks'. The pitch was in a desperately poor condition by now, and for the local derby with Leeds United on 27 February it was described as having 'virtually no grass on the playing surface'.

March brought gale-force winds, but they failed to blow away Huddersfield's sprint for the finishing line. Home wins over Tottenham (3-1), Cup semi-finalists Manchester United (5-0), and Aston Villa (5-1) made it seven home wins in a row. The superlatives were trotted out week after week as Town established a stranglehold on the title race. After the Manchester United game, 'Observer' in *Athletic News* wrote: 'Town simply smothered United, who are for sheer effectiveness one of the strongest elevens of the season'.

George Brown continued to score profusely, and two goals in the Aston Villa game took his season's total to 33. In March he won his first representative honour when he was selected, along with Roy Goodall, for the Football League team's 2-0 win over the Scottish League at Celtic Park. *Athletic News* wrote of his performance: 'he did not do his powers justice'. But Brown's consistency was certainly undimmed by the arrival at Leeds Road of another centre-forward to challenge for his position, Willie Devlin from Scotland.

'Demon' Devlin, as he was nicknamed, had scored 38 goals for Cowdenbeath that season and 69 goals in 68 matches for the club in total. Nowadays, Cowdenbeath find themselves in the lowest division of the Scottish League, but in the 1920s they were a powerful force in Scottish football, finishing fifth (just behind Celtic) in 1924-25. Town paid £4,000 for Scotland's leading scorer, sparking rumours that George Brown would be sold, but officials at Leeds Road denied the stories.

Devlin was a native of Bellshill, a small town near Motherwell in the Lanarkshire minefields, an area that produced a conveyor-belt of Scottish international footballers, such as Alex James, Hughie Gallacher, Matt Busby, Billy McNeill, Gary McAllister and Ally McCoist. Devlin was quick on the ball and a good passer, as well as having the traditional Scottish strength as a dribbler. His greatest ability, however, and the one which gained him most of his goals, was his propensity to shoot on sight at every opportunity.

Following the Maine Road FA Cup disaster, increasing numbers of Huddersfield supporters harboured doubts about their team's defence. Two away victories in Town's winning run, however, convinced the pessimists that all was well again. At St James' Park, with the gates closed on a massive 56,000 crowd, Huddersfield soaked up everything the Magpies could muster and after winning 2-0 were accused of being 'the thieving magpies'. Two weeks later at Anfield, Town rode their luck somewhat but showed Liverpool how to take half-chances. Devlin netted his third goal in three games. In the press, Huddersfield were described as 'the wonder team of the age'.

'Demon' Devlin had been signed to replace Charlie Wilson, who had joined Stoke. The size of Devlin's fee, however, required more funding and Joe Williams was sold to the Potters as well – the pair raising around £4,500, which was more than enough to pay for the Scottish striker. Stoke's new purchases could not halt the club's slide into Division Three (North) at the end of the season, but both played key roles in the successful promotion campaign that followed. Wilson went on to score 118 goals in 167 games for Stoke over the next five years, while Williams performed consistently well before his former manager, Herbert Chapman, paid £3,000 to take him to Highbury in 1929.

On 27 March, following Huddersfield's 5-1 home win over Aston Villa, Town had a commanding lead:

	P	W	D	L	F	A	Pts
Huddersfield	35	20	10	5	81	49	50
Arsenal	34	18	7	9	72	52	43
Sunderland	35	18	6	11	83	64	42

Huddersfield's winning ways were checked at Leicester's Filbert Street on Easter Saturday, where a large crowd saw the home side deservedly win 2-0. Sam Wadsworth was given another torrid time by his namesake, but no relation, Harry Wadsworth on Leicester's right wing. Football followers across the whole country wanted to see this extraordinary Town team which was on the verge of making history, and two days later a Bank Holiday crowd of 27,000 packed into Bury's Gigg Lane 'enclosure' to witness a goalless draw.

Home crowds were also on the up, with four 25,000-plus Saturday crowds at Leeds Road. A new ground record for a league game of 34,871 was established for Easter Tuesday's clash with Blackburn Rovers – a fixture which doubled as Wadsworth's benefit game. London-born reserve player Bert Smith was selected for his first game in over two years. He was not fielded in his usual wing-half position, but as a centre-forward in a reshuffled forward line necessitated by injury to Clem Stephenson. Bert Smith scored a glorious header and hit the bar in what would be his last appearance in Town's colours before a summer move to Bradford City. Town's other two goals in the 3-1 victory were scored by George Brown, who thus equalled Sammy Taylor's record of 35 goals in a season.

From 1925 onwards, all Football League clubs were required to return attendance data to the League after every home game. Prior to this, information on attendances is sporadic and relies heavily on estimates from contemporary newspaper reports. In the 1925-26 season, Town's average crowds were up again – from 18,215 in 1924-25 to 19,569 – but they were still only sixteenth in the list of best supported clubs. Huddersfield's gates were even 4,000 below those recorded at Yorkshire rivals Hillsborough, to see a Wednesday team playing in Division Two. For the second year running, however, Town were proving to be the most attractive visiting club, drawing an average away crowd of 27,130. League attendances across the country in general were slightly up, reversing the downward trend since the peak of the first post-War season of 1919-20. Curiously, the best-supported club in the country was Second Division Chelsea, who attracted an average home gate of 32,355.

Huddersfield's home attendances would fall by a few hundred the following season, and would decline dramatically through the 1930s. In 1932-33 their average of 11,965 was the lowest in the First Division, and thereafter the mini-boom in crowds in the immediate pre-World War II seasons bypassed Huddersfield. After 1945, however, in common with all clubs, Huddersfield's crowds rocketed as the post-War demand for leisure in general and football in particular ensured all-time record attendances. Between 1946 and 1956 Huddersfield's average crowds were never below 20,000, and they peaked in 1953-54 when an average 30,820 poured through the Leeds Road turnstiles.

The long-serving Harry Cawthorne had been admirably filling David Steele's right-half position. A native of Darnall, near Sheffield, Cawthorne had been at Leeds Road for six years but his first-team opportunities had been restricted to 29 games in five years, owing largely to the imperious form of Steele. Once again, however, the strength of the club's reserves proved to be the key to a successful championship challenge. Cawthorne dovetailed beautifully into the Town system, and Steele's long absence was barely noticed. *Athletic News* summed up Harry's game perfectly: 'a man who has a future though he may never be an artist'.

Cawthorne's reward for his loyalty was a benefit game against West Ham, a match that, coincidentally, could virtually seal the championship for Town. Other correspondents were more complimentary about Harry. The *Examiner* praised his efforts: 'The work of Cawthorne was also outstanding. This player began last season as a useful and hard-working but rather clumsy member of the team; such a judgement no longer applies, last night at any rate Cawthorne was still hard-working but he was also nimble and stylish to a degree.'

All week, Town's followers were doing their arithmetic as to the various outcomes. The bottom line was that if Arsenal faltered at Roker Park, and Town beat the Hammers, the lead over the Gunners would be eight points. Huddersfield would then have to lose their last three games whilst Arsenal would need to win their last four, and significantly improve their goal average. Only such a scenario could deny Town their third successive championship.

On a defining day in the title race, Huddersfield beat West Ham with a Jackson brace, and Arsenal helpfully lost at Sunderland after their goal-keeper, Dan Lewis, and Sunderland's prolific scorer Halliday were sent off for fighting. The championship race was as good as over. A point on the Monday evening against Bolton would make the title mathematically secure for Town.

Bolton, however, had a Wembley FA Cup final date with Manchester City ten days hence, and rested some key players for the 5.30 kick-off, but it is unlikely that their restoration would have made any difference. With only just over half of the eventual 21,000 crowd inside Leeds Road by the kick-off, thousands of fans arriving late from work missed Town's two goals inside the first fifteen minutes. Wadsworth's exquisite forward pass found Cook, who touched the ball sideways for Smith, whose drive into the roof of the net was so fierce that it shook the uprights. Four minutes later it was 2-0 when Smith's perfect centre hit the bar and fell neatly on to Alex Jackson's head. Just before half-time Smith was again the creator. Jackson headed his cross into the area and Stephenson nudged the ball home to complete the scoring. The second half was dull but did nothing to dampen the enthusiasm at the final whistle as Town were given a three-minute standing ovation.

Later that night, several Town players were presented to the audience at the second house at the Huddersfield Hippodrome theatre. Later in the week, the whole team were guests at the theatre, where the manager, Mr Ernest Naylor, had arranged a special 'Football Carnival' and decorated the theatre in Town's colours. According to George Binns in *Huddersfield Town 75 Years On*: 'Eleven members of the chorus appeared in blue and white jerseys, and Jackson Owen, the principal comedian, told with great effect a number of stories about a certain gentleman from Aberdeen whom he and Alex Jackson knew. A feature of the show was a sketch called "The Dustman's Wedding", and the audience laughed itself hoarse when they discovered that Sam Wadsworth and his wife were taking part. They were quite unrehearsed but it is on record that there was a good deal of horseplay and that Wadsworth threw sausages and fruit about "with the easy grace of a professional revue artist".'

Shoals of telegrams poured into the ground over the next few days. Among them was one from India, signed by well-wishers in Madras. Another came from Czechoslovakia, which read: 'The Czechoslovakian sporting people have read with enthusiasm the news of Huddersfield Town's great success.'

Club chairman Mr A Brook Hirst put the success down to the team, the team spirit and the character of the boys: 'No matter how good a player may be, it is his character that counts at Leeds Road.' Manager Cecil Potter attributed the achievement to wonderful team spirit. 'I have never had to deal with a better or more loyal set of players.' The *Huddersfield Examiner* was euphoric, unlike the previous year, describing the success as 'monumental' and one which 'no spurt of individual brilliance will eclipse'.

Two matches remained for Huddersfield's tired heroes and they both ended in defeat. At Highbury, Town – deprived of the services of Ted Taylor, Roy Goodall and Alex Jackson (all playing in the England versus Scotland game at Old Trafford) – lost 1-3 to Herbert Chapman's League runners up. All of Town's three internationals performed well as Scotland beat England 1-0, Jackson scoring the goal. Goodall, in his first international, 'so young, yet so cool, confident and clean', impressed. *Athletic News* described Taylor as having 'no peer in English custodian realms'. The 39-year-old Teddy's eighth cap would unknowingly be his last. His days as Town's first-choice custodian were also numbered; three days after the international it was reported that Hugh Turner – a goalkeeper from Gateshead High Fell – had signed for Huddersfield. In six months' time, Turner would be first choice.

Back at Leeds Road, over 5,000 watched Town's reserves clinch their second successive Central League title by beating Wolves 3-0, thanks to two Bert Smith goals. A week later, on Cup final day, 12,000 watched Town's reserves draw 0-0 with Bolton at Burnden Park. The majority had turned up because it was the easiest way of keeping in touch with matters at Wembley Stadium, where Bolton's first team were winning the FA Cup against Manchester City.

With a General Strike looming, Huddersfield wrapped up their season at Meadow Lane where, in front of a rain-soaked crowd of under 5,000, the already-relegated home side ran out 4-2 winners, as Town took their foot off the pedal.

Not everyone praised the club for their unique feat. The sports editor of the *Sunday News*, William Bouchier, criticised Town for buying the league title by signing Willie Devlin in March. The *Examiner*, defending the club, pointed out that Devlin played a very small part in the title win: 'The truth is that Town had spent all season looking for a replacement for Charlie Wilson, whose illness had meant he was not up to the rigours of a Division 1 campaign. If they had found one before Devlin they would have signed him.'

The board minutes confirmed the club's interest in other forwards before Devlin was signed. The names included Kelly of Burnley and Grimsby's Joe Robson, both of whom later joined Town. The statistics do not support the *Sunday News* either: Devlin played only four games for the club from the eleven available to him after he signed.

Another critic suggested that Town had been lucky with injuries. The facts again dispute this. Injuries to key players Steele, Goodall, Taylor, Charlie Wilson and Billy Smith would have decimated many clubs, but Huddersfield's excellent reserve strength ensured that the effects of the injuries were minimised.

The final margin over second-placed Arsenal was five points and an unfashionable club from a small Yorkshire mill town had accomplished a feat denied to all the previous giants of the English game. Preston, Sunderland, Aston Villa, Sheffield Wednesday and Liverpool had all won back-to-back titles, but none had managed the glorious hat-trick.

Huddersfield's players were rewarded with an end-of-season, five-game tour of Switzerland. The club was guaranteed £1,200 for their participation. The board minutes show that the club had received several touring offers, but rejected at least two – from Argentina and Spain – and asked the players to choose between Scandinavia and Switzerland.

By the season's close, the impact of the changes to the offside laws could be more objectively considered. The number of goals scored in Division One was up by a massive 43 per cent to 1703, an average of 3.68 per game. In other countries, however, the impact was less dramatic. In Scotland and Sweden, for instance, the increase was 12 per cent, whilst in Austria goals increased by 16 per cent.

From a defensive point of view, however, too many goals were being conceded and it was inevitable that there would be a tactical response to the forwards' new-found freedom. Many commentators credit Herbert Chapman and Charles Buchan at Highbury for being the first to plug the 'hole' in defence, following Arsenal's 0-7 defeat at Newcastle in October 1925. Chapman's response was to withdrew his centre-half, Jack Butler, from his roving attacking role, and converted him into an out-and-out defender to mark the opposing centre-forward. Contemporary match reports, however, dispute Chapman's pioneering role in this respect. *Athletic News* points out that several clubs – notably Tottenham, Birmingham, Newcastle and West Ham – experimented by using the centre-half as a dedicated defender right from the start of the season. *Topical Times*, a football magazine of the era, considered the new tactics were introduced by Birmingham.

The change in role for the centre-half was just one of several possibilities explored by clubs in the early weeks of 1925-26. As the season took shape, the model of what is now referred to as the 'classic' formation was established. The full-backs moved outwards to the flanks to mark the wingers. This allowed the 'centre-back' to drop back between them as the third back. The wing half-backs, previously responsible for marking the wingers, turned inwards to midfield, where they linked with the inside-forwards, who now lay a little deeper than in the past. In attack, the 'W' formation came about with the wingmen and the centre-forward forming a three-pronged attack, when formerly it had been a five-pronged attack.

In *Herbert Chapman on Football*, the Arsenal manager expounded his views on wingers: 'We have ceased to use our wing-forwards in the old style in which they hugged the sidelines and centred from the corner flag. In my judgement this is fatally out of date. At Arsenal it is the aim of Hulme and Bastin (the Arsenal wing-men) to come inside when the Arsenal attack, but the two wing-halves do the same thing, which means seven men going up and converging on goal.'

The well-known football writer Ivan Sharpe summed up the impact in *Athletic News* of 21 December 1925: 'The off-side change has relieved the public of much of the boredom that accrued from breaking up play, from the spoiling tactics of a team that is fearful of the consequences of defeat and plays for safety first. It has eased the grip of defence. It has extended the scope of forwards sufficiently to cause a change of scene and a goal to come at any moment. The atmosphere of the "new football" is electrified by the feeling that, wherever the ball may be, one never knows what may happen in the moment ahead. The critics are quiet, the off-side change is rapidly making good. Its attendant increase in scoring, on the whole, has been beneficial. Let us be thankful that the goalless draw is far less common.'

By the start of the 1930s, however, the offside trap was coming back as Chapman describes: 'Offside tactics are creeping back, and backs, in understanding with their halves, are moving up and trapping the centre-forward and the wing-men just as in the old days.'

Chapter 9

~ How the Mighty Fell ~
(From 1926)

In May 1926, Huddersfield Town FC were without peers in the English domestic game yet, amazingly, when one considers their hat-trick of League championships, the club would not win a major honour throughout the remainder of the twentieth century.

Huddersfield would remain a major force in the country up until the mid-1930s but would then begin a decline that would gradually but inexorably accelerate until, in the 1970s, the club found itself in the Fourth Division. The half-century following the triple championships would not be without its moments – three FA Cup finals, all lost, promotions, big cup-ties – but nothing would ever compare to the three exhilarating seasons between 1923 and 1926. Huddersfield's fall from grace was not theirs alone. Once-powerful provincial clubs could no longer dine at the top table, and many found themselves in lower divisions – some, like Huddersfield, in the lowest.

Nothing stands still in football, however, and three months after Town's third championship was clinched the shock news was announced that manager Cecil Potter was leaving the club with immediate effect. The timing of the announcement was strange. The *Huddersfield Examiner* broke the story on 24 August – just four days before the new season commenced – and in the same bulletin revealed that the board had appointed first-team trainer Jack Chaplin to the manager's position. The reason publicly given for Potter's resignation was 'the ill-health of him and his family'. The players were at their annual pre-season golf outing at Meltham Golf Club that day, and the *Examiner* noted that 'opportunity was taken of the gathering at lunch to make the official announcement of the changes in management'.

The summer had been uneventful on the football scene; in fact in the *Huddersfield Examiner* the previous Saturday an editorial commented on the quietness: 'never has the curtain gone up on the drama of the "soccer" season with less beating of drums and blowing of trumpets than it will do this year. One reason for the calm is the fact that the question "will Huddersfield Town win the championship again?" cannot arouse quite the overpowering interest.'

The article seems almost to suggest that football followers were getting bored with Town's domination of English football and looked forward to a different name on the championship trophy. Similar disenchantment could be discerned in the 1970s and 80s when Liverpool were all-powerful, and again since the introduction of the Premier League, when Manchester United have swept all before them. The *Examiner* went on to say, however: 'The very calm of the start of the voyage may be the prelude to a journey as exciting as any that has gone before.'

All this tranquillity was about to be shattered by the news of Potter's departure. It is now known that Potter's departure was at the club's instigation, not the manager's.

The first inkling of problems surfaces in the minutes of a special board meeting convened on 10 August. The routine weekly meeting had taken place the previous day, and the minutes – in Potter's hand – record that 'the next meeting will take place on 16 August'. The following day four of the club's six directors met at chairman Amos Brook Hirst's offices. (This was unlike formal board meetings, which normally took place at Leeds Road.) The minutes of that meeting are briefer and in a new hand, believed to be that of assistant secretary Harry Beever. There is only one item recorded in the minutes and it reads as follows:

'Mr Potter produced correspondence which he had had with the Llandudno FC and also undertaking which he had signed to take the first team to Llandudno the first or second week in September.

'Mr Potter was asked to retire and after a long discussion it was resolved that the firm's solicitors write the Llandudno club's solicitors pointing out that Mr Potter had produced the correspondence which had passed and reported the result of his visit to Llandudno on the 20th April for the first time at this meeting, that the club would provided [sic] all allegations against the club were withdrawn, and any records against the club either returned to us or expunged, permit the team to go to Llandudno and play a match on the 1st September, *to get Mr Potter out of the trouble which he had created for himself.* [author's italics]

'It was further resolved that Mr Potter be instructed to write no further letters of any moment without submitting them to the chairman.'

Six days later, on 16 August, following the next weekly board meeting, the minutes record what appears at first sight to be a routine discussion. The minutes, again written in what is assumed to be Beever's handwriting, cover items such as plans for the celebration dinner the following Saturday, the signing of a reserve-team player, and a request from local schools for a trophy. According to these minutes, near the end of the meeting, the subject reverted to Potter's predicament:

'Mr Potter was asked to retire and after a long discussion as to his position with the club it was resolved that Mr Hirst and Mr Dawson (deputy chairman) interview him at once, with a view to terminating his agreement.

'Mr Hirst and Mr Dawson reported that Mr Potter would be willing to terminate his agreement at once if the club paid him £400.

'Resolved unanimously that Mr Potter be paid £400 to immediately terminate his agreement with the club.'

Potter had a year left to run on his contract at a salary worth £600 *per annum*. The termination payment, therefore, was approximately eight months salary.

As there had been no rumours about Potter's resignation, that says much for the discretion of the directors and Beever, who clearly knew of Potter's exit. The next meeting took place at Mr Dawson's office four days later on 20 August. This time there was only one item discussed, the new manager: 'The position of secretary-manager was fully discussed and it was left with Mr Hirst, Mr Dawson and Mr Barlow to make certain enquiries and report at the next meeting.'

Three days later, after what sounds like a hectic few days, the board met again and the minutes of their discussions are as follows:

'Mr Hirst stated the position regarding Clem Stephenson and also details regarding his interview with Mr J F Chaplin. A resolution was then passed appointing Mr H Beever as secretary to the club at a salary of £312 per annum. A further resolution was passed appointing Mr J F Chaplin as manager of the club at a salary of £10 per week plus bonus. At this stage Mr Chaplin joined the meeting.'

It is clear from this that the directors had split Potter's secretary-manager's role between Jack Chaplin and Harry Beever, but what was not recorded in the minutes was that the real reason for Potter's departure was explicitly not to be revealed. As far as the press and supporters were concerned, he was resigning for reasons of health in order to be allowed to save face.

The following morning the world was informed. The players were briefed over lunch at the golf course and the *Examiner* carried the story in its early editions. 'Center', writing in the newspaper, was not totally surprised: 'they [the changes] will cause some surprise naturally but the observant would have possibly noticed that Mr Potter was not present at the celebration of the winning of the championship which took place at the Town Hall on Saturday evening last.'

More details came to light in the *Examiner* on 28 August, when the 'health myth' was further reinforced by the local soccer reporter who relayed a conversation with Potter: 'The health of his children had been a constant worry since he had been in Huddersfield. He had a terrible time last winter owing to their ill-health and he will get them away to the south as soon as possible.' The club was presumably happy for this version of events to be made public, for it distracted – and continued to distract for over 75 years – from what really happened.

The details of what really happened, of course, are lost to us. What the minutes make clear is that on Tuesday, 20 April, three days after Town had played at Highbury – and after the title had been secured – Potter travelled to north Wales on personal or club business. What transpired between Potter and Llandudno FC resulted in correspondence between the two, which escalated into an exchange of solicitors' letters between the two football clubs regarding allegations of an unknown nature against Huddersfield Town. Mysteriously, the source of these allegations appears to have taken over four months to come to light. Whatever their nature, Potter was evidently the author of his own misfortune.

Huddersfield Town were guests of honour at a triple-championship celebratory dinner at the Town Hall. The original event, planned for May, had been postponed because of travel disruption caused by the General Strike. Football League Vice-President Charles Sutcliffe stood in for the president, Mr John McKenna, to present the silverware and medals, not only to the first team, but also to the successful reserves who had won the Central League for the second successive season. In addition, the club received Football League permission to present gifts to a value of £30 to each player. This time Clem Stephenson chose a canteen of silver cutlery in a hand-carved wooden box on legs.

Sutcliffe's witty and admiring speech went down well. He described himself as 'tired of proposing the toast to this team', then became more serious as he added: 'There was something I have always admired about the club – I thought it would be characteristic of the town – it seemed that when they made up their minds to do a thing, they did it, and the "beggar" of it was there was no stopping them.' The jovial townsfolk, well fed and watered, appreciated Sutcliffe's flattering tributes and warmed to the promise that a more permanent token of the club's remarkable achievement would be given at a later date. This transpired to be a large commemorative shield which today takes pride of place in the foyer of the McAlpine Stadium.

Potter returned to Sussex but four months later he was back in football, accepting an offer to become manager of Norwich City, for whom he had once played. Cecil was unable to inspire the Third Division club to any great success and left after two seasons in charge. He never managed again in football after leaving Norwich, and it is believed he returned to Sussex. The stress of football management did not, however, seem to have any long-term effects – he lived to the ripe old age of 86.

Whatever the real reason for Potter's departure, it is surprising that a man who had led Huddersfield Town to the League championship was not greatly sought after. Perhaps clubs on the lookout for a top manager believed that Potter had merely ridden to success on the coat-tails of his illustrious predecessor.

It footballing terms, it is hard to imagine a situation more dramatic than the manager of the League champions quitting overnight. It is no less puzzling to find the event all but ignored by both the local and national press. It seems incredible that the story did not cause a bombshell in Huddersfield, if nowhere else.

When Herbert Chapman resigned a year earlier, Huddersfield Town had not considered the possibility of promoting from within, and the fact that the title had been won for a third time vindicated the decision to look for outside inspiration. Now, after Potter's departure, Jack Chaplin's promotion to the management post seemed equally logical. It provided continuity – he knew all the players and the players knew and trusted him – and he had been involved throughout all the club's successes.

The decision to elevate Chaplin might not, however, have been cut and dried. The reference to Clem Stephenson at the board meeting on 23 August is vague, but it may be the case that Stephenson was the directors' first choice. If so, perhaps the 36-year old indicated his preference to continue playing. The fact that Stephenson became manager upon hanging up his boots three years later might indicate some form of agreement between Clem and the directors dating back to this time.

For the moment, Jack Chaplin was the new manager of Huddersfield Town, and he must have been a happy man. Not only was Jack given a pay rise to take him to £10 per week; the board minutes also reported that a home telephone had been installed at the club's expense!

The role of secretary-manager was split in two, as it had been prior to Chapman. Chaplin would concentrate on playing matters, while assistant secretary Harry Beever was promoted to secretary and would focus on administration. This division of duties acknowledged that the huge brief previously undertaken by Chapman was too much for one man and Town would never again employ a joint secretary-manager.

At the same time, Town's reserve-team trainer and former player, Jack Foster, was moving to Bradford City to become their assistant manager. Dick Murrell was Chaplin's choice as first-team trainer, but the board minutes state that he could be appointed only 'on condition that he was prepared to give up his public house in Huddersfield'. Presumably Murrell did not think that swapping his public house for the trainer's job was worthwhile, because in early September Archie Taylor was appointed to the post of first-team trainer.

Only two senior players had been added to the club's roster in the close season – Hugh Turner, a young goalkeeper from Gateshead amateur side High Fell, and Johnny Dent, a powerfully built centre-forward from Durham City. Turner would displace veteran Ted Taylor before the season was over and go on to make almost 400 appearances for Town over the next ten years.

In February 1927 Taylor became the first big-name player to leave the champions when he signed for his hometown club Everton. Although just weeks from his 40th birthday, Taylor went straight into Everton's first team and a year later won another League Championship medal with the Toffees. After winding down his career at Wrexham, Taylor retired to live in Huddersfield.

In the same month that Taylor left, Harry Cawthorne joined Sheffield United. David Steele had recovered from his injuries and Harry was surplus to requirements. The board minutes for December 1926 mention an unspecified breach of discipline by three players, one of whom was Cawthorne. That may have had something to do with his departure. At Bramall Lane he failed to perform to the high standards he had reached at Huddersfield and within two years was playing non-league football with Welsh club Connah's Quay.

Needless to say, Huddersfield's players were in big demand by other clubs, the three Georges – Brown, Cook and Shaw – being the most sought after. Brown was the automatic centre-forward by this time, and although Newcastle made strong overtures the club never wavered from their insistence on keeping him.

George 'Teapot' (on account of his stick-out ears) Shaw was a full-back whose Town career was spent mostly in the reserves and whose first-team appearances were restricted to deputising for Goodall or Wadsworth. Shaw played 24 games over the three championship seasons without winning a medal, and Derby and West Bromwich Albion courted him strongly in the autumn of 1926. Albion offered £2,000, a fair sum for a reserve player in those days. Town, not desperate to sell, held out for more and in December 1926 Albion raised their offer to £4,100, a fee which illustrates the value of Town's strong reserve set up. The board minutes reveal Shaw's cut from the transfer was £222 13s 4d, in lieu of benefit monies unpaid. Shaw went on to play 425 games for the Midlands club, helping them to win the FA Cup and promotion to Division One in 1931. He was also capped once by England in 1932.

The board minutes for that autumn record many similar enquiries for players. At the same time, Huddersfield were always on the lookout for new players. Jack Chaplin, Clem Stephenson and Billy Watson all undertook scouting missions to various parts of England and Scotland at various times.

Defending their three championships and heading for a fourth, Town might well have pulled it off. Instead, despite losing only eight games all season, they finished runners-up to Newcastle in the final table. Yet the five-point margin that separated them from the Magpies might have been much closer had they done better than win only one of their last seven games – ironically a 1-0 victory over their rivals from Tyneside. Town's defence was inconsistent: despite conceding only 60 goals, the same number as the previous season, and keeping fourteen clean sheets, the defence had some serious off-days. At the other end of the pitch, George Brown, whilst not as prolific as in 1925-26, still managed 27 goals, but his supporting players were less successful. Devlin disappointingly mustered only ten goals in 28 appearances. That was considered a failure and he left for Liverpool, where he briefly rediscovered his goal-touch before fading into obscurity. Alex Jackson's six goals were ten fewer than he scored in the previous campaign.

The bottom line, however, was the total points gathered. During the championship years Town had been remarkably consistent, earning in sequence 57, 58, and 57 points. This makes it hard to settle arguments about which of the three constituted Huddersfield's best team. Had Town accumulated 57 points in 1926-27 they would indeed have been champions for a fourth time, since Newcastle gathered only 56. Instead Town fell five short, with just 51.

Huddersfield's occasional inconsistency followed them into the FA Cup, where they suffered a surprise 1-3 defeat at the ground of Millwall from Division Three (South). The Cup shock prompted swift changes by the new manager. Veteran Billy Watson, who had missed only three games in the three championship campaigns, was axed after playing over 300 first-team games in a fourteen-year career. The hard-working and honest servant of the club could not win his place back but stayed on the playing staff for a further twelve months before joining the coaching staff. He severed his links with Huddersfield in 1929, but his two sons,

Albert and Willie, later joined the Town's playing staff and Willie went on to achieve the rare distinction of representing England at both football and cricket in the 1950s.

The month after the Millwall defeat was the busiest in terms of transfer activity in Town's history. In addition to Taylor, Shaw, Devlin and Cawthorne leaving, George Cook – who had fewer and fewer first-team opportunities – joined Villa, and wing-half Tom Meads arrived from Stockport County. Cook, by this time aged 31, would go on to play First Division football for a further five years with Villa and later, Spurs.

The out-going activity was necessary to fund the major purchase of England international Bob Kelly from Sunderland. In December 1925 the Wearsiders had outbid Town when the talented inside-forward, with twelve England caps, had been put up for sale by Burnley. When it was plain that his move to Roker Park had not worked out, Town swooped to strengthen their forward line, which was now not only the finest in the club's history but could also make strong claims to be one of the best club forward lines ever seen in British football. With Clem Stephenson now 37 years old, Kelly was bought as his replacement, but nobody told Clem and he played on for a further two years. Like Clem, Kelly had wonderful vision and superb ball-playing skills. His partnership with Alex Jackson was an instant success – Kelly scored a hat-trick on his debut against Sheffield Wednesday – and almost emulated the telepathic combination of Clem and Billy Smith. It is hardly surprising that over the years George Brown scored so many goals, playing between four such talented players.

If there was one season since the triple championships that Town deserved to win honours it was in 1927-28. On 14 April 1928, Town stood on the verge of becoming the first club to win the League and Cup double in the twentieth century. Those fans who can remember those days tend to agree that this was the finest Huddersfield team of them all. In the league with five games remaining, they led second-placed Everton by one point with a game in hand. A week later they tasted Wembley for the first time, in the FA Cup final with Blackburn Rovers. Town were favourites following a thrilling Cup run. Reports describe the 6-1 quarter-final victory over Tottenham as a classic. In the semi-final, Huddersfield and Sheffield United required three games to separate them, watched by an aggregate attendance of over 192,000 spectators. These included over 69,000 at Old Trafford, the third highest crowd ever at that stadium. Huddersfield eventually progressed by virtue of a Jackson goal.

Like other clubs before and afterwards, Huddersfield fell between the League and Cup stools. At Wembley they were stunned by a Blackburn goal in the first minute which, had it been scored in the modern game would surely have been disallowed. Town keeper Billy Mercer was shunted into his goal by Blackburn's Puddefoot, allowing Roscamp to drive the loose ball into the net. Town, despite their star-studded attack, never recovered and lost 1-3.

Five league games squeezed into fourteen days after the final proved to be too many for Huddersfield's tired heroes. In an unprecedentedly tight season, just seven points separated fourth-placed Derby from bottom-placed Middlesbrough. Consequently, there were no dead games and there was something at stake in virtually every game of the closing weeks. Two defeats in three days for Huddersfield in the final midweek handed the trophy to the men from Goodison, although Everton's finishing surge of six wins out of eight – with Dixie Dean netting fifteen goals on his way to an all-time record of 60 – might have proved unstoppable.

Billy Smith, with seventeen goals, had enjoyed his most prolific season. A match report from that season sums up his rare talent: 'Another delightful feature was the virility of WH Smith. Time after time he travelled along the touchline like a racehorse, centered [sic] accurately and varied the practice by doubling in towards goal in his inimitable style.'

In *Huddersfield Town 75 Years On*, George Binns describes Smith's style, 'His method basically was to move on to his opposing full-back until the defender was forced to make a challenge. Whereupon with the back committed Smith would sidestep the tackle, make his way with tremendous speed down the wing to near the goal line before crossing the ball almost invariably with such accuracy and pace that numerous scoring opportunities were thereby created for his team mates.'

In appreciation of Billy's talents, Charles Buchan noted that such methods ensured Huddersfield's forwards were unlikely to be caught in an offside trap. This was a matter of particular importance during the first part of Smith's playing career, when the offside law required there to be three opponents and not just two between a player and the goal when receiving the ball. Smith's outstanding club form earned him a recall to the England team six years after his first two caps. In early March 1928 his wing play was a major reason for the Football League's 6-2 win over the Scottish League at Ibrox, and secured his place for the annual battle with Scotland three weeks later at Wembley. Fearing another drubbing, the Scots drafted in several 'Anglos' – Scots playing their football in England – including Town's Alex Jackson and the diminutive forwards Hughie Gallacher and Alex James.

It was an auspicious occasion for Huddersfield Town as, in addition to Smith and Jackson, they provided three further Englishman for the game – Goodall, the regular right-back, Bob Kelly at inside-right, and Tommy Wilson finally earning international recognition after years on the fringes. The Football League refused to allow Town to postpone their game at Bury on the same day and a makeshift Huddersfield side (there were several first-teamers injured) containing nine reserves won 3-2. It would be 1960 before the League relented on this perennially contentious issue and allowed clubs to call off games if they had two or more players on international duty.

Scotland's tiny forwards – Jackson at 5ft 9½in was the tallest and James and Gallacher were under 5ft 6in – destroyed England on a wet and slippery surface to become collectively known as the 'Wembley Wizards'. It was Jackson's finest moment and he netted a hat-trick in his team's shock 5-1 win to earn a place in Scottish football history.

Town's team was inevitably ageing, and the following 1928-29 season proved to be Stephenson's last as a player. On retiring, he took over as manager, with Chaplin – a reluctant manager in 1926 – standing down and reverting to trainer's duties. There was no question of Chaplin being sacked. A conversation with Chaplin's granddaughter, Pat Armer, throws some light on Jack's dilemma.

Pat recalls that it was common knowledge in the family and amongst the players of the time that Jack's wife, Eva, held him back in his career. Eva apparently resented his absences for away games, Cup preparations and social engagements, which were the inevitable duties of any club manager. Pat Armer believes that her grandfather was hampered career-wise and that he may have been relieved by no longer having to juggle an unhappy home life with the pressures of club management.

Chaplin continued as trainer until the outbreak of war in 1939, whereupon at the age of 57 he retired to Blackpool where he and Eva bought a house. They later returned to Yorkshire to live at Warmsworth, near Doncaster, where they both died on the same Easter weekend in 1952 in suspicious circumstances. Pat Armer relates the story: 'My grandfather had some diabetes problems but was not seriously ill. As an eight-year-old I went to their house and discovered them in bed unconscious. My grandmother was dead and my grandfather died in hospital the following day.'

Both died as a result of barbiturate poisoning. At the ensuing inquest it was affirmed that Eva had committed suicide. An open verdict was reached on Jack, 'there being insufficient evidence to show how the poison was administered.' (see page 192) She was only 62 and he 69. Pat Armer suspects that her grandfather was murdered by his wife. Either way, it was a sad end to a fine life.

Also in 1929, David Steele, now 35, was given a free transfer after 203 appearances and joined Preston North End. Steele played only one season at Deepdale before moving into coaching, first with Bury, then non-league Ashton National, then in Denmark. Steele returned to England in 1934 to become a coach with Sheffield United before becoming manager of Bradford Park Avenue.

Steele returned to Leeds Road as manager in 1943, although at the time he was technically in the position of managing both Bradford and Huddersfield simultaneously. He offered to look after the affairs of Park Avenue for two months until they appointed a new manager. Steele was unable to restore Town's fortunes and was sacked in the summer of 1947 after the side finished twentieth (though escaping relegation by a clear eight points) in the first post-War season. Bradford City tempted him back to club management in 1948, whereupon he joined the rare breed to have been in charge of both Bradford clubs. In the mid-1950s he returned to Huddersfield as a scout and when he died in May 1964, aged 69, he was running a pub in Stanningley.

Following the Cup final defeat in 1928, Billy Mercer never played for Huddersfield again, and within a few weeks had joined Second Division Blackpool. Hugh Turner became the club's regular goalie, hardly missing a game over the next eight seasons, and was selected for England on one occasion. Another Wembley man, Ned Barkas, lost his place to a fit-again Wadsworth and soon afterwards left to join Birmingham for £4,000. Ned, a more than adequate full-back, had his opportunities restricted by England defenders Goodall and Wadsworth, and had played only 131 games in eight seasons. At St Andrews he immediately became first-choice full-back and went on to captain the Blues to the FA Cup final in 1931. In 1937, at the age of 35, he surprisingly joined Chelsea and retired just before the outbreak of war. His war was spent in a Birmingham factory and managing non-league Solihull Town. He died in the Birmingham area in 1962.

Jack Chaplin's third and final season in charge, 1928-29, ended in terrible anticlimax. A dreadful slump in form after February saw Town finish sixteenth in the table, clear of relegation, but thirteen points behind champions Sheffield Wednesday. George Brown led Town's goalscoring charts with fifteen goals, but his haul was his lowest since 1924. Brown's feats had won him eight England caps and the nickname 'Bomber'. His value on the transfer market was probably at its peak when Town sold him to Aston Villa for £5,000 in August 1929. His prowess in front of goal did not desert him in the Midlands and he netted 36 goals in his first season and 35 in 1932-33 as Villa finished League runners-up. When

Brown finally retired from playing in 1938, after further service with Burnley, Leeds and Darlington, he had amassed a remarkable career total of 273 goals in 440 games. He later settled in the Aston district of Birmingham and, like many of his contemporaries, ran a pub. George Brown died young, aged 45, in 1948.

In Clem Stephenson's first season as Huddersfield manager, it was soon apparent that the club would not be challenging for League honours, but the FA Cup gave Town an opportunity for glory. After defeating highly-placed Aston Villa away in the quarter-finals, they were drawn against runaway League leaders Sheffield Wednesday in the semi-final. Almost 70,000 watched at Old Trafford as Alex Jackson, with his knack of rising to the big occasion, scored twice to send Town through to their second Wembley final in three years, this time against Herbert Chapman's Arsenal. Once again Huddersfield started as favourites and enjoyed many of the game's better moments. However, the wily Chapman with his shrewd tactics, and Alex James, the diminutive Arsenal schemer who carried out the great man's instructions on the pitch, put paid to Town's hopes with a 2-0 win.

Sam Wadsworth, by now 33 years old, had left Leeds Road soon after Stephenson's appointment as manager. Wadsworth returned to his native Lancashire to sign for Burnley but played only a handful of games before being forced to retire through injury. In total, Sam won nine England caps and is recognised as one of the finest full-backs of his era. In 1935 he became a pioneer for English coaches by moving to the Continent to take up a post as coach at PSV Eindhoven. Whilst PSV were not the force in European football that they are today, they nevertheless were a relatively big club in the then amateur game in Holland.

In 1938 Wadsworth switched to DWS Amsterdam, another top Dutch club, and led them to their regional league title in his first season. In early 1940 with Hitler's forces on the verge of invading the Low Countries, Wadsworth became – according to Ian Thomas in *Leeds Road: Home of My Dreams*, 'one of twelve British coaches to escape on the last boat to leave Holland.' Sam was quoted as saying: 'I lost everything when the Germans kicked me out of Holland. I left "Jerry" my football boots, but remembered at the last minute to bring my international caps.'

After the War, Sam returned to Holland and led PSV to the Dutch Cup in 1950 and the League Championship in 1951. That year he brought PSV to Huddersfield for a friendly to commemorate the Festival of Britain, which Town won 4-1. PSV reciprocated soon afterwards with a game in Holland and the British arm of Philips (the huge electronics firm that owns PSV) presented Town with an electronic scoreboard, the first of its type in Britain. Wadsworth lived in Holland until his death at the age of 64 in 1961.

In 1938, to celebrate the 50th Anniversary of the Football League, a poll was taken to find the best 'team' from all players from 1888 to 1938. Sam Wadsworth was included in this eleven, along with two other members of the great Huddersfield team, Billy Smith and Clem Stephenson.

Early in the 1930-31 season, Alex Jackson hit one of his hot patches. Having netted nine times in the previous season's FA Cup run, he started the new season at centre-forward and scored seven goals in the first four games, including a hat-trick in a 6-0 win at Old Trafford which had the press corps drooling. Huddersfield had never adequately replaced George Brown at centre-forward, and now eyed Grimsby's prolific scorer Joe Robson, a player they had coveted four years previously. The only way for the club to afford Robson, valued at £8,000, was to sell one of their own stars, and when newly-promoted Chelsea offered a massive £8,750 for Alex Jackson, Town accepted. Robson would score eighteen goals in 23 games, including a hat-trick in the 10-1 club record win over Blackpool that winter. A final position of fifth, however, was not good enough for supporters weaned on championships. The average crowd at Leeds Road slipped to under 14,000, almost 6,000 below the average in 1925-26.

At Stamford Bridge, the 'Gay Cavalier' as Alex Jackson had become known, joined two fellow Scottish internationals – legendary centre-forward Hughie Gallacher, and inside-forward Alec Cheyne. Over 50,000 watched Jackson's Stamford Bridge debut and crowds flocked to see Chelsea's team of all-stars. Overall, however, the stars failed to gel as a team and in keeping with Chelsea's Music Hall tradition the club failed to get amongst the honours. Jackson lost his Scottish place and never added to his seventeen caps after leaving Leeds Road. Remarkably he was only once on the losing side for his country. After two seasons at the Bridge, Jackson had a dispute over money with the Chelsea board and was put on the transfer list for £4,500. With no club willing to spend big money on a player who had earned something of a reputation as a pay-rebel, Alex drifted out of League football. He signed for Lancashire non-league side Ashton National who, not being bound by the maximum wage, happily paid Jackson £15 a week when the League's maximum was £8.

Jackson later moved to France and played for Nimes, Le Touquet and Nice. He died in a motor accident whilst serving in the Army in Egypt in 1946, aged 41.

Tommy Wilson, at 32, had lived through big changes in the game in his twelve-year career at the top. He had made the transition from the old-pivot style centre-half to the defensive 'extra man' required after the new offside law in 1925. Beforehand, many of his contemporaries in that position had been on the short side, and as a result lacked the height needed to do justice to the new 'blocker' centre-half role. They had been selected for the position more for their skill than for their size or tackling ability.

Wilson adapted superbly by curtailing his forward runs and becoming a rugged but skilful 'stopper'. There was rarely a suspicion that Wilson was finding the heavier defensive burden excessive. In a career of almost peerless performances, it was strange that for so long Tommy was unable to attract the attentions of the England selectors. And when at last the call did come – for the England v Scotland game of 1928 – he was confronted by one of the greatest forward lines in Scottish history. Tommy was never chosen for his country again.

At Leeds Road, Wilson was for three seasons under pressure from understudy Alf Young. In January 1931, following a third round FA Cup defeat at Leeds, Tommy lost his place to Young and the following autumn he joined Division One strugglers Blackpool. After a month with his new club, Tommy returned to Leeds Road, only to see Blackpool beaten 5-0. At least his presence in the Seasiders' defence was enough to help them avoid relegation. In the summer of 1932 he returned to Huddersfield as assistant trainer to Jack Chaplin, a role he performed until the outbreak of war. In 1945 he became trainer at Barnsley, where he died, aged 51, in 1948. In total, Tommy Wilson made 500 League and Cup appearances for Huddersfield, a record only bettered by Billy Smith.

In 1931 Billy Smith overtook Tommy Wilson's appearance total and set a Football League record by becoming the first forward to ever to play 500 League games. He kept his place until February 1934, by which time the 38-year-old had amassed 574 first-team games for Town, a club record that still stands. Billy Smith's career stretched from 1913 until 1934 and he was awarded an unprecedented *four* benefits by the club. He was awarded the League's long-service medal by President John McKenna in 1934. On 10 February 1934 he made his final appearance in a Town shirt at Bramall Lane, Sheffield.

At the end of that season, the Huddersfield Town chairman, Amos Brook Hirst, wrote this letter of appreciation to Billy Smith:

'6 May 1934

My Dear Billy,

I wish on behalf of myself, my co-directors and the Management and Staff of the club to convey to you our sincere and hearty appreciation of the services you have rendered to the club, over the last 21 years. You have at all times been a devoted and loyal player. You have never at any time given the management a moment's uneasiness. Your football career should be taken as an example by all young players that might, if they take the same care of themselves and apply themselves as seriously and thoroughly as you have done, have some little hope of emulating your wonderful career. We are all sorry that Anno Domini plays such an important part in the career of a football player and would wish that we could go back, at any rate in your life, some 15 years so that we might, instead of parting with you as a player at the present time, be looking forward to another 15 years of the benefit of your wonderful skill and ability on the field of play. We wish you and your family all the best of luck and hope that you may soon acquire a post as a Manager, in which capacity I have no doubt that the ability which you could bring to bear in such a position would most certainly make a success of the situation.

Yours sincerely

Amos Brook Hirst, Chairman'

The early 1930s, whilst not as successful as the halcyon era of the mid-20s, still saw Huddersfield Town as one of the top sides in the country. In the four seasons between 1930-34 the team always finished in the top six. In 1932, another Wembley appearance looked possible, until the quarter-final paired Town with the, by now, mighty Arsenal.

Herbert Chapman had led Arsenal to their first trophy – a 2-0 Cup final victory over Town – in 1930. With a little help from the chequebook, he had moulded the Gunners into a superb team which had then waltzed away with the 1930-31 championship with a record 66 points. Arsenal had three of the biggest stars in the game in David Jack – who had cost a record £10,890 in 1928, Scottish international Alex James, another costly signing, and boy wonder Cliff Bastin. Chapman had his sights set on the elusive League and Cup double which no club had achieved since Aston Villa in 1897.

The quarter-final between Chapman's present and former clubs was a Cup-tie that the whole of Yorkshire wanted to see. A Leeds Road ground record crowd of 67,037, paying receipts of £4,883, watched as the Gunners won 1-0. The result wrecked Huddersfield's fantastic FA Cup home record. In 26 home ties dating back to 1913 they had previously won 25 and drawn one!

Chapman's Gunners, however, were destined to finish second in the League in 1932 and lose to Newcastle at Wembley. By this time, Town were just not in the same league, figuratively speaking. This was illustrated a few weeks after the Arsenal Cup-tie, when a crowd of under 3,000 attended Leeds Road for a midweek game with Manchester City.

Arsenal would recover from the disappointment of 1932 and – between 1932 and 1935 – emulate Town's feat of winning the League title in three successive seasons. As at Huddersfield, Chapman would not be around to celebrate the last leg of the hat-trick. On 6 January 1934 he was taken ill with a chill and died, two weeks before his 56th birthday. His death came as a massive shock, and many of the Arsenal players only heard about it as they arrived at Highbury for the game with Sheffield Wednesday that afternoon.

Several thousand people lined the streets of Hendon four days later to watch the funeral cortege travel from Chapman's home in Haslemere Avenue to nearby St Mary's Parish Church. In *Herbert Chapman: Football Emperor*, Stephen Studd wrote: 'The parish magazine later recorded that the crowds outside the church kept within "the bounds of reverent remembrance" for the burial, but Reverend A Hunt Cooke, an acquaintance of Chapman at St Mary's, remembers the scene as a shocking affair. "There were people climbing all over the graves with cameras. Mr Chapman would not have approved".'

Chapman is buried in the peaceful and pretty graveyard at St Mary's Church, Hendon, which has the character of a village churchyard, with ancient cedar and yew trees. His tomb, shared by his wife Annie Bennett Chapman, lies only a few yards from the Rundell Mausoleum, a landmark which inspired a scene in the novel *Dracula*. Its author, Bram Stoker, is thought to have visualised the mausoleum for the staking through the heart of Lucy the vampire. Herbert Chapman might turn in his grave if he knew of such things, much as Lucy turned (and screeched) in hers.

An obituary in *The Times* spoke effusively about the man: 'His sides won matches not because Chapman was watching them from the stand but because he knew how to choose the players that would win the matches for him and, just as important, he knew how to get the best out of them once he had got them. A lot of nonsense has been talked about his "blackboard lectures" on tactics but he did his side the inestimable service of making them think about the game, and the results of his teachings were obvious on the field of play. He was an autocrat – he had to be to accomplish so much and he lived for his work and expected others to do the same. But for all that, he had an innate Yorkshire geniality which showed itself at unexpected moments.'

Chapman's years at Highbury were not without controversy, as once again he sailed very close to the winds of financial misconduct. His time at Leeds City had been tarnished by accusations of impropriety, the terms of Clem Stephenson's signing for Huddersfield suggest the player received rewards not mentioned in his contract and, within weeks of arriving at Highbury, Chapman was entangled in yet more shenanigans.

Chapman had been closely involved in the signing of top England player Charlie Buchan from Sunderland. One stumbling block to the player's move south was the fact that Buchan would lose income from his Sunderland sports shop. It later became known that Arsenal had made a large, illegal payment to compensate Buchan and persuaded him to sign. In 1929, chaiman Sir Henry Norris was charged by an FA commission of various offences, including offering financial inducements to players and diverting club funds to his private account.

Norris sued the Football Association when they published details of their enquiry and, in court – according to Stephen Studd in *Herbert Chapman: Football Emperor* – Norris openly accused Chapman of 'lying' when the manager denied knowing anything about illegal payments. Norris alleged that Chapman had pleaded with him to pay Buchan what he wanted, but had carefully left the room while the deed was actually done. The court upheld the FA's verdict and Sir Henry turned his back on football for good. His successor at Arsenal, Sir Samuel Hill-Wood, was content to leave Chapman with a free rein and his power was now absolute.

The Norris court case leaves in the air a number of unanswered questions. It is hard to believe, for example, that Chapman – who made the first approach to Buchan by visiting him at his shop – knew nothing of this possible stumbling block. As secretary-manager at Highbury, any financial arrangements with Buchan would surely have been authorised or accounted for by Chapman. It seems that Chapman might have been fortunate not to have been 'in the dock' with Norris in 1929.

Another contentious issue arose when Alex James arrived from Preston North End that same year. According to John Harding in *Alex James: Life of a Football Legend*, Arsenal and Preston had agreed a fee for James's move to Highbury, but the player had not signed. It was common knowledge in the football world that several other clubs had failed to meet James's 'illegal' demands for under-the-counter payments. James was allegedly contacted by Tom Paton – a director of Bradford City and a friend of Chapman's – and asked to travel to Bradford to meet Paton. When James entered the room, to 'his amazement' he was confronted by Chapman. Paton suggested that he and Chapman had arranged an alternative way of solving James's 'past difficulties'. Chapman divulged that he had fixed up a two-year contract for James to be a sports demonstrator at Selfridges in Oxford Street for £250 *per annum*. Chapman explained that the job would get round the League's restrictions on 'illegal induce-ments', as it was the store and not Arsenal who would apparently be offering him the job.

The wily Chapman, conscious of the scrutiny any transfer involving the infamous James would attract, requested an official Football League enquiry, once he had acquired the player's signature. The League smelt a rat but could prove nothing and the deal went ahead with James picking up an extra £5 per week for a sinecure at Selfridges. Many of these facts did not come to light until 1937, three years after Chapman's death, when James 'sold' his story to the *News of the World*; a story which portrayed Chapman in a less than perfect light.

Chapman's impact on Arsenal, however, was enormous and Hill-Wood, chairman of Arsenal from 1927 to 1949, had the highest regard for his manager: 'He was the most outstanding man I ever met, and if Herbert Chapman had not been a football manager he would have made an excellent Prime Minister. He persuaded the authorities to change the name of the [nearest] tube station from Gillespie Road to Arsenal.'

Chapman's legacy at Highbury is marked today by a marble bust, by famed sculptor Sir Jacob Epstein, which graces the main entrance hall at Arsenal Stadium. It stands as an epitaph to one of the greatest football managers of all time.

In this connection, one wonders why no comparable statue graces the McAlpine Stadium. Chapman did no more for Arsenal than he did for Huddersfield and, given that he enjoyed material resources at Highbury denied to him at Leeds Road, his achievements at Huddersfield are all the greater.

But life moved on, for Arsenal as for Huddersfield. Billy Smith was appointed player-manager at Rochdale, but life in the lower reaches of Division Three (North) was not agreeable to him. Forced to play inferior players and sell his best, he lasted less than eighteen months before being sacked. After leaving Rochdale he ran a shop in Doncaster. He died in 1951 – another of Town's heroes to pass away before their allotted span – aged 56. His son, Conway Smith, also played for Huddersfield and made 30-odd appearances for the club in the late 1940s.

Billy Smith's departure in 1934 left Roy Goodall as the only remaining triple championship member on the playing staff. Roy had won 25 caps at full-back for England and captained his country eleven times. One of his finest moments came in Rome in 1933 when, despite blood stream-ing from a cut above his eye, he rallied his defence to fend off the bril-liant Italian attackers and earn England a 1-1 draw. Ironically, the FA had put Goodall's former boss, Herbert Chapman, in temporary charge of the England team, the first time such an appointment had been made. Goodall was undoubtedly one of the finest full-backs ever to pull on England colours, and his partnership with Sam Wadsworth was unrivalled in domestic football. In 1926 Syd Puddefoot, the then famous West Ham and England forward, claimed they were 'the best pair of backs playing football anywhere today'.

The last cap for the tall, angular Goodall came later in 1933, and he left Huddersfield in 1937 – after 440 appearances for Town – to become trainer at Nottingham Forest. During the War he served in the Army as a company quartermaster and was working at a local hospital when Mansfield Town sought his services in 1945. He failed to make an impact at Field Mill, and Mansfield were forced to apply for re-election in the first post-War season. In 1949 Goodall returned to Leeds Road on the coaching staff and stayed until his retirement in 1965. He was a regular visitor to Leeds Road until his death in 1982.

Clem Stephenson carried on as Town's manager until June 1942. The club's slide continued after finishing third in Division One in 1935-36. But, despite the team's deficiencies, Clem led them to a further FA Cup final in 1938, when Town lost in controversial circumstances to Preston North End. In the first Wembley final decided by a penalty goal, Town's captain Alf Young was adjudged to have fouled Preston's Mutch inside the area, when photographic and newsreel evidence later showed that the challenge was outside. Despite losing, as on previous special occasions a motorcade was used to ferry the Huddersfield contingent from the railway station to a civic reception at the Town Hall. This occasion, however, marked the end of a long and golden era for Huddersfield Town.

Guide to Seasonal Summaries

Col 1: Match number (for league fixtures); Round (for cup-ties).
      e.g. 4R means 'Fourth round replay.'

Col 2: Date of the fixture and whether Home (H), Away (A), or Neutral (N).

Col 3: Opposition.

Col 4: Attendances. Home gates appear in roman; Away gates in *italics*.
      Figures in **bold** indicate the largest and smallest gates, at home and away.
      Average home and away attendances appear after the final league match.

Col 5: Respective league positions of Town and opponents after the game.
      Town's position appears on the top line in roman.
      Their opponents' position appears on the second line in *italics*.
      For cup-ties, the division and position of opponents is provided.
      e.g. 2:12 means the opposition are twelfth in Division 2.

Col 6: The top line shows the result: W(in), D(raw), or L(ose).
      The second line shows Town's cumulative points total.

Col 7: The match score, Town's given first.
      Scores in **bold** show Town's biggest league win and heaviest defeat.

Col 8: The half-time score, Town's given first.

Col 9: The top line shows Town's scorers and times of goals in roman.
      The second line shows opponents' scorers and times of goals in *italics*.
      A 'p' after the time of a goal denotes a penalty; 'og' an own-goal.
      The third line gives the name of the match referee.

Team line-ups: Town line-ups appear on top line, irrespective of whether
      they are home or away. Opposition teams are on the second line in *italics*.
      Players of either side who are sent off are marked !
      Town players making their league debuts are displayed in **bold**.

LEAGUE DIVISION 1 — Manager: Herbert Chapman — SEASON 1923-24

No	Date	Att	Pos	Pt	F-A	H-T	Scorers, Times, and Referees	1	2	3	4	5	6	7	8	9	10	11
1	H MIDDLESBROUGH 25/8	20,000	- / -	W 2	1-0	0-0	Wilson C 68 — Ref: J Sharpe	Taylor	Barkas	Wadsworth	Smith A	Wilson C	Watson	Richardson G	Islip	Wilson C	Stephenson	Smith W
								Clough	*Freeman*	*Maitland*	*Harris*	*Ellerington*	*Slade*	*Botterill*	*Birrell*	*Wilson A*	*Elliott*	*Urwin*
2	A PRESTON 27/8	18,331	- / -	W 4	3-1	0-1	Smith W 51, Wilson C 54, Sapsford 33 [Stephenson 70] — Ref: H Hopkinson	Taylor	Barkas	Wadsworth	Smith A	Wilson T	Watson	Walter	Islip	Wilson C	Stephenson	Smith W
								Branston	*Hamilton*	*Yates*	*Gilchrist*	*Mercer*	*Crawford*	*Rawlings*	*Woodhouse*	*Roberts*	*Sapsford*	*Quantrill*
3	A MIDDLESBROUGH 1/9	20,000	5 / 18	L 4	0-2	0-1	Birrell 27, Cochrane 60 — Ref: J Sharpe	Taylor	Barkas	Goodall	Smith A	Wilson T	Watson	Richardson G	Islip	Wilson C	Stephenson	Smith W
								Clough	*Freeman*	*Maitland*	*Harris*	*Webster*	*Pender*	*Birrell*	*Elliott*	*Wilson A*	*Cochrane*	*Urwin*
4	H PRESTON 4/9	14,000	3 / 21	W 6	4-0	2-0	Smith W 25, Wilson C 45,75, Steph' 65 — Ref: H Hopkinson	Cowell	Barkas	Wadsworth	Smith A	Wilson T	Watson	Cook	Johnston	Wilson C	Stephenson	Smith W
								Branston	*Hamilton*	*Yates*	*Duxbury*	*Marshall*	*Crawford*	*Rawlings*	*Marquis*	*Roberts*	*Laird*	*Quantrill*
5	A NOTTS CO 8/9	20,000	6 / 4	L 6	0-1	0-1	Hill 20 — Ref: C Lines	Cowell	Barkas	Wadsworth	Smith A	Wilson T	Watson	Cook	Islip	Wilson C	Stephenson	Smith W
								Iremonger	*Ashurst*	*Cope*	*Flint*	*Dinsdale*	*Kemp*	*Daly*	*Cooper*	*Cock*	*Hill*	*Price*
6	H NOTTS CO 15/9	16,000	8 / 6	D 7	0-0	0-0	Ref: C Lines	Taylor	Barkas	Wadsworth	Smith A	Wilson T	Watson	Walter	Islip !	Wilson C	Stephenson	Smith W
								Iremonger	*Ashurst*	*Cope*	*Flint !*	*Dinsdale*	*Kemp*	*Daly*	*Cooper*	*Cock*	*Hill*	*Barry*
7	A EVERTON 22/9	35,000	9 / 7	D 8	1-1	0-1	Brown 58, Chadwick 37 — Ref: W Brearley	Taylor	Barkas	Wadsworth	Smith A	Wilson T	Watson	Walter	Cook	Brown	Stephenson	Smith W
								Fern	*McDonald*	*Livingstone*	*Brown*	*McBain*	*Hart*	*Chedgzoy*	*Irvine*	*Cock*	*Chadwick*	*Troup*
8	H EVERTON 29/9	16,500	5 / 12	W 10	2-0	2-0	Brown 19, Stephenson 30 — Ref: W Brearley	Taylor	Barkas	Wadsworth	Cawthorne	Wilson T	Watson	Walter	Cook	Brown	Stephenson	Smith W
								Fern	*McDonald*	*Livingstone*	*Brown*	*McBain*	*Hart*	*Parry*	*Irvine*	*Cock*	*Chadwick*	*Harrison*
9	A WEST BROM 6/10	17,041	4 / 12	W 12	4-2	3-2	Smith W 20, 80, Cook 26, 31, Davies 24, Carter 25 — Ref: J Forshaw	Taylor	Barkas	Wadsworth	Cawthorne	Wilson T	Watson	Walter	Cook	Brown	Stephenson	Smith W
								Ashmore	*Smith*	*Adams*	*Magee*	*Bowser*	*McNeal*	*Spencer*	*Carter*	*Davies*	*Jones*	*Fitton*
10	H WEST BROM 13/10	18,800	5 / 11	D 13	0-0	0-0	Ref: J Forshaw	Taylor	Barkas	Wadsworth	Steele	Wilson T	Watson	Walter	Cook	Brown	Stephenson	Smith W
								Ashmore	*Smith*	*Adams*	*Magee*	*Bowser*	*McNeal*	*Glidden*	*Carter*	*Davies*	*Morris*	*Fitton*

Match reports

1. Ex-town man Slade gets a warm ovation. Town are well on top and Stephenson's thunderbolt rattles the bar right on half-time. Wilson's header from Richardson's cross deservedly wins the points. Wadsworth superb with his mighty clearances. Ted Taylor rarely troubled by Boro.

2. A deluge of rain has left the pitch very wet. Sapsford's goal looks offside but is deserved. Billy Smith levels after a stunning move and sets up Wilson. Cook ploughs through the mud to set up the third as Preston's defence falls apart. Preston fan rushes on to dispute Town goal with ref.

3. Boro gain revenge against a poor Town. Charlie Wilson's challenge unsights Taylor and Billy Birrell's shot creeps in. Birrell later sets up Cochrane. Town's smooth play deserts them and they rarely trouble Boro. Sam Wadsworth, out with a twisted ankle, is badly missed.

4. The Bank holiday and the 6pm kick-off keeps the crowd low. Tricky Johnston is called up for a rare game. Wilson and Cook force a poor Preston team into errors for the first and third goals and a bigger win would not have flattered Town. Taylor misses the game with severe flu.

5. Newly promoted County are unbeaten but their physical game and one-back tactics catch Cook constantly offside. A sunny day is spoilt by a rough game. Wadsworth is tricked by Daly, and Hill heads in from close range. Cook heads against the bar but Smith's crosses go to waste.

6. With bad feeling hanging over from last week. Islip is sent off for felling Iremonger and Flint for an off-the-ball challenge on Billy Smith in the first half. The crowd's call for some football falls on deaf ears as the robust challenges continue in a disgraceful game. Football is the loser.

7. Islip has two broken ribs from last week's battle and Wilson has a cold. Mickley-boy Brown is recalled and celebrates with a stunning goal. Slick Everton are on top for long periods and Chadwick's goal is a clever move. Walter hits the bar and Taylor's double save denies Everton.

8. Cawthorne comes in for Bert Smith who has a knee injury. In a period of intense Town pressure Smith and Stephenson are dazzling with deft one-twos and corner king Billy Smith sets up Brown. Stephenson dribbles through a bamboozled defence for No 2. Everton rarely threaten.

9. England keeper Taylor makes a brilliant save to deny Davies in the early minutes before Albion take an early lead. Five goals in 12 minutes leave the fans breathless. Stephenson and Smith are again in dazzling form, the former creating the first three and Smith scoring two stunners.

10. Steele returns after long illness and does well. Islip is banned for a month after Notts Co game. Determined Albion are a good match and create chances. Ashmore punches Cook's header onto the bar and it looks a goal. Wadsworth's penalty for a foul on Clem is well saved by Ashmore.

Match results and line-ups (Huddersfield Town)

#	Venue	Opponent	Date	Att	Opp Pos	Pos	Res	Pts	Score	HT	Scorers	Referee
11	A	BIRMINGHAM	20/10	18,000	19	3	W	15	1-0	1-0	Smith W 43	Ref: A Fogg
12	H	BIRMINGHAM	27/10	12,000	20	1	W	17	1-0	0-0	Stephenson 73	Ref: A Fogg
13	A	LIVERPOOL	3/11	30,000	12	2	D	18	1-1	1-0	Stephenson 8, Chambers 68	Ref: F Todman
14	H	LIVERPOOL	10/11	15,400	14	2	W	20	3-1	0-0	Cook 46, 47, Wad W 48(og), Chambers 53	Ref: F Todman
15	A	BOLTON	17/11	17,630	3	2	L	20	1-3	0-1	Wilson C 87, Smith J 9, Smith JR 61, Jack 85	Ref: T Crew
16	H	BOLTON	24/11	18,000	4	2	W	22	1-0	0-0	Cook 80	Ref: T Crew
17	A	SUNDERLAND	1/12	29,000	4	3	L	22	1-2	0-1	Wilson C 48, Marshall 25, Buchan 90	Ref: A Rothwell
18	H	SUNDERLAND	8/12	18,600	4	3	W	24	3-2	2-0	Wilson C 35, 86, Smith W 43, Buchan 60, Ellis 70p	Ref: A Rothwell
19	A	ARSENAL	15/12	25,000	17	2	W	26	3-1	1-0	Wilson C 22, 49, 75, Young 46	Ref: A Kirby
20	H	ARSENAL	22/12	15,000	17	2	W	28	6-1	1-0	Cook 11, Wilson C 47, 82, 86, Baker 88 [Stephenson 49, 63]	Ref: A Kirby
21	A	TOTTENHAM	25/12	44,274	9	3	L	28	0-1	0-0	Lindsay 57	Ref: F Procter

Line-ups (Town in roman, opponent in italic)

#	Boot	Barkas	Goodall	Steele	Wilson T	Watson	Walter	Cook	Wilson C	Stephenson	Smith W
11	Boot	Barkas	Goodall	Steele	Wilson T	Watson	Walter	Cook	Wilson C	Stephenson	Smith W
11	*Tremelling*	*Ashurst*	*Jones*	*Liddell*	*McClure*	*Barton*	*Harvey*	*Crosbie*	*Rawson*	*Linley*	*Clarke*
12	Taylor	Barkas	Wadsworth	Steele	Smith A	Watson	Walter	Cook	Wilson C	Stephenson	Smith W
12	*Tremelling*	*Ashurst*	*Womack*	*Liddell*	*Cringan*	*Barton*	*Harvey*	*Crosbie*	*Bradford*	*Lane*	*Clarke*
13	Taylor	Barkas	Wadsworth	Steele	Wilson T	Watson	Walter	Cook	Wilson C	Stephenson	Smith W
13	*Scott*	*Lucas*	*McKinlay*	*McNab*	*Wadsworth W*	*Pratt*	*Wadsworth H*	*Forshaw*	*Walsh*	*Chambers*	*Hopkin*
14	Taylor	Barkas	Wadsworth	Steele	Wilson T	Watson	Walter	Cook	Wilson C	Stephenson	Smith W
14	*Scott*	*Lucas*	*McKinlay*	*Bamber*	*Wadsworth W*	*Pratt*	*Wadsworth H*	*Forshaw*	*Walsh*	*Chambers*	*Hopkin*
15	Taylor	Barkas	Wadsworth	Steele	Wilson T	Watson	Walter	Cook	Wilson C	Stephenson	Smith W
15	*Pym*	*Howarth*	*Finney*	*Nuttall*	*Rowley*	*Jennings*	*Butler*	*Jack*	*Smith JR*	*Smith J*	*Vizard*
16	Taylor	Goodall	Wadsworth	Steele	Wilson T	Watson	Walter	Cook	Wilson C	Stephenson	Smith W
16	*Pym*	*Howarth*	*Finney*	*Nuttall*	*Seddon*	*Jennings*	*Butler*	*Jack*	*Smith JR*	*Smith J*	*Vizard*
17	Taylor	Goodall	Wadsworth	Steele	Wilson T	Watson	Walter	Cook	Wilson C	Stephenson	Smith W
17	*McInroy*	*Cresswell*	*England*	*Clunas*	*Parker*	*Andrews*	*Prior*	*Marshall*	*Buchan*	*Hawes*	*Ellis*
18	Taylor	Goodall	Wadsworth	Steele	Wilson T	Watson	Walter	Cook	Wilson C	Stephenson	Smith W
18	*McInroy*	*Cresswell*	*England*	*Clunas*	*Parker*	*Andrews*	*Grimshaw*	*Marshall*	*Buchan*	*Hawes*	*Ellis*
19	Taylor	Goodall	Wadsworth	Steele	Wilson T	Watson	Walter	Cook	Wilson C	Stephenson	Smith W
19	*Robson*	*Mackie*	*Whittaker*	*Graham*	*Butler*	*Blyth*	*Rutherford*	*Earle*	*Young*	*Woods*	*Paterson*
20	Taylor	Goodall	Wadsworth	Steele	Wilson T	Watson	Walter	Cook	Wilson C	Stephenson	Smith W
20	*Robson*	*Mackie*	*Kennedy*	*Graham*	*Butler*	*Blyth*	*Rutherford*	*Woods*	*Young*	*Baker*	*Haden*
21	Taylor	Goodall	Wadsworth	Steele	Wilson T	Watson	Walter	Cook	Wilson C	Stephenson	Smith W
21	*Maddison*	*Clay*	*Forster*	*Smith*	*Lowe*	*Grimsdell*	*Walden*	*Seed*	*Lindsay*	*Elkes*	*Handley*

11. Taylor and Wadsworth are away on England duty as is Birmingham's Joe Bradford, who is sorely missed. Tom Wilson almost scores twice from corners before Smith rifles home after good work by Walter. Tremelling pulls off four brilliant saves whilst Len Boot has a quiet debut.

12. An uninspiring performance takes Town top against Blues who have not won in nine. Smith is no replacement for Tom Wilson who has a cold and sorely missed. The hero Tremelling is finally beaten by cool Clem. Attendance kept down by Huddersfield v Halifax Rugby League game.

13. Prime Minister Baldwin watches his first professional game. The sponges are needed as the champions go for a physical approach. Town have the strong wind in the first half and lead through Clem's brilliant shot. Taylor is unsighted for England man Chambers' goal. Town end on top.

14. No dull moments in a classic game. Frantic start to the second half sees Town three up with virtually no Pool players touching the ball. Super football with Cook netting two and Wadsworth heading in trying to clear his lines. Chambers is the first visiting player to score at Leeds Road.

15. Bolton are a bogey side for Town – only one win in 11 games. Town start well but the muddy pitch does not suit Town and Joe Smith's goal rocks them. Jack Smith hits the second after a rebound and a limping David Jack does likewise for the third. Taylor keeps the score down.

16. The slippery, icy pitch is a great leveller. Herbert Chapman runs the line until the linesman arrives at half-time. In an excellent game Bolton match Town until last quarter. The quiet Cook lobs Pym for the goal and Bolton have no chance to respond. Goodall replaces Barkas in style.

17. A fine game on a sticky pitch. Ellis misses a twice-taken penalty after Goodall fouls Hawes but atones by crossing for league's leading scorer Charlie Buchan to head the winner. Cook misses a great chance before Wilson's low shot goes in. Sunderland's seventh successive home win.

18. The ref loses control of a rough game. Tom Wilson sets up the first and Clem the second after intense pressure. Taylor fumbles Buchan's shot and the ref says it is over the line before Watson pushes Buchan for a penalty. Wilson nets a stunner from outside the box for a deserved win.

19. An outclassed Arsenal wilt on a slimy pitch after a strong first half. Wilson swivels to slide home the first. Young looks offside for the Arsenal goal. Wilson heads in Smith's centre and the keeper is rooted as he thumps home his third from 18 yards with his supposed poor right foot.

20. Poor Arsenal are seven without a win and are routed in a second-half blitz. Cook finishes off a five-man move for No 1. Robson is given little cover as Stephenson turns on the style, scoring two and making another three goals. Walter's speed on the wing is also crucial to the success.

21. The players find standing up difficult on the frosty surface. A massive holiday crowd goes home happy. Ex-Spur Charlie Wilson is closely marked by Lowe. Goodall, hampered with an eye injury, misjudges Clay's long ball and Lindsay's header sails past Taylor for the only goal.

LEAGUE DIVISION 1   Manager: Herbert Chapman   SEASON 1923-24

No	Date		Att	Pos	Pt	F-A	H-T	Scorers, Times, and Referees	1	2	3	4	5	6	7	8	9	10	11
22	H 26/12	TOTTENHAM	28,600	3 / *10*	30 W	2-1	0-0	Smith W 65p, 79 *Handley 52* Ref: F Procter	Taylor *Maddison*	Goodall *Clay*	Wadsworth *Forster*	Steele *Smith*	Wilson T *Lowe*	Watson *Grimsdell*	Walter *Walden*	Cook *Thompson*	Wilson C *Lindsay*	Stephenson *Elkes*	Smith W *Handley*

A snowbound pitch is treacherous but Town keep their feet well. Charlie Wilson limps off after 15 mins with a leg injury and Spurs' Walden is off for the second half. Elkes handles for a penalty before Smith and Clem's double one-two creates Billy's winner. A big crowd roar Town on.

No	Date		Att	Pos	Pt	F-A	H-T	Scorers, Times, and Referees	1	2	3	4	5	6	7	8	9	10	11
23	A 29/12	BLACKBURN	18,000	3 / *6*	30 L	0-1	0-0	*Harper 74* Ref: F Hall	Taylor *Sewell*	Goodall *Rollo*	Wadsworth *Wylie*	Steele *Roscamp*	Wilson T *Healless*	Watson *McKinnell*	Walter *Crisp*	Cook *McIntyre*	Brown *Harper*	Stephenson *McKay*	Smith W *Byers*

Town miss Clem, thigh strain, and Charlie Wilson, leg injury, in a poor game they deserve to lose. Taylor saves well from McKay but Ted Harper taps in a rebound, the eleventh goal of his debut season. Brown's last-minute shot clearly strikes a hand but the referee waves play on.

No	Date		Att	Pos	Pt	F-A	H-T	Scorers, Times, and Referees	1	2	3	4	5	6	7	8	9	10	11
24	H 5/1	BLACKBURN	16,300	4 / *7*	32 W	1-0	0-0	Stephenson 51 Ref: F Hall	Taylor *Sewell*	Goodall *Rollo*	Wadsworth *Wylie*	Steele *Roscamp*	Wilson T *Healless*	Watson *McKinnell*	Walter *Crisp*	Johnston *McIntyre*	Brown *Harper*	Stephenson *McKay*	Richardson E *Byers*

Smith excused following the death of his father and Cook has a toe injury. Sewell defies Town with good saves as Rovers are pummelled. Stephenson's mazy dribble ends with a goal from an acute angle. Brown fluffs his shot when clear through. Whistle-happy ref spoils the game.

No	Date		Att	Pos	Pt	F-A	H-T	Scorers, Times, and Referees	1	2	3	4	5	6	7	8	9	10	11
25	H 19/1	CHELSEA	14,200	4 / *20*	32 L	0-1	0-0	*Ferguson 90* Ref: F Slater	Taylor *Marsh*	Goodall *Smith*	Wadsworth *Harrow*	Steele *Priestley*	Wilson T *Wilding*	Watson *Meehan*	Cook *Castle*	Johnston *Armstrong*	Brown *Wilson*	Stephenson *Miller*	Smith W *Ferguson*

A shock result: it is only Chelsea's third win in 23 games. The disjointed attack lacks sting and is badly off-colour. Smith hits the post twice but their luck is out too. Castle's swerving shot deflects off Wadsworth and Taylor spills it to Ferguson. Cook looks uneasy on the right wing.

No	Date		Att	Pos	Pt	F-A	H-T	Scorers, Times, and Referees	1	2	3	4	5	6	7	8	9	10	11
26	A 26/1	CHELSEA	33,500	4 / *20*	34 W	1-0	0-0	Stephenson 56 Ref: F Slater	Taylor *Marsh*	Barkas *Smith*	Wadsworth *Harrow*	Cawthorne *Priestley*	Wilson T *Wilding*	Watson *Meehan*	Cook *Castle*	Johnston *Armstrong*	Brown *Wilson*	Stephenson *Miller*	Smith W *Ferguson*

Revenge, but Town are lucky to win. Three changes as Goodall and Steele are dropped and Walter returns from injury. Andy Wilson is in top form and hits the woodwork twice. Chelsea bombard Town but Taylor is superb. Walter's free-kick is hit home first time by a limping Clem.

No	Date		Att	Pos	Pt	F-A	H-T	Scorers, Times, and Referees	1	2	3	4	5	6	7	8	9	10	11
27	A 9/2	NEWCASTLE	25,000	3 / *8*	36 W	1-0	0-0	Stephenson 70 Ref: T Scholey	Taylor *Mutch*	Goodall *Russell*	Wadsworth *Hudspeth*	Cawthorne *McIntosh*	Wilson T *Spencer*	Watson *Gibson*	Walter *Aitken*	Johnston *Clark R*	Wilson C *Keating*	Stephenson *McDonald*	Smith W *Mitchell*

Newcastle have a Cup replay in two days and rest several stars. Town just do enough to win. Clem's goal is a cunning job after Russell's error, against the run of play and after a dire first half. The second period is more lively but driving wind, drizzle and poor light hamper good play.

No	Date		Att	Pos	Pt	F-A	H-T	Scorers, Times, and Referees	1	2	3	4	5	6	7	8	9	10	11
28	H 16/2	WEST HAM	12,500	4 / *12*	37 D	1-1	0-0	Smith W 70 *Ruffell 50* Ref: I Baker	Taylor *Hampson*	Barkas *Henderson*	Wadsworth *Young*	Steele *Bishop*	Wilson T *Kay*	Watson *Cadwell*	Walter *Edwards*	Johnston *Collins*	Wilson C *Brown*	Stephenson *Williams*	Smith W *Ruffell*

The Hammers are an attractive team but Town should have won easily. Ruffell leaves Barkas for dead as he races through to score a solo goal. Smith's goal is a beats three men in a run from the halfway line to score with a thunderous shot. Snow and mud hinder play.

No	Date		Att	Pos	Pt	F-A	H-T	Scorers, Times, and Referees	1	2	3	4	5	6	7	8	9	10	11
29	H 27/2	NEWCASTLE	6,000	4 / *9*	38 D	1-1	1-1	Stephenson 42 *Seymour 32* Ref: T Scholey	Taylor *Mutch*	Shaw *Hampson*	Wadsworth *Hunter*	Steele *McKenzie*	Wilson T *Spencer*	Watson *Mooney*	Walter *Low*	Johnston *Cowan*	Wilson C *Harris*	Stephenson *McDonald*	Smith W *Seymour*

Only 3,000 are present as the midweek afternoon game starts. Seymour's header sneaks past Taylor. Brown breaks through and crosses for Clem to level. Brown and Wilson go close after the break but Newcastle's vulnerable defence is not troubled. Shaw makes a nervous debut.

No	Date		Att	Pos	Pt	F-A	H-T	Scorers, Times, and Referees	1	2	3	4	5	6	7	8	9	10	11
30	H 1/3	CARDIFF	18,000	3 / *1*	40 W	2-0	2-0	Brown 25, 33 Ref: W Harper	Taylor *Kneeshaw*	Barkas *Nelson*	Shaw *Blair*	Cawthorne *Evans H*	Wilson T *Keenor*	Watson *Hardy*	Steele *Lawson*	Brown *Gill*	Wilson C *Davies L*	Stephenson *Clemell*	Smith W *Evans J*

The game goes ahead despite Friday night's blizzard and rumours that it is off keep the gate low. Cardiff are outclassed and barely have a shot in what is only their fourth defeat of the season. Brown heads in Smith's corner and scores after a mix-up. Snow mounds surround the pitch.

No	Date		Att	Pos	Pt	F-A	H-T	Scorers, Times, and Referees	1	2	3	4	5	6	7	8	9	10	11
31	A 15/3	SHEFFIELD UTD	29,000	4 / *5*	42 W	1-0	1-0	Brown 6 Ref: T Rothwell	Boot *Gough*	Barkas *Cook*	Shaw *Milton*	Cawthorne *Pantling*	Wilson T *Waugh*	Watson *Green*	Steele *Partridge*	Brown *Boyle*	Wilson C *Menlove*	Stephenson *Hoyland*	Smith W *Evans*

Thrilling game on dry, hard pitch. Brown fires in Smith's cross past an unsighted Gough. Town's defence is outstanding and Boot makes five good saves. Wilson hits the post as Town threaten to increase their lead. Cardiff lose at home to Notts County and the title race is hotting up.

Season results grid — matches 32–42 (Huddersfield Town). Top name in each position = Town player; italic name below = opponent.

#	Date	H/A	Opponent	Att	Pos	Res	Opp Pos	Pts	Score	HT	Town scorers	Opp scorers	Referee
32	22/3	H	SHEFFIELD UTD	19,500	3	W	5	44	1-0	0-0	Wilson C 75	—	Ref: T Rothwell
33	27/3	A	WEST HAM	15,000	1	W	12	46	3-2	1-1	Smith W 30, Wilson C 65, 80	*Young 5p, 55p*	Ref: I Baker
34	5/4	H	ASTON VILLA	26,280	3	W	7	48	1-0	1-0	Smith W 20p	—	Ref: W Brearley
35	12/4	H	MANCHESTER C	11,000	2	D	14	49	1-1	0-0	Brown 65	*Roberts 68*	Ref: I Baker
36	14/4	A	CARDIFF	30,000	1	D	2	50	0-0	0-0	—	—	Ref: W Harper
37	18/4	A	BURNLEY	25,000	2	D	17	51	1-1	1-0	Brown 12	*Waterfield 20*	Ref: H Hopkinson
38	19/4	A	MANCHESTER C	40,000	2	D	13	52	1-1	0-1	Wilson C 54	*Warner 12*	Ref: I Baker
39	22/4	H	BURNLEY	**33,178**	1	W	17	54	1-0	1-0	Smith W 43	—	Ref: H Hopkinson
40	26/4	A	NOTT'M FOREST	12,000	2	D	20	55	1-1	1-0	Cook 6	*Nelis 47*	Ref: H Hopkinson
41	30/4	A	ASTON VILLA	14,000	2	L	6	55	1-3	1-2	Smith W 10	*Walker 12, Capewell 39, Dorrell 47*	Ref: G Watson
42	3/5	H	NOTT'M FOREST	19,000	1	W	20	57	3-0	1-0	Cook 32, 57, Brown 67	—	Ref: H Hopkinson

Line-ups (Town / *opponents*):

- **32 Sheffield Utd:** Boot, Shaw, Wadsworth, Cawthorne, Wilson T, Watson, Steele, Brown, Wilson C, Stephenson, Smith W / *Blackwell, Cook, Milton, Pantling, Waugh, Green, Mercer, Boyle, Menlove, Gillespie, Tunstall*
- **33 West Ham:** Boot, Shaw, Wadsworth, Cawthorne, Wilson T, Watson, Steele, Brown, Wilson C, Stephenson, Smith W / *Hampson, Henderson, Young, Bishop, Kay, Cadwell, Edwards, Proctor, Campbell, Moore, Ruffell*
- **34 Aston Villa:** Taylor, Shaw, Wadsworth, Cawthorne, Wilson T, Watson, Steele, Brown, Wilson C, Stephenson, Smith W / *Jackson, Smart, Mort, Moss, Milne, Johnstone, York, Mackay, Capewell, Walker, Dorrell*
- **35 Manchester C:** Boot, Barkas, Goodall, Cawthorne, Wilson T, Watson, Steele, Brown, Wilson C, Stephenson, Smith W / *Mitchell, Cookson, Fletcher, Carroll, Elwood, Wilson, Morris, Warner, Roberts, Johnson, Murphy*
- **36 Cardiff:** Taylor, Cawthorne, Wadsworth, Steele, Wilson T, Watson, Walter, Brown, Wilson C, Cook, Smith W / *Farquharson, Nelson, Page, Wake, Keenor, Hardy, Gill, Jones, Davies, Clennell, Evans J*
- **37 Burnley:** Taylor, Shaw, Wadsworth, Cawthorne, Wilson T, Watson, Steele, Brown, Wilson C, Stephenson, Smith W / *Dawson, Smelt, Taylor, Bassnett, Hill, Parkin, Bennie, Kelly, Beel, Cross, Waterfield*
- **38 Manchester C:** Taylor, Shaw, Wadsworth, Cawthorne, Wilson T, Watson, Steele, Brown, Wilson C, Stephenson, Richardson E / *Mitchell, Cookson, Calderwood, Sharp, Elwood, Wilson, Morris, Warner, Roberts, Johnson, Daniels*
- **39 Burnley:** Taylor, Cawthorne, Wadsworth, Steele, Wilson T, Watson, Richardson E, Brown, Wilson C, Stephenson, Smith W / *Dawson, Wheelhouse, Taylor, Parkin, Hill, Robinson, Bennie, Kelly, Beel, Cross, Waterfield*
- **40 Nott'm Forest:** Taylor, Cawthorne, Wadsworth, Steele, Wilson T, Watson, Walter, Cook, Brown, Stephenson, Richardson E / *Bennett, Bulling, Barratt, Belton, Morgan, Wallace, Gibson, Flood, Walker, Nelis, Martin*
- **41 Aston Villa:** Taylor, Shaw, Wadsworth, Cawthorne, Wilson T, Watson, Steele, Johnston, Brown, Stephenson, Smith W / *Jackson, Smart, Mort, Moss, Milne, Blackburn, York, Kirton, Capewell, Walker, Dorrell*
- **42 Nott'm Forest:** Taylor, Barkas, Wadsworth, Steele, Wilson T, Watson, Richardson E, Brown, Cook, Stephenson, Smith W / *Bennett, Bulling, Barratt, Belton, Parker, Wallace, Gibson, Flood, Walker, Nelis, Martin*

Match notes:

32. Spring-like day as Town leapfrog Cardiff. Very tight game with little to choose between the sides. Clem sets up the winning goal with a defence-splitting pass that leaves Wilson unmarked. After the goal United crumble. Clem and Billy thrill the crowd with scintillating football.

33. Off-colour Town are slightly lucky to win. A choppy wind makes football difficult and West Ham twice lead with penalties, given for Shaw's dubious handball and Wadsworth's fist out. Stephenson and Steele set up opportunistic goals for Charlie Wilson, back to his poaching best.

34. Villa are fresh from an FA Cup semi-final victory last week. Dr Milne pushes Wilson down for the spot-kick. England captain Moss is over-physical with Clem, which makes this a hard-won victory. Villa push Town hard but can't breach the solid defence. Dry pitch and a lively ball.

35. Taylor and Wadsworth are playing for England v Scotland. A ragged game after a promising start. Town do everything but score but finally take the lead. Heavy rain makes conditions hard and keeps the crowd low. City's Roberts is seen to handle the ball before scoring a lucky goal.

36. The top two clash. The teams are level on points but Town have two games in hand. A titanic struggle with grim, determined defences on top. Clennell twice and Davies miss good first-half chances on a greasy pitch. Cardiff pile on pressure in second half but Taylor is magnificent.

37. A draw is fair from a strenuous game but there is no revenge for the Cup defeat. In the last minute Charlie Wilson shoots against the keeper's legs and Brown fires over as the whistle goes. Sunderland go top again but have played more games than Town and Cardiff. Smith is crocked.

38. Town play in red at City's new ground. Shaw hesitates and Warner nets. Clem has a goal ruled out. Richardson has a fine shot tipped over but crosses for the unmarked Wilson to score a deserved goal. Cardiff win to draw level again. After a fourth game in eight days Town look weary.

39. For the first time Town are title favourites after probably the worst display of season in Billy Smith's benefit game. Charlie Wilson hobbles after a clash with Hill. Dawson keeps Burnley in the game before Richardson makes Smith's goal. A deserved win against plucky opponents.

40. On the day that Newcastle beat Villa in the Cup final, Town fail to beat struggling Forest. Cook scores after the ball pin-balls around the Forest area. Tom Wilson impedes Taylor and the ball skids off Nelis for a lucky goal. Cardiff beat 10-man Birmingham 2-0 but miss crucial chances.

41. Villa make amends for the Cup final defeat on a quagmire pitch. Town are unlucky, as they play some great football. Villa take their chances and their solid defence soaks up incessant second-half pressure. Cardiff are now title favourites, as off-form Birmingham have little to play for.

42. Forest without a win in eight are never in with a shout as Town do the necessary and wait for the score from St Andrews. Heavy rain falls after half-time but Town raise their game. The crowd wait expectantly for the Cardiff score and a 0-0 draw hands the title to Town on goal-average.

Home Average 17,565
Away 23,846

LEAGUE DIVISION 1 (CUP-TIES) Manager: Herbert Chapman SEASON 1923-24

FA Cup			F-A	H-T	Scorers, Times, and Referees	1	2	3	4	5	6	7	8	9	10	11
1 H BIRMINGHAM 4 W 12|1 30,924 17			1-0	1-0	Johnston 7 Ref: A Fogg	Taylor *Tremelling*	Goodall *Ashurst*	Wadsworth *Womack*	Steele *Dale*	Wilson T *Cringan*	Watson *Barton*	Cook *Harvey*	Johnston *Lane*	Brown *Bradford*	Stephenson *Islip*	Smith W *Linley*

Blues look better than their league position but lack a cutting edge and Town deserve the win, their third 1-0 win over Blues this season. Islip is their best forward against his old club but England man Bradford is well held by T Wilson and Dan Tremelling is in top form. Clem injured.

2 A MANCHESTER U 4 W 2|2 66,678 2:10			3-0	2-0	Wilson C 14, 84, Stephenson 28 Ref: F Todman	Taylor *Steward*	Barkas *Silcock*	Wadsworth *Moore*	Steele *Bennion*	Wilson T *Barson*	Watson *Hilditch*	Walter *Spence*	Johnston *Mann*	Wilson C *Henderson*	Stephenson *Lochhead*	Smith W *McPherson*

Over 20,000 Town fans in one of United's biggest ever crowds see their heroes progress comfortably. Gale-force winds make football difficult and United persist in the high balls. Johnston creates a masterful first and also has a hand in Clem's goal. It is no contest after the break.

3 A BURNLEY 4 L 23|2 54,775 15			0-1	0-1	Weaver 22 Ref: J Sharpe	Taylor *Dawson*	Barkas *Smelt*	Wadsworth *Taylor*	Steele *Bassnett*	Wilson T *Hill*	Watson *Morgan*	Walter *Bennie*	Johnston *Kelly*	Wilson C *Beel*	Stephenson *Cross*	Smith W *Weaver*

A record crowd watch as Burnley raise their mediocre league form to shock Town, who miss early chances and rarely threaten after the goal. Wilson skims the bar in the first minute but is otherwise dwarfed by the lanky Hill. Beel looks offside as he sets up Weavers' winning goal.

			Home					Away					
		P	W	D	L	F	A	W	D	L	F	A	Pts
1	HUDDERSF'D	42	15	5	1	35	9	8	6	7	25	24	57
2	Cardiff	42	14	5	2	35	13	8	5	8	26	21	57
3	Sunderland	42	12	7	2	38	20	10	2	9	33	34	53
4	Bolton	42	13	6	2	45	13	5	8	8	23	21	50
5	Sheffield U	42	12	5	4	39	16	7	7	7	30	33	50
6	Aston Villa	42	10	10	1	33	11	3	10	8	19	26	49
7	Everton	42	13	7	1	43	18	5	6	10	19	35	49
8	Blackburn	42	14	5	2	40	13	3	6	12	14	37	45
9	Newcastle	42	13	5	3	40	21	4	5	12	20	33	44
10	Notts Co	42	9	7	5	21	15	5	7	9	23	34	42
11	Manchester C	42	11	7	3	34	24	4	5	12	20	47	42
12	Liverpool	42	11	5	5	35	20	4	6	11	14	28	41
13	West Ham	42	10	6	5	26	17	3	9	9	14	26	41
14	Birmingham	42	10	6	5	25	19	3	9	9	16	30	39
15	Tottenham	42	9	6	6	30	22	3	8	10	20	34	38
16	West Brom	42	10	6	5	43	30	2	8	11	8	32	38
17	Burnley	42	10	5	6	39	27	2	7	12	16	33	36
18	Preston	42	8	4	9	34	27	4	6	11	18	40	34
19	Arsenal	42	8	5	8	25	24	4	4	13	15	39	34
20	Nott'm Forest	42	3	9	9	19	15	3	3	15	23	49	32
21	Chelsea	42	7	9	5	23	21	2	5	14	8	32	32
22	Middlesbro	42	6	4	11	23	23	1	4	16	14	37	22
		924	232	132	98	725	418	98	132	232	418	725	924

	Appearances		Goals		
	Lge	FAC	Lge	FAC	Tot
Barkas, Ned	21	2			
Boot, Len	5				
Brown, George	22	1	8		8
Cawthorne, Harry	16				
Cook, George	25	1	9		9
Cowell, Billy	2				
Goodall, Roy	14	1			
Islip, Ernie	3				
Johnston, Billy	8	3			
Richardson, Ted	5			1	1
Richardson, George	2				
Shaw, George	9				
Smith, Bert	8				
Smith, Billy	39	3	13		13
Steele, David	31	3			
Stephenson, Clem	40	3	11	1	12
Taylor, Ted	35	3			
Wadsworth, Sam	37	3			
Walter, Joe	26	2			
Watson, Billy	42	3			
Wilson, Charlie	31	2	18	2	20
Wilson, Tommy	41	3	1		1
(own-goals)					
(22 players used)	462	33	60	4	64

Odds & ends

Double wins: (4) Preston, Birmingham, Arsenal, Sheffield U.
Double losses: (0).

Won from behind: (4) Preston (a), WBA (a), Spurs (h), West Ham (a).
Lost from in front: (1) Aston Villa (a).

High spots: Clinching the title in a dramatic finale.
Thrilling win at West Brom.
FA Cup win at Old Trafford.
Form of Stephenson and Smith on the left wing.
Defensive solidity throughout.

Low spots: FA Cup exit at Burnley.
Defeat at Villa Park when the title looked secure.
Shock home defeat to lowly Chelsea.
Disgraceful scenes against Notts County.

Hat-tricks: (2) Charlie Wilson v Arsenal (2).
Opposing hat-tricks: (0).
Ever-presents: (1) Watson.
Leading scorer: Charlie Wilson (20).

LEAGUE DIVISION 1 — Manager: Herbert Chapman — SEASON 1924-25

No	Date		Att	Pos	Pt	F-A	H-T	Scorers, Times, and Referees	1	2	3	4	5	6	7	8	9	10	11
1	A 30/8	NEWCASTLE	47,000	-	W 2	3-1	1-1	Brown 20, C Wilson 55, Steph'son 62 / Cowan 25 / Ref: F Hall	Taylor	Goodall	Wadsworth	Steele	Wilson T	Watson	Williams	Brown	Wilson C	Stephenson	Smith W
									Mutch	*Hampson*	*Hudspith*	*Mooney*	*Spencer*	*Gibson*	*Low*	*Cowan*	*Harris*	*McDonald*	*Seymour*

A massive crowd watches the Champions play the FA Cup winners. Newcastle look stronger until Brown's headed goal from Smith's cross. Cowan equalises in a scramble but Town's dominance is rewarded with a Wilson rocket and a sweet Clem header from Billy Smith's corner.

No	Date		Att	Pos	Pt	F-A	H-T	Scorers, Times, and Referees	1	2	3	4	5	6	7	8	9	10	11
2	H 2/9	NOTT'M FOREST	13,500	-	W 4	3-0	3-0	Wilson C 10, 25, 41 / Ref: J Ashworth	Taylor	Goodall	Wadsworth	Steele	Wilson T	Watson	Williams	Brown	Wilson C	Cook	Smith W
									Hardy	*Bulling*	*Barratt*	*Belton*	*Parker*	*Wallace*	*Gibson*	*Morris*	*Walker*	*Miller*	*Martin*

Forest are beaten by a super display. Wilson's first is a sweet move with Forest reduced to statues. His second, a volley, almost breaks the stanchion and bounces out 20 yards. His third, set up by Cook, is a delicious lob. New man Tiny Williams leaves full-backs on the floor.

No	Date		Att	Pos	Pt	F-A	H-T	Scorers, Times, and Referees	1	2	3	4	5	6	7	8	9	10	11
3	H 6/9	SHEFFIELD UTD	20,200	2 *16*	W 6	2-1	2-1	Wilson C 11, Brown 32 / Boyle 29 / Ref: I Josephs	Taylor	Goodall	Wadsworth	Steele	Wilson T	Watson	Williams	Brown	Wilson C	Stephenson	Smith W
									Blackwell	*Cook*	*Milton*	*Pantling*	*Waugh*	*Green*	*Mercer*	*Boyle*	*Johnson*	*Gillespie*	*Tunstall*

Bank Holiday weekend keeps crowd down. Town find it hard to break down the tight Blades. Brown sets up Wilson. Tunstall's teasing cross is headed in by Boyle before Brown's similar header wins the game. Stephenson limps off with strained ligaments after some rough treatment.

No	Date		Att	Pos	Pt	F-A	H-T	Scorers, Times, and Referees	1	2	3	4	5	6	7	8	9	10	11
4	A 8/9	NOTT'M FOREST	12,000	1 *21*	W 8	1-0	0-0	Cook 65 / Ref: J Ashworth	Taylor	Goodall	Wadsworth	Steele	Wilson T	Watson	Williams	Brown	Wilson C	Cook	Smith W
									Hardy	*Thompson*	*Barratt*	*Wallace*	*Morgan*	*Burton*	*Morris*	*Flood*	*Walker*	*Nelis*	*Martin*

Four defeats in a row for Forest and they will struggle. They deserve more for a strong midfield performance but they lack punch. 41-year-old Sam Hardy's career is coming to an end and his weak punch goes to Cook whose ground shot is inch perfect. Below-par Town are lucky to win.

No	Date		Att	Pos	Pt	F-A	H-T	Scorers, Times, and Referees	1	2	3	4	5	6	7	8	9	10	11
5	A 13/9	WEST HAM	28,103	3 *3*	D 9	0-0	0-0	Ref: D Asson	Taylor	Goodall	Wadsworth	Steele	Wilson T	Watson	Williams	Brown	Wilson C	Cook	Richardson E
									Hampson	*Henderson*	*Young*	*Tresarden*	*Kay*	*Cadwell*	*Edwards*	*Earle*	*Watson*	*Jennings*	*Ruffell*

An even contest ends with a fair result. West Ham are unbeaten, have not conceded a goal, and a big crowd wants to see this game. Defences are on top but goal chances go begging. Williams is behind Town's best moves. Edwards hits the underside of the bar for the Hammers.

No	Date		Att	Pos	Pt	F-A	H-T	Scorers, Times, and Referees	1	2	3	4	5	6	7	8	9	10	11
6	H 20/9	BLACKBURN	18,000	1 *4*	D 10	0-0	0-0	Ref: J Forshaw	Taylor	Goodall	Wadsworth	Steele	Wilson T	Watson	Williams	Brown	Wilson C	Cook	Smith W
									Sewell	*Roxburgh*	*Wylie*	*Roscamp*	*Pool*	*Campbell*	*Hulme*	*McKay*	*Harper*	*McIntyre*	*Crisp*

Town are the only unbeaten side in Division 1. A dazzling sun affects some players but defences are always on top. Breakaways create some excitement but, Williams apart, Town's clueless attack is bottled up. Town's late bombardment is fruitless and Rovers deserve their point.

No	Date		Att	Pos	Pt	F-A	H-T	Scorers, Times, and Referees	1	2	3	4	5	6	7	8	9	10	11
7	A 27/9	LEEDS	41,600	1 *11*	D 11	1-1	0-1	Smith W 65 / Swan 34 / Ref: A Ward	Taylor	Goodall	Wadsworth	Steele	Wilson T	Watson	Williams	Brown	Wilson C	Cook	Smith W
									Down	*Duffield*	*Menzies*	*Sherwin*	*Hart*	*Baker*	*Coates*	*Whipp*	*Thorn*	*Swan*	*Harris*

A record crowd is crammed in to see the first Div 1 derby between the clubs, with hundreds around the pitch perimeter. Swan capitalises on Goodall's mistake to net and the crowd go wild. Smith dribbles through, only for the keeper to fumble the ball and hand Billy a goal on a plate.

No	Date		Att	Pos	Pt	F-A	H-T	Scorers, Times, and Referees	1	2	3	4	5	6	7	8	9	10	11
8	A 4/10	ASTON VILLA	42,500	1 *8*	D 12	1-1	0-0	Cook 66 / Walker 80 / Ref: J Fowler	Taylor	Goodall	Wadsworth	Steele	Wilson T	Watson	Williams	Brown	Wilson C	Cook	Smith W
									Spiers	*Smart*	*Mort*	*Moss*	*Milne*	*Blackburn*	*York*	*Kirton*	*Capewell*	*Walker*	*Dorrell*

Town are unlucky not to win comfortably. George Brown has a good goal ruled offside; then scores, but the ref gives a penalty. Spiers saves Smith's kick, but finally Villa score from an unjust corner – Billy Walker heading a soft goal to cancel out Cook's effort from Williams' cross.

No	Date		Att	Pos	Pt	F-A	H-T	Scorers, Times, and Referees	1	2	3	4	5	6	7	8	9	10	11
9	H 11/10	ARSENAL	15,500	1 *7*	W 14	4-0	2-0	Smith W 33, Cook 35, Wilson C 73, [Brown 84] / Ref: W Harper	Taylor	Goodall	Cawthorne	Steele	Spence	Watson	Williams	Brown	Wilson C	Cook	Smith W
									Robson	*Mackie*	*Kennedy*	*Milne*	*Butler*	*John*	*Blyth*	*Neil*	*Woods*	*Ramsey*	*Haden*

Robson is the Gunners' hero as he saves them from a cricket score in a one-sided game. Smith is the first player ever to score direct from a corner. Cook scores a super second after a sweeping move involving Brown and Smith. Wilson has an easy third and Brown heads a corner in.

No	Date		Att	Pos	Pt	F-A	H-T	Scorers, Times, and Referees	1	2	3	4	5	6	7	8	9	10	11
10	A 18/10	MANCHESTER C	50,000	1 *6*	D 15	1-1	0-0	Brown 48 / Barnes 51 / Ref: R Sharp	Taylor	Goodall	Wadsworth	Steele	Wilson T	Watson	Williams	Brown	Wilson C	Cook	Smith W
									Mitchell	*Cookson*	*Fletcher*	*Sharp*	*Elwood*	*Pringle*	*Austin*	*Roberts*	*Johnson*	*Barnes*	*Murphy*

Taylor is injured just before half-time and Watson goes in goal. Chapman's brave tactics are to attack and Town are applauded by City's fans. Smith's outswinging cross finds Mitchell in two minds and Brown smashes home. Watson makes fine saves and is not at fault for the goal.

Match-by-match record (matches 11–21)

#	Venue	Opponent	Date	Result	Score (FT)	HT	Attendance	Pos	Opp Pos	Pts
11	H	BIRMINGHAM	25/10	L	0-1	0-1	20,500	2	1	15
12	A	WEST BROM	1/11	L	0-1	0-1	15,683	5	2	15
13	H	TOTTENHAM	8/11	L	1-2	1-0	18,500	9	16	15
14	A	LIVERPOOL	12/11	W	3-2	3-1	25,000	3	11	17
15	A	BOLTON	15/11	L	0-1	0-1	35,000	5	10	17
16	H	NOTTS COUNTY	22/11	D	0-0	0-0	12,300	7	1	18
17	A	EVERTON	29/11	W	2-0	1-0	27,500	6	19	20
18	H	SUNDERLAND	6/12	W	4-0	0-0	18,000	2	5	22
19	A	CARDIFF	13/12	D	2-2	2-2	25,000	4	15	23
20	H	PRESTON	20/12	W	1-0	1-0	15,000	2	22	25
21	A	BURNLEY	25/12	W	5-1	2-0	26,332	2	20	27

11 — H BIRMINGHAM, 25/10 (L 0-1)
Town: Boot, Goodall, Wadsworth, Steele, Wilson T, Watson, Williams, Brown, Cook, Stephenson, Smith W
Birmingham: Tremelling, Womack, Jones, Liddell, Cringan, Barton, Harvey, Crosbie, Bradford, Islip, Scriven
Scorers: Bradford 38
Ref: W Turnbull

Town finish the match with nine men bombarding Brum's goal. Taylor absent with knee injury and Charlie Wilson is dropped allowing Clem to return. Bradford punishes slack defending with a shot from Harvey's free-kick with Boot looking at fault. Birmingham go top of the league.

12 — A WEST BROM, 1/11 (L 0-1)
Town: Boot, Goodall, Wadsworth, Steele, Wilson T, Watson, Williams, Brown, Cook, Stephenson, Smith W
West Brom: Ashmore, Smith, Perry, Magee, Reed, Richardson, Jones, Carter, James, Wilson, Byers
Scorers: James 20
Ref: W Brearley

The gate is affected by pouring rain, with most of the fans crammed under the covered terracing. The poor light forces the ref to kick-off ten minutes early. James' glancing header wins the game. Speedy Albion are in top form. Town press hard in the second half but can't equalise.

13 — H TOTTENHAM, 8/11 (L 1-2)
Town: Boot, Goodall, Wadsworth, Steele, Wilson T, Smith N, Williams, Wilson C, Cook, Stephenson, Smith W
Tottenham: Hinton, Forster, Poynton, Smith, Walters, Skinner, Thompson, Seed, Hargreaves, Elkes, Handley
Scorers: Wilson C 24; Seed 57, Thompson 90
Ref: J Hickling

Spurs play five reserves and pull off a shock. Wilson scores a clever goal against his old club from Billy Smith's cross. Jimmy Seed's diving header makes it 1-1. Boot makes a hash of a one-on-one with Thompson and is made to look foolish. Watson axed after 90 consecutive games.

14 — A LIVERPOOL, 12/11 (W 3-2)
Town: Boot, Goodall, Wadsworth, Steele, Wilson T, Watson, Williams, Cook, Wilson C, Stephenson, Smith W
Liverpool: Scott, Lucas, McKinlay, McNab, W Bromilow, Rawlings, Forshaw, Chambers, Shone, Hopkin
Scorers: Smith W 23, Cook 31, Wilson C 43; Forshaw 30, McNab 69
Ref: J Telford

Smith is on song as Town put on their best display of the season for their first ever win at Anfield. Boot protests that he is fouled for the first Pool goal. Bromilow is caught napping in his own area by Smith. Cook scores a good second and Clem sets up Charlie Wilson for the third.

15 — A BOLTON, 15/11 (L 0-1)
Town: Boot, Goodall, Wadsworth, Steele, Wilson T, Watson, Williams, Cook, Wilson C, Stephenson, Smith W
Bolton: Pym, Howarth R, Finney, Nuttall, Seddon, Jennings, Butler, Jack D, Cassidy, Smith Joe, Vizard
Scorers: Cassidy 28
Ref: A Caseley

A game between two of the league's most skilful sides fails to live up to expectations. Town players appeal for offside after Len Boot's mad rush, but Cassidy's goal stands. Wanderers deserve the win as Town create few chances. Notts County and Birmingham lead Div 1 with 20 pts.

16 — H NOTTS COUNTY, 22/11 (D 0-0)
Town: Mercer, Goodall, Wadsworth, Steele, Wilson T, Watson, Williams, Cook, Wilson C, Stephenson, Smith W
Notts County: Iremonger, Ashurst, Cornwell, Wren, Dinsdale, Kemp, Daly, Widdowson, Cock, Davis, Barry
Ref: E Westwood

County's mean defence – they have conceded only seven goals in 16 games – is rock solid but they are no attacking force and Town should have got both points. Willie Mercer, a new signing from Hull, has a quiet debut. Drizzling rain and poor visibility keeps the crowd down.

17 — A EVERTON, 29/11 (W 2-0)
Town: Mercer, Goodall, Wadsworth, Steele, Wilson T, Watson, Williams, Cook, Wilson C, Stephenson, Smith W
Everton: Harland, McDonald, Livingstone, Peacock, McBain, Hart, Chedgzoy, Irvine, Cock, Chadwick, Troup
Scorers: Cook 18, Wilson C 70
Ref: G Nunnerley

Mercer gives Town's defence a stronger look, handling some difficult shots and keeping up with Clem but he was superb. Billy Watson is back to his best with his brilliant anticipation. Steele's brief absence appears to have made him stronger.

18 — H SUNDERLAND, 6/12 (W 4-0)
Town: Mercer, Goodall, Wadsworth, Steele, Wilson T, Watson, Williams, Cook, Wilson C, Stephenson, Smith W
Sunderland: McInroy, Cresswell, England, Clunas, Ferguson, Andrews, Grimshaw, Buchan, Marshall, Hawes, Ellis
Scorers: Wilson C 48, 76, Stephenson 49, [Smith W 75]
Ref: W Harper

McInroy spoils a brilliant first half by miskicking for Williams to set up the first goal. Tiny crosses for Clem to head No 2. Then Billy scores a brilliant solo goal and sets up Wilson's second. The joint league leaders suffer their biggest defeat of the season and Town look like champs.

19 — A CARDIFF, 13/12 (D 2-2)
Town: Mercer, Goodall, Wadsworth, Steele, Wilson T, Watson, Williams, Cook, Wilson C, Stephenson, Smith W
Cardiff: Farquharson, Nelson, Blair, Wake, Keenor, Hardy, Lawson, Davies L, Davies W, Beadles, Evans
Scorers: Cook 35, 36; Davies L 10, Beadles 30
Ref: A Kingscott

Cook scores two from close range to cancel out impressive Cardiff's start. After the break, with rain making the surface treacherous, Town look more likely, with their half-backs' superb tackling and spoiling upsetting Cardiff's rhythm. Clem shoots just wide in the dying minutes.

20 — H PRESTON, 20/12 (W 1-0)
Town: Mercer, Goodall, Wadsworth, Steele, Wilson T, Watson, Williams, Cook, Wilson C, Stephenson, Smith W
Preston: Branston, Wade, Cook, Forrest, McCall, Williamson, Aitken, Paterson, Woodhouse, Barnes, Harrison
Scorers: Wilson C 12
Ref: W Turnbull

Preston have only three wins all season. They play well and fight hard but lack cutting edge. Stephenson is out with a thigh injury. Wilson has an easy task of breasting the ball into the net after Branston's parry. Cook is harshly adjudged to have handled but Smith misses from the spot.

21 — A BURNLEY, 25/12 (W 5-1)
Town: Mercer, Goodall, Wadsworth, Steele, Wilson T, Watson, Williams, Cook, Wilson C, Stephenson, Smith W
Burnley: Dawson, Smelt, Fergus, Bassnett, Armitage, Tresadern, Tonner, Cross, Roberts, Greenhalgh, Waterfield
Scorers: Wilson C 32, 40, 56, 73, Brown 70; Cross 72
Ref: R Kelso

Burnley, still reeling from recent death from pneumonia of manager John Haworth aged 48, are demolished by Charlie Wilson's slick shooting. In dreadful muddy conditions Jerry Dawson keeps the score down but Charlie just seems to be on the spot to capitalise on woeful defending.

LEAGUE DIVISION 1 — Manager: Herbert Chapman — SEASON 1924-25

No	Date	Team	Att	Pos	Pt	F-A	H-T	Scorers, Times, and Referees	1	2	3	4	5	6	7	8	9	10	11
22	H 26/12	BURNLEY	30,300	W 2 / 20	29	2-0	2-0	Smith W 22, Cook 25 — Ref: R Kelso	Mercer / Dawson	Goodall / Smelt	Wadsworth / Waterfield	Steele / Bassnett	Wilson T / Hill	Watson / Tresadern	Williams / Tonner	Cook / Cross	Wilson C / Roberts	Stephenson / Beel	Smith W / Lancaster
23	H 27/12	NEWCASTLE	13,500	D 2 / 5	30	0-0	0-0	Ref: J Pennington	Mercer / Bradley	Goodall / Hudspeth	Shaw / Maitland	Steele / McKenzie	Wilson T / Spencer	Watson / Curry	Williams / Urwin	Brown / Cowan	Wilson C / Loughlin	Stephenson / McDonald	Smith W / Seymour
24	A 3/1	SHEFFIELD UTD	28,500	D 2 / 16	31	1-1	1-0	Smith W 17*, Johnson 90 — Ref: I Josephs — * some sources credit Pantling	Mercer / Sutcliffe	Goodall / Cook	Shaw / Milton	Steele / Pantling	Wilson T / King	Watson / Green	Williams / Partridge	Cook / Boyle	Wilson C / Johnson	Stephenson / Gillespie	Smith W / Tunstall
25	H 17/1	WEST HAM	14,000	L 3 / 12	31	1-2	0-1	Watson 33, Ruffell 84 — Ref: D Asson	Mercer / Hampson	Goodall / Henderson	Wadsworth / Young	Steele / Carter	Wilson T / Kay	Watson / Cadwell	Walter / Yews	Cook / Moore	Binks / Watson	Stephenson / Williams	Smith W / Ruffell
26	A 24/1	BLACKBURN	12,000	W 3 / 18	33	3-2	1-1	Brown 25, 65, Walter 72 — McIntyre 23, Crisp 80 — Ref: J Forshaw	Mercer / Sewell	Goodall / Rollo	Shaw / Wylie	Steele / Roscamp	Wilson T / Healless	Watson / McKinnell	Walter / Hulme	Brown / McKay	Binks / McIntyre	Stephenson / McCleery	Smith W / Crisp
27	H 31/1	LEEDS	10,500	W 2 / 17	35	2-0	1-0	Smith W 8, Brown 61 — Ref: G Watson	Mercer / Russell	Goodall / Duffield	Shaw / Menzies	Steele / Baker	Wilson T / Hart	Watson / Atkinson	Walter / Coates	Brown / Whipp	Wilson C / Powell	Stephenson / Swan	Smith W / Harris
28	H 7/2	ASTON VILLA	19,500	W 1 / 14	37	4-1	1-1	Brown 11, 73, 85, Stephenson 80 — Walker 1 — Ref: J Fowler	Mercer / Spiers	Goodall / Smart	Shaw / Bowen	Steele / Johnstone	Wilson T / Dennington	Watson / Muldoon	Walter / York	Brown / Kirton	Wilson C / Walker	Stephenson / Stephenson	Smith W / Dorrell
29	A 14/2	ARSENAL	25,000	W 2 / 18	39	5-0	3-0	Brown 8, Stephenson 15, [Wilson C 29, 65, 80] — Ref: W Harper	Mercer / Lewis	Goodall / Baker	Shaw / Mackie	Steele / Young	Wilson T / Blyth	Watson / John	Walter / Hoar	Brown / Brain	Wilson C / Woods	Stephenson / Ramsey	Smith W / Toner
30	H 21/2	MANCHESTER C	19,300	D 1 / 10	40	1-1	0-1	Smith W 63 — Roberts 9 — Ref: R Sharp	Mercer / Mitchell	Goodall / Cookson	Shaw / Fletcher	Steele / Pringle	Wilson T / Cowan	Watson / Wilson	Walter / Austin	Brown / Sharp	Wilson C / Roberts	Stephenson / Johnson	Smith W / Daniels
31	A 28/2	BIRMINGHAM	12,000	W 1 / 7	42	1-0	1-0	Brown 4 — Ref: W Turnbull	Mercer / Tremelling	Goodall / Ashurst	Wadsworth / Liddell	Steele / Jones	Wilson T / Cringan	Watson / Dale	Williams / Harris	Brown / Bradford	Wilson C / Briggs	Stephenson / Islip	Smith W / Linley

22 — BURNLEY: Burnley's four changes improve their defence a little but they lack bite in attack. Smith capitalises on Bassnett's bad mistake. Dawson errs for the second with Smith the creator. Burnley's Hill has cocaine injected into an eye injury. Town ease up after the goals and are barely troubled.

23 — NEWCASTLE: The pitch is practically under water as the rain pours down. The stand is packed, but on the uncovered bank only 30 or 40 fans brave the elements. Town adapt better than the Magpies in a mistake-riddled game. In a desperate onslaught United hang on bravely to get a point.

24 — SHEFFIELD UTD: Town playing against the wind in the first half let the Blades off the hook. Williams' cross is hit home by Smith of Pantling's boot. Town's caution is punished in the last minute when George Shaw, in for out-of-form Wadsworth, is out of position and Partridge crosses for Johnson.

25 — WEST HAM: Walter returns after injury for Williams and Charlie Wilson is axed to the fans' ire. Reserve Syd Binks disappoints. Ref blocks a sure Hammers goal before Vic Watson heads in Ruffell's cross for a soft goal. Town have a Cup hangover and struggle against West Ham's offside tactics.

26 — BLACKBURN: Off-form Wadsworth and Cook are dropped. A lethargic Town are lucky to win as the sun's eclipse affects the light. Hulme almost pulls it out of the fire for Rovers after Brown's clever free-kick sets up Walter's goal. Mercer looks good but frightens fans with his two-fisted punches.

27 — LEEDS: Leeds' good start has evaporated and relegation is looking possible. Heavy morning rain keeps the crowd down and leaves large areas of the pitch under water. Smith scores when debutant Russell spills Brown's shot and crosses for Brown's header. Recalled Wilson unsettles Leeds.

28 — ASTON VILLA: The spring-like weather is too late to help a sodden pitch. Walker heads in after York hits the bar. A deserved victory, with Town well on top after an early shock. Brown scores with two headers and a tap-in. Clem ends up on his back scoring no.3. WBA lose at home and Town go top.

29 — ARSENAL: Hailstorm before the kick-off turns the pitch into a quagmire. Charlie Wilson's second hat-trick at Highbury in successive years, including a magnificent leap for his second, has home fans applauding. He is set to score a sixth when a barking dog seems to make him fall over the ball.

30 — MANCHESTER C: On a dry and firm pitch the league's leading scorer nets his 26th goal after fooling Goodall and Shaw. Wilson's shot is only half-held by Mitchell and Smith sweeps the ball and Mitchell into the net. City miss two open goals and have another disallowed as Town live dangerously.

31 — BIRMINGHAM: The start delayed for 24 minutes because of a rainstorm and then a haze descends making visibility poor. Dale's mis-kick in the cloying mud lets in Brown for a soft goal. Ashurst's early injury means Birmingham play with ten men. The game ends in semi-darkness with Town on top.

Huddersfield Town — season record, matches 32–42

No.	V	Opponents	Date	Att.	Pos	Res	Score	Opp Pos	Pts
32	H	WEST BROM	11/3	15,400	1	D	1-1	2	43
33	A	TOTTENHAM	14/3	32,500	1	W	2-1	8	45
34	H	BOLTON	21/3	29,287	1	D	0-0	5	46
35	H	EVERTON	4/4	15,500	1	W	2-0	20	48
36	A	BURY	10/4	31,772	1	W	1-0	5	50
37	A	SUNDERLAND	11/4	35,000	1	D	1-1	6	51
38	H	BURY	14/4	28,440	1	W	2-0	6	53
39	H	CARDIFF	18/4	15,500	1	D	0-0	12	54
40	A	PRESTON	25/4	12,634	1	W	4-1	21	56
41	A	NOTTS COUNTY	29/4	8,000	1	D	1-1	8	57
42	H	LIVERPOOL	2/5	19,800	1	D	1-1	4	58

Home average 18,215 — Away average 27,291

---

32 — H WEST BROM (11/3)
Brown 37; Carter 83. Ref: W Brearley
Huddersfield: Mercer, Goodall, Wadsworth, Steele, Wilson T, Watson, Williams, Brown, Wilson C, Stephenson, Smith W
West Brom: *Ashmore, Smith, Baugh, Magee, Reed, Richardson, Glidden, Carter, James, Wilson, Gregory*
The top two clash in a Wednesday afternoon game. Defences are on top and a draw is fair in an unexciting game. Steele makes the opening for Wilson to set up Brown. Goodall's error lets in England player Carter. Albion's run of six away wins is ended. Wadsworth back in favour.

33 — A TOTTENHAM (14/3)
Stephenson 22, Brown 80; Lane 30. Ref: J Hicking
Huddersfield: Mercer, Goodall, Wadsworth, Steele, Spence, Watson, Williams, Brown, Wilson C, Stephenson, Smith W
Tottenham: *Hinton, Forster, McDonald, Smith, Skitt, Grimsdell, Thompson, Seed, Lane, Handley, Dimmock*
Town survive Spurs' bombardment. Brown heads in after Smith's lob is flicked on by Williams. Town are only second side to win at Spurs, whose six-game winning run is over. Smith's corner is hooked in by Clem, then Dimmock makes a goal for Lane. Town lead WBA by a point.

34 — H BOLTON (21/3)
Ref: A Caseley
Huddersfield: Mercer, Goodall, Wadsworth, Steele, Wilson T, Watson, Williams, Brown, Wilson C, Stephenson, Smith W
Bolton: *Pym, Howarth R, Greenhalgh, Nuttall, Seddon, Howarth N, Butler, Jack R, Jack D, Smith Joe, Vizard*
Snowflakes, sunshine and a bitter wind, but a brilliant attacking game and a miracle there are no goals. Seddon gives Charlie Wilson a hard time but doesn't break the rules. Sam Wadsworth back to his best and Mercer has little to do. Town deserve to win. Large away following.

35 — H EVERTON (4/4)
Wilson C 14, 38p. Ref: G Nunnerley
Huddersfield: Mercer, Goodall, Shaw, Steele, Wilson T, Watson, Williams, Brown, Wilson C, Stephenson, Smith W
Everton: *Harland, McDonald, O'Donnell, Brown, McBain, Reid, Chedgzoy, Irvine, Dean, Kennedy, Troup*
Weeks after being dropped by Town, Wadsworth captains England. A windy day and a poor Everton team. This is Dixie Dean's third Everton game, a week after his first goal, but Wilson keeps him quiet. Smith is brought down and Charlie's vicious spot-kick bounces back out to him.

36 — A BURY (10/4)
Smith W 31. Ref: H Clayton
Huddersfield: Mercer, Goodall, Wadsworth, Steele, Wilson T, Watson, Williams, Brown, Wilson C, Stephenson, Smith W
Bury: *Harrison, Smith, Adamson, Porter, Bradshaw, Turner, Robbie, Stage, Finney, Ball, Amos*
Bury, back in Division 1 after 12 years absence, have crept into the title race with a great run. Billy Smith's cool finish inflicts their first home loss since December. A tough match with no quarter given by either side was watched by one of Bury's biggest ever crowds. Town top again.

37 — A SUNDERLAND (11/4)
Brown 35; Hawes 75. Ref: W Harper
Huddersfield: Mercer, Goodall, Wadsworth, Steele, Wilson T, Watson, Williams, Brown, Wilson C, Stephenson, Smith W
Sunderland: *McInroy, Cresswell, England, Clunas, Parker, Andrews, Grimshaw, Buchan, Marshall, Hawes, Ellis*
Sunderland have a strong home record and a draw is a good result. Brown's thunderous shot reminds the locals of Charlie Buchan at his best. Sunderland's pressure finally pays dividends. Willie Mercer handicapped by leg injury. West Brom draw at home and Town lead by one point.

38 — H BURY (14/4)
Brown 33, Wilson C 52. Ref: H Clayton
Huddersfield: Mercer, Goodall, Wadsworth, Steele, Wilson T, Walter, Williams, Brown, Wilson C, Stephenson, Smith W
Bury: *Harrison, Adamson, Ogden, Brooks, Bradshaw, Turner, Stage, Robbie, Burkinshaw, Amos, Matthews*
Injury-hit Bury make five changes and their title tilt is over. Both sides look tired on the grassless surface. Unmarked Brown heads in Walter's cross. Harrison fumbles Wilson's header from Walter's corner. Tom Wilson's benefit match. Now virtually a two-horse race after Bolton lose.

39 — H CARDIFF (18/4)
Ref: A Kingscott
Huddersfield: Mercer, Goodall, Wadsworth, Steele, Wilson T, Watson, Williams, Brown, Wilson C, Stephenson, Smith W
Cardiff: *Farquharson, Nelson, Blair, Wake, Sloan, Hardy, Gill, Collins, Nicholson, Hagan, Lawson*
Cardiff are Cup finalists. Cardiff have three men on Welsh international duty and two injured. Goodall and Stephenson are injured. In a gusty wind Steele plays well but Town are pretty lethargic. A scrappy game against a resolute defence. WBA win at Forest to draw level on points.

40 — A PRESTON (25/4)
Wilson C 30, Brown 65, 80, 89; Barnes 70p. Ref: W Turnbull
Huddersfield: Mercer, Cook, Shaw, Steele, Wilson T, Watson, Williams, Brown, Wilson C, Stephenson, Smith W
Preston: *Prout, Hamilton, Phizacklea, Woodward, Forrest, Crawford, Woodhouse, Paterson, Marquis, Barnes, Sapsford*
Preston are down and manager Lawrence resigns after the match but they fight hard until 20 minutes from time. Then Smith's glorious run rips open the defence and Brown taps in. Shaw fouls Barnes for a penalty before Brown takes advantage of errors. One point needed for the title.

41 — A NOTTS COUNTY (29/4)
Wilson C 55; Kemp 75. Ref: E Westwood
Huddersfield: Mercer, Cook, Shaw, Steele, Wilson T, Watson, Williams, Brown, Wilson C, Stephenson, Smith W
Notts County: *Iremonger, Ashurst, Cope, Flint, Dinsdale, Kemp, Daly, Staniforth, Widdowson, Davis, Barry*
Town survive a tense opening with County forcing six corners. Williams' teasing free-kick is headed in by Wilson. Kemp's shot ends the game with injuries. unsighted Mercer from a corner. Dramatic finish sees Town kicking for touch at every opportunity. Several players end the game with injuries.

42 — H LIVERPOOL (2/5)
Cawthorne 37; Wilson T 3 (og). Ref: J Telford
Huddersfield: Mercer, Goodall, Wadsworth, Cawthorne, Wilson T, Watson, Williams, Brown, Wilson C, Stephenson, Smith W
Liverpool: *Scott, Lucas, Parry, McNab, Cockburn, Bromilow, Rawlings, Forshaw, Chambers, Shone, McKinlay*
Wilson nets an own goal trying to clear a Chambers' cross. Cawthorne leaps like a salmon to head in Smith's corner. The crowd invade the pitch at the end to see League President McKenna present trophies to Stephenson and Spence, captain of the victorious Central League side.

LEAGUE DIVISION 1 (CUP-TIES)   Manager: Herbert Chapman   SEASON 1924-25

FA Cup		F-A	H-T	Scorers, Times, and Referees	1	2	3	4	5	6	7	8	9	10	11
1 A BOLTON	2 L	0-3	0-2	Jack 2, Smith Joe 22p, Vizard 84	Mercer	Goodall	Wadsworth	Steele	Wilson T	Watson	Williams	Cook	Wilson C	Stephenson	Smith W
10|1	50,412 3			Ref: G Nunnerley	*Pym*	*Chambers*	*Finney*	*Nuttall*	*Seddon*	*Howarth N*	*Butler*	*Jack D*	*Smith JR*	*Smith Joe*	*Vizard*

In muddy conditions another defeat at Burnden. Williams is limping after getting an early knock. 10,000 Town fans see Bolton start like a train and Jack nets after an attack is not cleared. Cook is the villain, handling for the penalty and then having a penalty saved after Seddon handles.

		P	W	D	L	F	A	W	D	L	F	A	Pts	Odds & ends
				Home					Away					
1	HUDDERSF'D	42	10	8	3	31	10	11	8	2	38	18	58	Double wins: (6) Nott'm For, Burnley, Arsenal, Everton, Bury, Preston.
2	West Brom	42	13	6	2	40	17	10	4	7	18	17	56	Double losses: (0).
3	Bolton	42	18	2	1	61	13	4	9	8	15	21	55	
4	Liverpool	42	13	5	3	43	20	7	5	9	20	35	50	Won from behind: (2) Blackburn (a), Aston Villa (h).
5	Bury	42	13	4	4	35	20	4	11	6	19	31	49	Lost from in front: (1) Tottenham (h).
6	Newcastle	42	11	6	4	43	18	5	10	6	18	24	48	
7	Sunderland	42	13	6	2	39	14	6	4	11	25	37	48	High spots: 10-game unbeaten start to the season.
8	Birmingham	42	10	8	3	27	17	7	4	10	22	36	46	17-game unbeaten run-in.
9	Notts County	42	11	6	4	29	12	5	7	9	13	19	45	Five-goal performances at Burnley and Arsenal.
10	Manchester C	42	11	7	3	44	29	6	2	13	32	39	43	Eleven away wins.
11	Cardiff	42	11	5	5	35	19	6	6	10	21	32	43	
12	Tottenham	42	9	8	4	32	16	6	4	11	20	27	42	Low spots: Three successive defeats in the autumn.
13	West Ham	42	12	7	2	37	12	3	5	13	25	48	42	FA Cup defeat at Bolton.
14	Sheffield Utd	42	10	5	6	34	25	3	8	10	21	38	39	
15	Aston Villa	42	10	7	4	34	25	3	6	12	24	46	39	
16	Blackburn	42	7	6	8	31	26	4	7	10	22	40	35	
17	Everton	42	11	4	6	25	20	2	7	13	15	40	35	
18	Leeds	42	9	8	4	29	17	2	4	15	17	42	34	
19	Burnley	42	7	8	6	28	31	4	4	13	18	44	34	
20	Arsenal	42	12	3	6	33	17	2	2	17	13	41	33	Hat-tricks: (5) Charlie Wilson (3); Brown (2).
21	Preston	42	8	2	11	29	35	2	4	15	8	39	26	Opposing hat-tricks: (0).
22	Nott'm Forest	42	5	6	10	17	23	1	6	14	12	42	24	Ever-presents: (0).
		924	234	127	101	756	436	101	127	234	436	756	924	Leading scorer: Charlie Wilson (24).

	Appearances Lge	FAC	Goals Lge	FAC	Tot
Barkas, Ned	1				
Boot, Len	5				
Binks, Syd	2				
Brown, George	32		20		20
Cawthorne, Harry	2		1		1
Cook, George	25	1			
Goodall, Roy	38	1	9		9
Mercer, Billy	27	1			
Richardson, Ted	1				
Shaw, George	11				
Smith, Norman	1				
Smith, Billy	41	1	9		9
Spence, Marshall	4				
Steele, David	38	1			
Stephenson, Clem	29	1	5		5
Taylor, Ted	10				
Wadsworth, Sam	33	1			
Walter, Joe	7				
Watson, Billy	41	1	1		1
Williams, Joe	35	1			
Wilson, Charlie	38	1	24		24
Wilson, Tommy	40	1			
(22 players used)	462	11	69		69

LEAGUE DIVISION 1   Manager: Cecil Potter   SEASON 1925-26

No	Date	Att	Pos	Pt	F-A	H-T	Scorers, Times, and Referees	1	2	3	4	5	6	7	8	9	10	11
1 H WEST BROM 29/8		21,975	-	-	D 1-1	0-0	Williams 47 / James 67 / Ref: A Fogg	Taylor / Ashmore	Goodall / Smith	Wadsworth / Baugh	Steele / Magee	Wilson T / Reed	Watson / Richardson	Jackson / Glidden	Brown / Carter	Wilson C / James	Stephenson / Wilson	Williams / Byers
2 A SHEFFIELD UTD 5/9		23,013	6 / 21	3	W 3-2	1-1	Wilson C 27, Jackson 66, Brown 86 / Johnson 43, Gillespie 46 / Ref: W Russell	Taylor / Alderson	Barkas / Harris	Wadsworth / Milton	Steele / Pantling	Wilson T / King	Watson / Green	Jackson / Mercer	Brown / Boyle	Wilson C / Johnson	Stephenson / Gillespie	Williams / Tunstall
3 H BURY 8/9		11,933	5 / 19	5	W 2-1	2-0	Binks 18, Brown 38 / Bullock 85 / Ref: C Lines	Taylor / Richardson	Barkas / Heap	Wadsworth / Adamson	Steele / Porter	Wilson T / Bradshaw	Watson / Turner	Jackson / Robbie	Brown / Stage	Binks / Bullock	Stephenson / Ball	Williams / Amos
4 H CARDIFF 12/9		19,033	4 / 19	6	D 1-1	0-0	Stephenson 60 / Davies W 59 / Ref: D Asson	Taylor / Farquharson	Barkas / Nelson	Wadsworth / Blair	Steele / Wake	Wilson T / Keenor	Watson / Hardy	Jackson / Lawson	Brown / Gill	Binks / Davies L	Stephenson / Davies W	Williams / Evans
5 A BIRMINGHAM 16/9		16,320	4 / 13	8	W 3-1	2-1	Cook 1, 10, Brown 70 / Scriven 40 / Ref: R Rudd	Taylor / Tremelling	Barkas / Womack	Wadsworth / Jones	Steele / Liddell	Wilson T / Cringan	Watson / Barton	Jackson / Harris	Cook / Crosbie	Brown / Briggs	Stephenson / Islip	Williams / Scriven
6 A TOTTENHAM 19/9		20,880	2 / 1	9	D 5-5	2-1	Jackson 4, 13, 70, Cook 62, Brown 86 / Elkes 7, 66, Dim' 51, Clay 60p, Osb' 65 Hinton / Ref: W Harper	Taylor / Hinton	Barkas / Clay	Wadsworth / Forster	Steele / Skinner	Wilson T / Smith	Watson / Grimsdell	Jackson / Osborne	Cook / Seed	Brown / Lindsay	Stephenson / Elkes	Williams / Dimmock
7 H MANCHESTER C 26/9		19,541	5 / 21	10	D 2-2	1-1	Cook 43, Williams 47 / Johnson 11, Warner 77 / Ref: J Fowler	Taylor / Mitchell	Barkas / Thompson	Wadsworth / McCloy	Steele / Coupland	Wilson T / Cowan	Watson / Benzie	Jackson / Austin	Cook / Warner	Brown / Browell	Stephenson / Johnson	Williams / Hicks
8 A EVERTON 3/10		35,665	3 / 15	12	W 3-2	2-0	Brown 28, 32, 73 / Troup 46, Chedgzoy 50 / Ref: J O'Donnell	Mercer / Harland	Barkas / McDonald	Wadsworth / O'Donnell	Steele / Brown	Wilson T / McBain	Watson / Hart	Jackson / Chedgzoy	Cook / Irvine	Brown / Dean	Stephenson / Kennedy	Williams / Troup
9 H BURNLEY 10/10		18,963	3 / 13	14	W 2-1	2-1	Brown 2, 17 / McCluggage 10p / Ref: J Head	Mercer / Dawson	Barkas / McCluggage	Wadsworth / Waterfield	Steele / Hill	Wilson T / Armitage	Watson / Parkin	Jackson / Kelly	Cook / Cross	Brown / Roberts	Stephenson / Beel	Williams / Page
10 A LEEDS 17/10		33,008	2 / 9	16	W 4-0	3-0	Cook 9, 89, Williams 14, Brown 27 / Ref: A Josephs	Mercer / Johnson	Barkas / Duffield	Wadsworth / Menzies	Shaw / Edwards	Wilson T / Hart	Watson / Baker	Jackson / Armand	Cook / Whipp	Brown / Jennings	Stephenson / Wainscoat	Williams / Jackson

Match reports

1. Jackson sets up Williams, only playing because Smith is ill, for the goal. The new offside law makes little difference, but there are only three stoppages for offside! Elsewhere goals flood in and Villa beat Burnley 10-0! Goodall suffers ankle injury and is off for most of the second half.

2. A miserable day in sooty Sheffield but the fans roll up to see the champs play the Cup winners. A great comeback in an injury-strewn game. Wilson's mid-air cartwheel is the pick of the goals but he ends up limping on the wing. Boyle is taken to hospital after a clash with Watson.

3. Joe Williams' crosses cause Bury problems and both goals stem from them. The slow Binks cannot miss the first and Brown coolly hits No 2. Bullock's late goal comes after the ref deflects it into his path. Bright football on a slippery surface. Bury smarting after 0-5 defeat to Bolton.

4. Taylor looks at fault when Davies' shot slips through his hands. Clem hits an unstoppable shot after good work by Jackson and Williams. Brown's header hits the post and Taylor atones with four good saves. Sam Wadsworth fouls Len Davies but Nelson's penalty sails over.

5. Super Town are applauded by a sporting crowd. Cook scores from Williams' cross after 30 seconds. Birmingham miss injured Joe Bradford. There is barely a chink in Town's armour. Town look skilful, well-balanced and well in control despite Scriven's goal. Brown also hits the bar.

6. Dreadful rain cuts the expected crowd by more than half but they see a classic with deadly finishing and crazy defending. Brown's brilliant late header is deserved as Spurs' defence collapses under fierce Town pressure and the run is maintained. Wadsworth booed for challenge on Seed.

7. Town slip up against struggling City but are the only unbeaten side. They look tired after two games in Scotland and miss chances. Sunderland and Spurs head league with 12 points. Williams looks to have lost the ball but springs up and wallops home. A physical game on a windy day.

8. Large crowd despite drizzly weather gives Town a massive welcome. Young prodigy Dixie Dean is shackled by Town's tough defence. Ted Taylor is dropped after recent boobs. Town well on top but two quick home goals throw the game wide before Brown hits a deserved winner.

9. More injuries as Wadsworth handles for the penalty then dislocates elbow and is off for some time. Steele also injured and Town play for a while with nine men. Brown scores an opportunist first and dribbles through for a second. This bulldog display extends the unbeaten run to 26.

10. Leeds' unbeaten home record falls as Town make it four away wins out of five. Cook scores from a rebound off the post. Williams adds No 2 in a scramble. Poor goalkeeping handed Brown his on a plate. Jackson sets up Cook for No 4. Shaw looks polished as Wadsworth's stand-in.

Match-by-Match Record (Matches 11–21)

#	V	Opponent	Date	Attendance	Pos	Res		Pts	Score	HT
11	H	NEWCASTLE	24/10	18,285	4	L	9	16	0-1	0-1
12	A	MANCHESTER U	31/10	37,213	2	D	9	17	1-1	1-0
13	A	ASTON VILLA	14/11	33,401	7	L	4	17	0-3	0-0
14	H	LEICESTER	21/11	14,386	6	W	18	19	3-0	2-0
15	H	LIVERPOOL	25/11	**7,285**	5	D	10	20	0-0	0-0
16	A	WEST HAM	28/11	13,914	5	W	13	22	3-2	2-0
17	H	ARSENAL	5/12	22,115	4	D	1	23	2-2	1-2
18	A	BOLTON	12/12	25,823	4	L	6	23	1-6	1-3
19	H	NOTTS COUNTY	19/12	7,972	3	W	17	25	2-0	1-0
20	H	SUNDERLAND	26/12	27,136	3	D	2	26	1-1	1-1
21	H	BIRMINGHAM	28/12	16,565	3	W	9	28	4-1	0-0

---

11. H NEWCASTLE — McDonald 11 — Ref: A Ward

- Town: Mercer; Barkas, Shaw; Steele, Wilson T, Watson; Jackson, Cook, Brown, Stephenson, Williams
- Newcastle: Wilson; Chandler, Hampson; McKenzie, Spencer, Mooney; Urwin, Cowan, Loughlin, McDonald, Seymour

The unbeaten run ends, three short of Burnley's 30-game record. Newcastle's massed ranks hold out against fierce pressure and deserve the win. Tom Wilson is off-form in a shaky Town defence.

12. A MANCHESTER U — Cook 22 / Thomas 48 — Ref: I Caswell

- Town: Mercer; Barkas, Shaw; Steele, Wilson T, Williams; Jackson, Cook, Brown, Stephenson, Smith W
- United: Steward; Moore, Silcock; Hilditch, Barson, Grimwood; Spence, Hanson, McPherson, Rennox, Thomas

Jackson plays for Scotland. Town are on top in the first half as Cook scores from Williams' cross and hits a post. Thomas scrambles a goal from a corner. United's kick and rush style upsets Town, who are lucky to survive. Smith looks rusty on his return but puts over good crosses.

13. A ASTON VILLA — Capewell 57, 65, 75 — Ref: T Rennie

- Town: Mercer; Barkas, Shaw; Steele, Wilson T, Watson; Jackson, Cook, Brown, Stephenson, Smith W
- Villa: Spiers; Smart, Mort; Johnstone, Talbot, Moss; York, Stephenson, Capewell, Walker, Dorrell

Len Capewell makes it 18 goals for the season. Taylor was expected to return but became indisposed overnight and Mercer continues. Villa's second-half pressure pays off as the fog descends. Town's attack never gets moving against a physical Villa side. Half the team are off-colour.

14. H LEICESTER — Brown 12, 80, Williams 25 — Ref: C Lines

- Town: Mercer; Goodall, Wadsworth; Steele, Wilson T, Watson; Williams, Brown, Jackson, Stephenson, Smith W
- Leicester: Campbell; Black, Osborne; Newton, Watson, Bamber; Adcock, Duncan, Chandler, Lochhead, Wadsworth

Town experiment with Jackson at centre-forward and Wadsworth returns. Smith makes all three goals. Brown scores from a rebound and heads in Smith's cross after a flowing move. Williams scores after fierce pressure.

15. H LIVERPOOL — (no scorers) — Ref: E Pinckston

- Town: Mercer; Goodall, Wadsworth; Steele, Wilson T, Watson; Williams, Brown, Jackson, Stephenson, Smith W
- Liverpool: Scott; Lucas, McKinlay; Jackson, Cockburn, Bromilow; Oxley, Chambers, Walsh, Baron, Hopkin

A cold, icy wind and a Wednesday afternoon kick-off keeps the crowd low. The pitch is rock hard and difficult to keep a grip on. Both sides hit woodwork in a first half dominated by Town. The pressure fails to produce a goal and Jackson and Smith are off-colour. Scott is Pool's hero.

16. A WEST HAM — Jackson 10, 44, Brown 71 / Ruffell 47, Watson 88 — Ref: D Asson

- Town: Mercer; Goodall, Wadsworth; Steele, Wilson T, Watson; Williams, Brown, Jackson, Stephenson, Smith W
- West Ham: Baillie; Hodgson, Hebden; Bishop, Barratt, Cadwell; Moore, Earle, Watson, Williams, Ruffell

A minute's silence for Queen Alexandra on a snow-covered pitch which proves treacherous, with four players suffering injuries and mistakes galore. West Ham finish with eight men but battle to the end after Vic Watson's solo goal. Billy Watson injures ankle and misses second half.

17. H ARSENAL — Jackson 11, 49 / Neil 5, Buchan 41 — Ref: H Stott

- Town: Mercer; Goodall, Wadsworth; Steele, Wilson T, Watson; Williams, Brown, Jackson, Stephenson, Smith W
- Arsenal: Harper; Mackie, John; Baker, Butler, Blyth; Hoar, Buchan, Brain, Neil, Haden

Town end league leaders' four-match winning run but Buchan look the better team. £100-a-goal Buchan is at the heart of all Arsenal's moves and scores a beautiful 13th. Braziers used to thaw icy pitch. Mercer misjudges Neil's shot and it creeps in. Jackson's thunderbolt levels scores.

18. A BOLTON — Brown 4 / Butler 9, Smith J 11, 83, Jack 37, [Smith JR 55, 88] — Ref: A Kingscott

- Town: Mercer; Goodall, Wadsworth; Steele, Wilson T, Cawthorne; Williams, Cook, Brown, Stephenson, Smith W
- Bolton: Pym; Haworth, Jennings; Cope, Round, Thornborough; Butler, Jack D, Smith JR, Smith J, Vizard

The Bolton bogey continues after Brown's header. Jack's superb header tops a stunning first half with Town rarely out of their own half. David Steele's temporary blindness means Town play second half with 10 men. Mercer saves Town from a bigger defeat but his days are numbered.

19. H NOTTS COUNTY — Wilson C 43p, Brown 67 — Ref: E Wood

- Town: Taylor; Goodall, Wadsworth; Cawthorne, Wilson T, Watson; Jackson, Brown, Wilson C, Stephenson, Smith W
- County: Iremonger; Ashurst, Cope; Flint, Dinsdale, Hilton; Taylor, Harris, Widdowson, Davis, Barry

County are fresh from a win over Sunderland. Taylor, Watson and Wilson return from injury. Snow on pitch and visibility poor. Jackson falls onto terracing and scrapes face. Wilson's shooting is awry but he nets from the spot after Jackson is upended. Fists fly as the game deteriorates.

20. H SUNDERLAND — Brown 9 / Halliday 33 — Ref: R Kelso

- Town: Taylor; Goodall, Wadsworth; Cawthorne, Wilson T, Watson; Jackson, Brown, Wilson C, Stephenson, Smith W
- Sunderland: Stoneham; Cresswell, England; Clunas, Marshall, McGorian; Prior, Kelly, Halliday, Andrews, Death

A sudden thaw means the pitch is like a mud flat. Charlie Wilson sets up Brown, and Taylor's double save from Halliday and Death is brilliant. League top scorer Halliday is penalised but Taylor parries. Defenders on top in an exciting game with Sunderland looking the better balanced side.

21. H BIRMINGHAM — Smith W 53, Steph' 60, Brown 70, [Jackson 73] / Bradford 85 — Ref: R Rudd

- Town: Taylor; Goodall, Wadsworth; Cawthorne, Wilson T, Watson; Jackson, Brown, Cook, Stephenson, Smith W
- Birmingham: Tremelling; Womack, Jones; Liddell, Hunter, Barton; Harris, Crosbie, Bradford, Briggs, Russell

Many fans are back to work and the gate is low. Jones' handball is penalised but Smith's penalty is saved. Despite rough treatment, Town are rampant after half-time and Smith's oblique shot is the pick of the goals. Blues argue that Clem's shot hasn't crossed the line, but it stands.

LEAGUE DIVISION 1

SEASON 1925-26

Manager: Cecil Potter

No	Date	V	Opponents	Att	Pos	Pt	Res	F–A	H–T	Scorers, Times, and Referees
22	2/1	A	WEST BROM	22,435	10	29	2 D	2–2	1–1	Williams 31, Brown 59; Reed 18, Glidden 89p. Ref: A Fogg
23	16/1	H	SHEFFIELD UTD	16,181	8	31	2 W	4–1	1–1	Goodall 26p, Cook 87, Brown 88, [Smith W 89]; Mercer 3. Ref: W Russell
24	20/1	A	SUNDERLAND	27,833	2	31	3 L	1–4	1–2	Brown 10; Prior 42, 75, Death 43, Halliday 65. Ref: A Kirby
25	23/1	A	CARDIFF	13,049	18	33	3 W	2–1	0–1	Cook 75, Jackson 77; Ferguson 42. Ref: D Asson
26	6/2	A	MANCHESTER C	36,645	21	35	1 W	5–1	0–0	Brown 53, 60, 90, Goodall 56p, [Smith W 75]; Roberts 89. Ref: J Fowler
27	11/2	A	BLACKBURN	21,434	17	35	2 L	1–2	1–1	Brown 35; Crisp 7, Healless 84. Ref: W Forshaw
28	13/2	H	EVERTON	17,278	8	37	1 W	3–0	2–0	Brown 15, 80, Raitt 25(og). Ref: J O'Donnell
29	20/2	A	BURNLEY	21,482	20	38	1 D	1–1	0–1	Smith W 65; Beel 7. Ref: E Westwood
30	27/2	H	LEEDS	26,248	19	40	1 W	3–1	1–0	Cook 20, Brown 60, Williams 83; Wainscoat 71. Ref: A Josephs
31	3/3	H	TOTTENHAM	13,005	12	42	1 W	2–1	0–1	Brown 55, 61; Elkes 20. Ref: A Ward

Line-ups (positions 1–11; Town listed first, opponents in italics)

22 — West Brom (A):
Taylor, Goodall, Wadsworth, Cawthorne, Wilson T, Watson, Williams, Brown, Jackson, Cook, Smith W
Ashmore, Smith, Adams, Richardson, Reed, Dutton, Glidden, Carter, James, Davies, Fitton

23 — Sheffield Utd (H):
Taylor, Goodall, Wadsworth, Cawthorne, Wilson T, Watson, Jackson, Cook, Brown, Stephenson, Smith W
Alderson, Sampy W, Birks, Sampy T, Waugh, Green, Mercer, Boyle, Johnson, Gillespie, Tunstall

24 — Sunderland (A):
Taylor, Goodall, Wadsworth, Cawthorne, Wilson T, Watson, Jackson, Cook, Brown, Stephenson, Smith W
Stoneham, Cresswell, England, Clunas, Parker, Andrews, Prior, Kelly, Halliday, Marshall, Death

25 — Cardiff (A):
Taylor, Goodall, Wadsworth, Cawthorne, Wilson T, Watson, Williams, Jackson, Brown, Cook, Smith W
Hills, Watson, Blair, Nicholson, Sloan, Hardy, Lawson, Davies W, Ferguson, Cassidy, McLachlan

26 — Manchester C (A):
Taylor, Goodall, Wadsworth, Hobson, Wilson T, Watson, Jackson, Raw, Brown, Cook, Smith W
Goodchild, Cookson, McCloy, Coupland, Cowan, Pringle, Austin, Browell, Roberts, Johnson, Hicks

27 — Blackburn (A):
Taylor, Goodall, Wadsworth, Hobson, Spence, Watson, Jackson, Raw, Brown, Cook, Smith W
Crawford, Rollo, Jones, Roscamp, Healless, McIntyre, Crisp, Puddefoot, Harper, Rigby, Mitchell

28 — Everton (H):
Taylor, Goodall, Wadsworth, Cawthorne, Wilson T, Watson, Jackson, Cook, Brown, Stephenson, Smith W
Hardy, Raitt, McDonald, Peacock, Bain, Hart, Chedgzoy, Irvine, Dean, Kennedy, Troup

29 — Burnley (A):
Taylor, Goodall, Wadsworth, Cawthorne, Wilson T, Watson, Jackson, Cook, Brown, Stephenson, Smith W
Dawson, McCluggage, Waterfield, Steel, Hill, Hughes, Bruton, Cross, Richards, Beel, Page

30 — Leeds (H):
Taylor, Goodall, Wadsworth, Cawthorne, Wilson T, Watson, Williams, Cook, Brown, Stephenson, Smith W
Potts, Allan, Menzies, Edwards, Townsley, Baker, Sissons, Whipp, Jennings, Wainscoat, Jackson

31 — Tottenham (H):
Taylor (Smith J), Goodall, Wadsworth, Cawthorne, Wilson T, Watson, Williams, Jackson, Brown, Cook, Smith W
Clay, Forster, Smith B, Skitt, White, Thompson, Seed, Osborne, Elkes, Hargreaves

Match notes

22. WBA have scored more goals than any other team at home and pummel Town early on. Reed scores when Taylor spills the ball. Williams' header goes in off the bar. Ashmore saves Jackson's penalty but is beaten by Brown from Smith's cross. Glidden's late penalty looks unfair.

23. Town bombard the Blades but only achieve a breakthrough three minutes from the end. Green handles and Goodall nets after Mercer's stinging shot. Goals 2 and 3 are scrambled efforts but Smith's goal brings the roof down. He darts between two men and unleashes an unstoppable shot.

24. Heavy going and a heavy ball in a game which should not have gone ahead. The mud suits title favourites Sunderland. Brown's clinical right-footer makes it seven successive scoring games. Halliday makes it 30 goals for the season and new signing Kelly assists for both Prior's goals.

25. Ferguson gets a surprise but deserved goal after he charges Taylor, who drops the ball. Cardiff fail to capitalise on their superiority and Town rally and Jackson heads an easy winner after Hills misses a free-kick. Arsenal and Sunderland both lose, so they and Town are level on points.

26. City again on top in first half but Town's defence looks more solid. Raw (ex-Tow Law) and former Yorkshire amateur George Hobson are debutants. After the break the wingers go to town, laying on Brown's super hat-trick as the mist descends. Cowan trips Jackson for the penalty.

27. Jack Carr's team record their first win in 7 which lifts them five places, but 29-goal Harper fails to score. Town lose one of their games in hand and are off the top on goal-average. Patchy snow but bitterly cold. Town well on top until Healless's scrambled goal when Ted Taylor slips up.

28. After five successive away games Town return home with a skilful display. George Brown outshines Dixie Dean and scores his 25th and 26th goals of the season. Raitt spoils the hat-trick by scoring past Hardy. Brown's second is a tap in after Hardy had saved well from Alex Jackson.

29. Another lowly team embarrass inconsistent Town and Burnley fans must wonder how Town are so high in the table. Taylor has one of his shaky days and Beel's shot foxes him. Superb Wadsworth, who will captain England v Wales, saves the day three times with goal-line clearances.

30. Williams is in for Jackson, playing for Scotland. There is virtually no grass on the playing surface. A big following from Leeds watch a wind-affected, scrappy game. Cook's powerful drive ends Leeds' resistance. Brown's delicious lob floats over Potts. Town beat a lowly club at last.

31. Town struggle against gale-force winds in first half but improve later. Many fans switch ends at half-time hoping to see home goals. Brown scores with Town's first long-range shot. Wind curls Williams' cross to an unmarked Brown. Elkes' thunderbolt deserves to win the game.

32 — A, 6/3 — NEWCASTLE · Att 56,496 · (12) · Div 1 · W · 44 · 2-0 (2-0)
Brown 30, 38 — Ref: A Ward
Town: Taylor, Goodall, Wadsworth, Cawthorne, Wilson T, Watson, Jackson, Brown, **Devlin**, Stephenson, Smith W
Newcastle: Wilson, Hampson, Crown, McKenzie, Curry, Harris, Urwin, Clark, Gallacher, McDonald, Mitchell
Another windy day and the gates are closed. Smith's great run and cross sets up Brown, who scores a second in a melee to make it 11 in seven games and 31 in total. Gallacher, a folk hero on Tyneside, is unlucky not to score. Stonewall defence clinches an important win. Devlin quiet.

33 — H, 13/3 — MANCHESTER U · Att 27,842 · (6) · Div 1 · W · 46 · **5-0** (1-0)
Cook 30, 57, Devlin 76, 80, [Smith W 88] — Ref: I Caswell
Town: Taylor, Barkas, Wadsworth, Cawthorne, Wilson T, Watson, Jackson, Cook, Devlin, Stephenson, Smith W
Manchester U: Mew, Moore, Jones, Bennion, Barson, Mann, Spence, Smith, Hanson, Rennox, Partridge
United, through to the semi-finals of the FA Cup, are outsiders for the title but are swept away. Devlin scores two opportunist goals on his home debut and deserves a hat-trick with a wicked shot which Mew pushed to the feet of Smith. Frank Barson tries to get tough but is out-smarted.

34 — A, 20/3 — LIVERPOOL · Att 35,255 · (12) · Div 1 · W · 48 · 2-1 (2-0)
Devlin 8, Stephenson 30, Forshaw 65 — Ref: E Pinckston
Town: Taylor, Goodall, Wadsworth, Cawthorne, Wilson T, Watson, Jackson, Brown, Devlin, Stephenson, Smith W
Liverpool: Scott, Lucas, McKinlay, McNab, Wadsworth, Bromilow, Oxley, Chambers, Hodgson, Forshaw, Hopkin
Liverpool are in transition but their domination is wasted by poor shooting. Town show them how to score in another great win. Devlin is left limping for the second half after a knock. Devlin nets after Clem's shot hits the bar then Town defend in depth after the skipper's screw-shot.

35 — H, 27/3 — ASTON VILLA · Att 28,442 · (10) · Div 1 · W · 50 · 5-1 (2-0)
Jackson 28, 44, Brown 56, 61, York 65 [Cook 80] — Ref: J Rennie
Town: Taylor, Goodall, Wadsworth, Cawthorne, Wilson T, Watson, Jackson, Cook, Brown, Stephenson, Smith W
Aston Villa: Jackson, Smart, Mort, Johnstone, Talbot, Moss, Armfield, Kirton, York, Walker, Chester
Devlin's foot injury rules him out. Its Clem's benefit and the band play 'For he's a jolly good fellow' as the teams come out. Jackson lashes in the first, then scores in a scramble. Brown scores two from close range before Billy Walker hits the bar from the spot. Town are irrepressible.

36 — A, 3/4 — LEICESTER · Att 29,903 · (10) · Div 1 · L · 50 · 0-2 (0-2)
Bell 11, Hine 33 — Ref: C Lines
Town: Taylor, Goodall, Wadsworth, Cawthorne, Wilson T, Watson, Jackson, Cook, Brown, Stephenson, Smith W
Leicester: Campbell, Black, Osborne, Duncan, Watson, Bamber, Findlay, Hine, Lochhead, Bell
Leicester's great second half to the season has pulled them away from the drop zone. Filbert Street is packed to see Town's super run ended. Ted Taylor fails to hold Bell's soft shot and Hine's unstoppable shot follows a flowing move. City deserve their win against lack-lustre Town.

37 — A, 5/4 — BURY · Att 27,144 · (4) · Div 1 · D · 51 · 0-0 (0-0)
Ref: T Brown
Town: Taylor, Goodall, Wadsworth, Cawthorne, Wilson T, Watson, Jackson, Cook, Brown, Stephenson, Smith W
Bury: Richardson, Heap, Adamson, Brooks, Bradshaw, Ward, Robbie, Stage, Bullock, Ball, Amos
A massive Bank Holiday crowd swelter in the heat. Bury are on top in early stages as Town play into the sun, but Taylor is in top form. Town come more into it after half-time but heat takes its toll and the game ends scrappily. Cook goes closest when he hits a post. Wilson is superb.

38 — H, 6/4 — BLACKBURN · Att **34,871** · (13) · Div 1 · W · 53 · 3-1 (2-0)
Brown 16, 27, Smith A 81 / Harper 87p — Ref: W Forshaw
Town: Taylor, Goodall, Wadsworth, Cawthorne, Wilson T, Watson, Jackson, Brown, Smith A, Cook, Smith W
Blackburn: Sewell, Rollo, Jones, Roscamp, Campbell, McIntyre, Crisp, Puddefoot, Harper, Rigby, Mitchell
Sam Wadsworth gets a marvellous ovation at the start of his benefit game. Bert Smith, playing his first game for two years, scores from Jackson's centre, and hits the bar in a good display. Goodall fouls Mitchell for a penalty. A record league crowd watches two tired teams.

39 — H, 10/4 — WEST HAM · Att 21,116 · (18) · Div 1 · W · 55 · 2-1 (0-1)
Jackson 59, 60 / Earle 7 — Ref: D Asson
Town: Taylor, Goodall, Wadsworth, Cawthorne, Wilson T, Watson, Jackson, Cook, Brown, Stephenson, Smith W
West Ham: Hufton, Hebden, Barratt, Carter, Kay, Collins, Yews, Watson, Earle, Moore, Ruffell
Town's win and Arsenal's defeat at Roker mean that the title is virtually secure. In Cawthorne's benefit, Hufton keeps overwhelmed Hammers in the game. Hufton spills the ball, allowing Cook to set up Jackson, who also volleys home No 2. Town pepper the Hammers right to the end.

40 — H, 12/4 — BOLTON · Att 20,829 · (7) · Div 1 · W · 57 · 3-0 (3-0)
Smith W 11, Jackson 15, [Stephenson 40] — Ref: A Kingscott
Town: Taylor, Goodall, Wadsworth, Cawthorne, Wilson T, Watson, Jackson, Cook, Brown, Stephenson, Smith W
Bolton: Pym, Haworth, Greenhalgh, Cope, Round, Butler, Thornborough, Baggett, Jack, Smith J, Vizard
Bolton have the FA Cup final in 12 days time. With the title clinched, Town are given a three-minute ovation at the end. A first half full of classy football was followed by 45 minutes of tedium. Joe Smith's Bolton, with several reserves, were swept aside by the triple champions.

41 — H, 17/4 — ARSENAL · Att 34,110 · (2) · Div 1 · L · 57 · 1-3 (0-2)
Devlin 75 / Hulme 8, Lawson 35, Parker 89p — Ref: H Stott
Town: Mercer, Barkas, Wadsworth, Cawthorne, Wilson T, Watson, Jackson, Cook, Devlin, Stephenson, Smith W
Arsenal: Lewis, Parker, John, Young, Blyth, **Dennis**, Buchan, Brain, Ramsay, Hulme
A hollow triumph for the Gunners over a tired Town. Chapman is away scouting. Town have three men in England v Scotland game, Arsenal one. Hulme scores after two brave saves by Mercer. Slick Buchan sets up No 2 and Wadsworth's brilliant save is at the expense of a penalty.

42 — A, 1/5 — NOTTS COUNTY · Att 4,715 · (22) · Div 1 · L · 57 · 2-4 (1-1)
Cook 24, Jackson 68 / Davis 19, 46, 48, Daly 84 — Ref: E Wood
Town: Mercer, Goodall, Wadsworth, Cawthorne, Wilson T, Watson, Jackson, Brown, Cook, Stephenson, Smith W
Notts County: Iremonger, **Smith G**, Kemp, Young, Dinsdale, Hilton, Daly, Kelly, Staniforth, Davis, Barry
40-year-old Iremonger makes his 601st and final appearance for relegated County. Town are given a warm welcome from a sparse crowd in pouring rain and hail. Notts adapt to dire conditions better than a tired Town. Alex Jackson's solo effort after a 50-yard run is the best goal.

Home Average 19,569 · Away 27,130

LEAGUE DIVISION 1 (CUP-TIES)

Manager: Cecil Potter

SEASON 1925-26

FA Cup				F-A	H-T	Scorers, Times, and Referees	1	2	3	4	5	6	7	8	9	10	11
3	A	CHARLTON	2 W	1-0	1-0	Goodall 32p	Taylor	Goodall	Wadsworth	Cawthorne	Wilson T	Watson	Jackson	Brown	Cook	Stephenson	Smith W
9/1		21,184 35:16				Ref: H Stott	*Preedy*	*Smith*	*Herod*	*Steele A*	*Armitage*	*Hardie*	*McGinn*	*Rankin*	*Millard*	*McCrorie*	*Cox*

A poor Cup-tie but Town go through courtesy of Goodall's penalty after Herod handled on the line. Town are superior but are sluggish until the last twenty minutes. Preedy saves Charlton from a heavy defeat. Charlie Wilson scores a hat-trick for the reserves but Brown's form is hot.

FA Cup				F-A	H-T	Scorers, Times, and Referees	1	2	3	4	5	6	7	8	9	10	11
4	A	MANCHESTER C	3 L	0-4	0-2	Hicks 21, 28, Roberts 50, Browell 62	Taylor	Barkas	Wadsworth	Cawthorne	Wilson T	Watson	Williams	Jackson	Brown	Stephenson	Smith W
30/1		74,799 18				Ref: A Timmins	*Goodchild*	*Cookson*	*McCloy*	*Coupland*	*Cowan*	*Pringle*	*Austin*	*Browell*	*Roberts*	*Johnson*	*Hicks*

Wobbly Town are deservedly dumped out by a lively City team. A Hicks drive sneaks past Taylor and he heads a second after a corner was not cleared. Wadsworth is at sea and Roberts mazy dribble ends in No 3. Browell heads a fourth. A crowd barrier gives way, leaving five fans hurt.

		P		Home					Away					Pts
			W	D	L	F	A	W	D	L	F	A		
1	HUDDERSF'D	42	14	6	1	50	17	9	5	7	42	43	57
2	Arsenal	42	16	2	3	57	19	6	6	9	30	44	52
3	Sunderland	42	17	2	2	67	30	4	2	13	29	50	48
4	Bury	42	12	4	5	55	34	8	3	10	30	43	47
5	Sheffield Utd	42	15	3	3	72	29	4	5	12	30	53	46
6	Aston Villa	42	12	7	2	56	25	5	4	12	30	51	44
7	Liverpool	42	9	8	4	43	27	4	5	12	27	36	44
8	Bolton	42	11	6	4	46	31	6	4	11	29	45	44
9	Manchester U	42	12	4	5	40	26	7	2	12	26	47	44
10	Newcastle	42	13	3	5	59	33	3	7	11	25	42	42
11	Everton	42	9	9	3	42	26	3	9	9	30	44	42
12	Blackburn	42	11	6	4	59	33	4	5	12	32	47	41
13	West Brom	42	13	5	3	59	29	3	3	15	20	49	40
14	Birmingham	42	14	2	5	45	25	2	6	13	31	56	40
15	Tottenham	42	11	4	6	45	36	4	5	12	21	43	39
16	Cardiff	42	8	5	8	30	25	8	2	11	31	51	39
17	Leicester	42	11	3	7	42	32	3	7	11	28	48	38
18	West Ham	42	14	2	5	45	27	1	5	15	18	49	37
19	Leeds	42	11	5	5	38	28	3	3	15	26	48	36
20	Burnley	42	7	7	7	43	35	6	3	12	42	73	36
21	Manchester C	42	8	7	6	48	42	4	4	13	41	58	35
22	Notts County	42	11	4	6	37	26	2	3	16	17	48	33
		924	259	104	99	1068	635	99	104	259	635	1068	924

Odds & ends

Double wins: (5) Sheffield U, Birmingham, Everton, Leeds, West Ham.
Double losses: (0).
Won from behind: (5) Sheffield U (h&a), Cardiff (a), Tottenham (h), West Ham (h).
Lost from in front: (2) Bolton (a), Sunderland (a).
High spots: 10-game unbeaten start.
Six straight wins in February-March, which virtually clinched the title.
Amazing 5-5 draw at Spurs.
International recognition for players.
Low spots: FA Cup defeat at Maine Road.
Heavy defeat at Bolton.
Hat-tricks: (3) Brown (2), Jackson (1).
Opposing hat-tricks: (2) Capewell (Aston Villa), Davis (Notts County).
Ever-presents: (0).
Leading scorer: George Brown (35).

	Appearances		Goals		
	Lge	FAC	Lge	FAC	Tot
Barkas, Ned	13				
Binks, Syd	2		1		1
Brown, George	41	2	35		35
Cawthorne, Harry	24	2			
Cook, George	29	1	14		14
Dennis, Harold	1				
Devlin, Willie	4		4		4
Goodall, Roy	29		2	1	3
Hobson, Robert	2				
Jackson, Alex	39	2	16		16
Mercer, Billy	13				
Raw, Harry	2				
Shaw, George	4				
Smith, Bert	1		1		1
Smith, Billy	28	2	6		6
Spence, Marshall	1				
Steele, David	18				
Stephenson, Clem	36	2	4		4
Taylor, Ted	29	2			
Wadsworth, Sam	38	2			
Watson, Billy	40	2			
Williams, Joe	23	1	6		6
Wilson, Charlie	4		2		2
Wilson, Tommy	41	2	1		1
(own-goals)					
(24 players used)	462	22	92	1	93

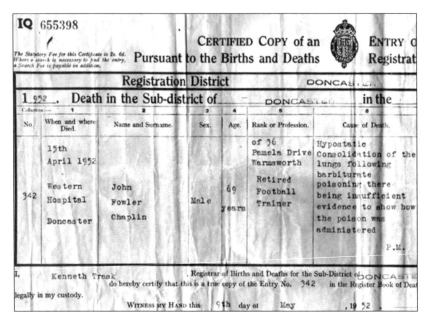

IQ 655398		CERTIFIED COPY of an			ENTRY O
The Statutory Fee for this Certificate is 2s. 6d. Where a search is necessary to find the entry, a Search Fee is payable in addition.	Pursuant to the Births and Deaths				Registrat

Registration District				DONCA	
1 952 . Death in the Sub-district of				DONCASTE	in the

No.	When and where Died.	Name and Surname.	Sex.	Age.	Rank or Profession.	Cause of Death.
342	15th April 1952 Western Hospital Doncaster	John Fowler Chaplin	Male	69 years	of 36 Pamela Drive Warmsworth Retired Football Trainer	Hypostatic Consolidation of the lungs following barbiturate poisoning there being insufficient evidence to show how the poison was administered P.M.

I, Kenneth Treak , Registrar of Births and Deaths for the Sub-District of DONCASTE do hereby certify that this is a true copy of the Entry No. 342 in the Register Book of Dea legally in my custody.

WITNESS MY HAND this 9th day of May , 19 52

The 1952 death certificate of Jack Chaplin, Town's trainer and manager. Death by poison

LIST OF SUBSCRIBERS AND VOTES FOR THE MOST IMPORTANT TOWN PLAYER 1923-26

Iain Ainley	Clem Stephenson	Neil Leeson	Clem Stephenson
Graham John Airs	Clem Stephenson	Trevor Marsden	George Brown
Steve Allen	Clem Stephenson	John Mason	Clem Stephenson
Stuart Ardrey		Paul Matthewman	Billy Smith
Mrs PR Armer	Jack Chaplin	Kevin McMahon	Clem Stephenson
David U Armitage	Clem Stephenson	Paul Miller	Billy Smith
Gary Ashton	Billy Smith	Andrew Moore	Clem Stephenson
Graham D Atkinson	Billy Smith	Ian Netherwood	
John Allen Beever	Billy Smith	Leigh Newby	Billy Smith
Alan M Beevers	Clem Stephenson	Scott Newby	Billy Smith
Jason Bellamy	George Brown	Martyn Norcliffe	Billy Smith
Simon Blakey	Billy Smith	Robert Pepper	Clem Stephenson
Dennis Bottomley	Billy Smith	Stuart M Perkins	
John Broadbent	Alex Jackson	Andrew Pollard	Charlie Wilson
Matthew Broadbent	Alex Jackson	Michael Raven	Billy Smith
Nigel Brook	Billy Smith	John David Raw	Alex Jackson
Ian Michael Carter	Herbert Chapman	David Rowbotham	Sam Wadsworth
Rachel Chambers		Irvine Shaw	Billy Smith
Anthony Claypole	Clem Stephenson	Robert Shaw	Billy Smith
Carl Crossland	Clem Stephenson	Gary Roy Skaczkowski	Roy Goodall
Stephen Dunning	Billy Smith	Richard Stocken	
Clark Eastwood	Billy Smith	Andrew R Swailes (Swazz)	Billy Smith
Andy Ellis	Clem Stephenson	Chris B Sykes	Clem Stephenson
Trevor & Colleen Ellis		SG Tattersfield	
Steve Exley	Billy Smith	Ben Thornes	Billy Smith
Eamonn Gallagher	Billy Smith	Jonathon Thorpe	
Marcus Garside	Alex Jackson	Trevor Howard Wardle	Clem Stephenson
Colin Gee	Clem Stephenson	The Revd David Wilding	Herbert Chapman
PJ Gooder	Billy Smith	John TC Wilkinson	Sam Wadsworth
Richard Green	Billy Smith	GM Wood	Clem Stephenson
Karl Hallos	Billy Smith		
Andrew Hepworth	Clem Stephenson	1ST	BILLY SMITH
Thomas Hepworth	Clem Stephenson	2ND	CLEM STEPHENSON
Andrew Kirk		3RD	ALEX JACKSON